Come
Stay
Celebrate!

Come
Stay
Celebrate!

Come
Stay
Celebrate!

THE STORY OF THE
SHELTER HOSTEL
IN EILAT, ISRAEL

Judith Galblum Pex

CLADACH
Publishing

Dedicated to all the Shelter volunteers

Contents

1. Who Wants to Run a Hostel, Anyway?

Asleep in our bed in the middle of the night, we were startled by a knocking on the window and a male voice calling, "John, John!"

For a few minutes we tried to ignore the disturbance, but the voice was persistent.

"John, I need help! I'm scared."

"Oh, no. It's Mike again," I muttered to John, nudging him out of bed. "He probably smoked and had a bad reaction with his pills. How'd he find our bedroom window?"

"I'm coming, go around to the front door," John called to Mike, then pulled on his jeans.

"Do I need this?" He looked at me. "Who wants to run a hostel, anyway?"

I was in no state for a deep discussion, and John didn't really expect an answer because in fact, we couldn't imagine life without our hostel.

John put on the kettle to make a cup of coffee for Mike and grabbed his keys to drive him to the hospital.

I lay in bed, awake now, remembering how we began our hostel here in the south of Israel.

הפסקה

Some ten years earlier on a scorching August afternoon, John was sitting outside the Peace Café drinking grapefruit juice. "Searching for a Heart of Gold" by Neil Young, one of John's favorite songs was playing, followed by "Mr. Tambourine Man" by Bob Dylan, bringing back memories of his early traveling days.

It was one of those days when you feel stuck in front of a hair dryer and think you'd collapse after walking a block. Anyone arriving in Eilat after the six-hour drive through the desert was struck by the dryness in his nostrils and burning in his throat.

The Peace Café provided little respite from the heat, being just a hole-in-the-wall with an awning out front. Located right off the town's main street, the Peace Café was the popular hangout for travelers in Eilat, a place to meet friends, get a cheap meal or drink, listen to music, or simply sit and watch the world go by. John often found a reason to drop by there, whether to quench his thirst or just strike up a conversation. Speaking five languages fluently plus bits of others, John was rarely at a loss for words and always found someone to talk to.

Fights often broke out at the Peace Café and people were known to throw chairs at each other, especially when the beer or vodka flowed. Eilat in 1978 was a frontier city, though it had tamed down since its beginning days when Israeli criminals were given the choice of going to jail or being exiled to Eilat. A small town squeezed between the Red Sea and the rugged Negev and Sinai deserts, Eilat for years had been a stopover on the hippie trail to India, the last place a person could find work to pay for the long overland trek east.

Guy, from France, had arrived in Eilat at about the same time as John. His Mediterranean coloring was a contrast to John's sun-bleached hair and reddish beard. As Guy approached his table John could tell from the smile on Guy's face that he had something important to share.

"Hey! Where've you been?" John motioned for his old friend to sit down. "Still living in the wadi?"

"I found a real place to stay!" Guy exclaimed, quickly downing a bottle of juice and ordering another round. "Enough living in a shack. It's hard to start paying rent, but this place is cheap and quiet."

"Great! In this heat those tin-roofed huts are unbearable," John said. "I can't believe how you stuck it out after the rest of us left. Amazing how we built them, though, scrounging around the dump for cardboard, plywood, tin sheeting, and all kinds of junk."

"Yeah, David's looked like a tepee," said Guy. "And I remember the lock on your door."

"At least we never stole anything to build our shacks. Do you remember the house that Dutch Alex built?" John asked.

"How could I forget?" laughed Guy. "It was the only place like that. And when we asked him where he got the new sheets of plywood, he never gave a straight answer. Everyone knew something was fishy."

"And then he actually invited his boss over for a cup of tea," chuckled John. "He took one look at Alex's hut and made him dismantle it right on the spot!"

"Now that I'm gone, I'm surprised too, that I lasted so long," said Guy, wiping his forehead with the back of his hand. "A few years ago there was always something to do, someone to talk to."

At its peak, hundreds of travelers lived in the dry rocky valley on the edge of town.

"So where d'you stay now?"

"Right around the corner. I can show you," said Guy. "I lived in this big house with an older Yemenite man, Rachamim, and his family. But after his kids grew up and moved out, Rachamin left too, and now I'm alone."

"Wow, I wonder if he'd be interested in renting it to us," John said, his blue eyes shining. "Things at our house are getting a bit out of hand. I was saying to Judy this morning we need a hostel for all our guests and friends. I trip over people on my way to work, and we've even had one guy sleeping in the kitchen lately. He seems to be always hungry; we hear him opening the fridge all night."

הכנסת אורחים

Having grown up in suburbia, for me life with a one-year-old child in a two bedroom apartment on the third floor felt claustrophobic. Especially with our constant stream of visitors as word of our hospitality spread. Although I enjoyed having people around, I would gladly give up morning lines for the bathroom and backpacks in every corner. A hostel was just what we needed.

2. From Igloos to Palm Trees

"My teacher told us that Jews aren't allowed to have a Christmas tree," I announced. My parents were busy unpacking boxes of ornaments and beginning to decorate our tree. At six years old, I was the oldest of four daughters.

My parents looked at each other and probably wondered what they'd gotten themselves involved in when they recently joined the synagogue. Although they didn't believe in God, being Jewish was a central part of their identity so having decided we needed to strengthen our Jewish roots, they became members of Temple Sinai. Attending religious school on Sunday mornings became part of our weekly schedule, and from then on we switched to celebrating Hanukkah instead of Christmas. A large percentage of our suburban Washington, D.C. neighborhood was Jewish, but to my non-Jewish friends I could boast that we received more presents than they did—on the first as well as the last nights of Hanukkah.

The other holiday I always looked forward to was Passover,

and I loved the yearly Seder meal at our cousins' house. Since they kept a kosher kitchen—separating meat and dairy dishes—they couldn't eat at our home. With the extended family gathered around a long table covered with traditional foods including matzos and sweet wine as well as gefilte fish, roast brisket and my aunt's famous chopped liver, growing up Jewish in America seemed the most natural thing to me.

As I grew older, however, my attitude began to change. "Why do I have to go to religious school anyway?" I argued with my parents. "I don't have any friends in my class, the teachers are boring, and learning to read prayers in Hebrew is a waste of time. At least in school we learn French, which makes more sense."

"Just one more year till your confirmation," my father insisted. "Everyone does that and then it's over." In our Reform synagogue, the confirmation ceremony celebrated our graduation from the Jewish studies program.

However it wasn't just against religious school that I was rebelling. Although outwardly I was still the model student and daughter, I went through times when I felt I had no reason to get out of bed in the morning. I wondered what was the purpose of all this studying, of my existence even. Wasn't there more to life than getting good grades, being accepted into a good university, getting a good job, and a good husband?

In my last year of high school a boy in my class invited me to a Jimi Hendrix concert. I didn't know what to expect, having never been to anything like that before. So I was surprised when on the way to the concert, he stopped the car, and pulling some cigarette papers and an envelope out of his pocket, said, "Let's smoke some of this first. We'll enjoy the concert more."

"I've never smoked before, not even cigarettes," I responded, while thinking that maybe it would help me loosen up and feel better about myself.

"That's okay, there's a first time for everyone," he said, already rolling a joint.

Although I did feel more open afterwards to stepping outside the boundaries my parents and society had set, I continued along the traditional path and began studying in university after I finished high school. Away from home, I met people with many different ideas and lifestyles, continued to smoke marijuana occasionally, and participated in demonstrations against the Vietnam War. Life was more interesting, but I had no idea what I wanted to study or what to make of my life.

המסעות

"Hey, why don't we do something really different this summer?" my boyfriend, Bob, suggested to me near the end of our first year at the University of Pennsylvania. "Let's hitchhike to Alaska."

That sounded like the kind of adventure I was seeking, and since I already had a job at Yellowstone National Park for a month, we decided he would pick me up and we'd continue from there.

Thumbing our way to Alaska over the ALCAN Highway was exactly the kind of experience I craved: empty spaces, rough roads, and friendly people. When we finally pulled into Fairbanks, a frontier town and the gateway to the large interior of Alaska, it was midnight and the sun had just grazed under the horizon. I found it strange to see people reveling and carrying on outside of bars when it was still light outside.

Finding a well-paying summer job was easy; I babysat for the four children of two nightclub dancers, and Bob worked as a firefighter. But we yearned to become acquainted with the "real Alaska" beyond the paved roads, so we took a flight to Kotzebue, an Eskimo town on the Chukchi Sea, above the Arctic Circle. Two ships came in during the summer with yearly supplies for its two-thousand inhabitants and for those from surrounding villages. While strolling along the wharf a couple of days later, we noticed an Eskimo man loading a pile of boxes into a boat, and stopped to watch.

"Hello, I'm Tommy Douglas and I have a store in Ambler, a

village five days upriver from here," he introduced himself. "If you two would help me load my boat, you can come up with me."

"When can we start?" we asked without hesitation. Now life was becoming really interesting.

Once in Ambler, the Eskimos received us warmly, and day by day we had less desire to return to the rat race of our former life at university.

"Many people long to live in a place like this—close to nature and cut off from civilization," I said to Bob as we sat on a blueberry covered knoll behind the village. "No phones, a mail plane twice a week, access only by boat in the summer, and snowmobile or dogsled in the winter."

"Yeah, it's definitely peaceful here—just what we've been looking for. I like that you can travel for days in any direction and never meet anyone," he said.

"So why don't we just stay and write our parents that we aren't coming back?"

Soon after, while walking outside the village on the ridge above the river, we met Oliver who was sitting in front of his house mending a fishing net. We were surprised to see a non-Eskimo, and yet looking at his house built into the side of a hill, his two huskies tied up outside, and his competence with the net, we thought he looked completely at home.

"Have a seat," Oliver said, motioning to two log stumps.

Chatting for a while, we shared our dilemma with him.

"Do you think we could make it through the winter?" we asked.

"Well, I've lived here for years. At first with my wife and children but now they've all gone back to the Lower Forty-Eight except for my daughter," Oliver said. "I could show you how to build a sod igloo like mine. You don't need much money because I can teach you to hunt caribou, to fish in the river with nets, and to trap rabbits and birds. To keep our feet warm in the winter we sew our own mukluks using sealskin for the soles and caribou skins for the uppers."

Bob and I looked at each other, hardly believing that our dream was coming true.

Oliver continued, "Another time I'll tell you how God brought me here. I plan to stay for as long as He tells me." That part sounded strange, but with all of Oliver's offers of help, I didn't let his religious quirks bother me.

Amidst the challenges and busyness of settling into a new environment, the fall passed quickly. We constructed a small pole house and covered it with plastic and sod. We shot and butchered a caribou and made a pile of the whitefish and salmon we'd caught, and froze them outside. We had enough firewood from trees we had felled to keep us warm and for cooking on through the winter. The snow began falling early.

In the winter, when the sun barely skimmed above the distant mountains and we didn't have much work to do, we had a lot of time to read books.

"Check out this book my sister sent me," I said to Bob. "It's written by an American professor who went to India and found a guru in the Himalayas. As soon as the guru met the professor he knew everything about him. It says he could read his thoughts and loved him with a pure love."

"What else does he write?" Bob asked, adding a log to the stove and flipping the sourdough pancakes.

"The professor claims we all have a guru someplace, waiting for us to find him. Makes me want to travel to India."

Oliver saw things differently.

"If you're really searching for the truth and the purpose of life, one day you'll start to believe in Jesus," he told me. Bob and I had braved the forty-below temperatures to press our way through the wind and snow to his house and were sharing with him a meal of dried caribou dipped in seal blubber oil.

"Oh, come on, Oliver," I laughed. "I thought you knew me better by now. I'm Jewish and Jesus is the last one I'll ever believe in."

I felt I could spend the rest of my life in Alaska, yet wanted to see more of the world before settling down. Bob and I also saw our futures differently. So three-and-a-half years after arriving in Fairbanks and with India as my goal, I flew to Portugal and began hitchhiking and working my way across Europe. A year later I reached Greece and took a boat to the island of Crete. Outside of Chania I met some backpackers who invited me to the abandoned house where they squatted.

"We don't have electricity or running water, but you can find grapes, figs, and cactus fruits nearby and find work in the vineyard," one of the guys told me. "Stay for a while. India will wait."

I had already tried living with a group of travelers, as we liked to call ourselves, distinct from tourists—those people who spent a lot of money to fly around the world, taking pictures and never getting involved with the locals—in a cave in Morocco, and on the Canary Islands. I believed that if we all had a non-materialistic and non-possessive attitude, a bunch of young people from different countries should be able to get along sharing their possessions and their lives. Yet why didn't it ever seem to work? Why were there so many divisions, arguments, and bickering about nothing? I hoped to find answers in India.

My parents flew over to meet me in Athens and we toured for a week around the Peloponnese Peninsula. They suggested I stop in Israel before making the long overland trip to India. I hadn't considered this before, but with distant relatives there and having heard from other backpackers about working on a kibbutz, I was quickly persuaded.

וַיְקַהֵל

Once planes began flying to Israel again following the Yom Kippur War, I landed in Ben Gurion Airport in Tel Aviv in October 1973. I could sense I was in a land where a conflict had barely ended. So many men as well as women, looking tan and healthy, were walking around in army uniforms with guns slung over their shoulders. Although buses weren't running regularly yet, that was no problem because hitchhiking was an acceptable means of transport in Israel, apparently not just in war time either. I joined the dozens at road junctions, stuck out my hand, and headed to Beer Tuvia, the moshav where my relatives lived.

My mother's first cousins, Aviva, Ben Ami, and Hannah, welcomed me warmly into their large, multigenerational family, and I had plenty of work to do on the farm with many men still away in the army. When I wasn't collecting eggs from their hens or picking up the pecans that fell after the mechanized tree shakers swept through, I helped Aviva in the kitchen. She had a gift of preparing food and making everyone who came to her door feel like a welcome and honored guest.

I loved Israel from the beginning—life was less rushed than in the U.S., and people were warm and took time for each other. I had accumulated stamps from many countries in my passport, but surprisingly, here I felt at home. Being in a country where nearly everyone was Jewish was a novel experience, though I felt embarrassed in front of my family by my complete lack of Scriptural knowledge. I learned in Israel that all children study the Bible in school beginning in the second grade; it's their history and literature book combined. I resolved to get ahold of a copy.

After two months on the moshav I wanted to see more of the country. Besides, winter was coming and as travelers we always migrated toward the warmth. I ended up in Nueiba, an oasis in the Sinai Peninsula which was part of Israel in those days. The wide open spaces and sparse population of the Sinai somehow reminded me of Alaska.

I felt I had come upon a desert paradise—palm trees scattered about in the white sand, rolling dunes, and transparent blue water with colorful coral reefs and fancifully shaped fish. The original Bedouin inhabitants added to the exotic picture—the men in ankle-length *jalabiyas* and white *keffiyehs* on their heads, women in heavy dark clothes and veils, and cute olive-skinned children with black eyes. A number of Israeli families had begun Moshav

Neviot, supporting themselves with a guest house and melon fields, and in the past few years travelers like me started moving in and camping.

Yet, within a few days I was feeling that even paradise can be boring if you're alone. Leaning against a palm tree and gazing over the Red Sea toward Saudi Arabia, I was trying to decide whether to stay longer or to leave. All options, too many, were open to me—back to the moshav, try Jerusalem, continue to India, or … something else?

I suddenly heard a voice and looked up to see a guy with sparkling eyes, a tanned leathery face, and a turban wrapped around his long hair.

"Parlez-vous Francais?" He sat down beside me. *"Je m'appelle Jacques."*

"Oui, un peu," I answered in French, waving flies away from my face. "I studied it in school and spent two months in Morocco. Where've you been to?"

"Africa," Jacques replied. "I spent a couple of years with the Pygmies and last year in Djibouti, on the Indian Ocean. I left my old life behind in Paris after I started to believe in Jesus Christ. Now I let Him lead me."

"Cool." Jacques had obviously been on the road for a while. He sounded weird with the Jesus stuff, but at least he was someone to talk to.

"Where d'you stay?" he asked.

"No place special, just hanging out. Thinking of moving on."

"Why don't you come and stay with me and my friends in our camp under the palm trees?" Jacques pointed to a distant clump of green fronds poking the sky.

Instinctively I knew I could trust Jacques, although his way of speaking was different than other travelers. And I soon realized that not only his words, but his behavior was different, nothing like that cave in Morocco and the house in Crete where we supposedly lived together in harmony but where tension ran beneath the surface. Jacques, by contrast, shared everything he owned.

During the day, he sat in the sun to make room for others in the shade, and in the evening around the campfire, he took the place in the smoke so that we didn't have to sit there.

Many folks found their way to Jacques's camp for different reasons. They certainly weren't there for luxurious accommodation because all he offered was a windbreak made of old sheets and palm branches, a few blankets spread over the sand, and a fire pit in the middle. Rather than a five-star rating you got a thousand stars because due to the absence of rain Jacques hadn't bothered constructing a roof.

When a guy named Dave showed up one day as we were sitting down to eat, Jacques immediately invited him to join us around our common pot. Dave told us that he had no money and asked if he might stay with us till he got things sorted out. Whereas most people contributed something towards the food expenses, obviously we couldn't expect anything from Dave.

Thus he surprised us some days later when he burst into our hut. "All my money's been stolen!" Dave exclaimed.

What money?

That was the day Jacques asked him to leave.

As Jacques continued on in a quiet way talking about Jesus, my desire to read the Bible grew stronger. But Jacques only had a copy in French.

I decided to go up to Jerusalem for a few days, thinking I'd surely find a Bible there. Moreover it was Christmas, and I had heard that Bethlehem was a popular gathering place for travelers. Arriving on Christmas Eve after hitchhiking up with Jacques, I joined the hundreds of young people milling among the local Arabs, Christian tourists, and foreign choirs. I sensed electricity in the air, or maybe it was just me and my expectation that something new was happening in my life.

I'd never given much thought to Jesus as an historical figure before. To me He was more of a legend, a Santa Claus figure, someone about whom people wrote songs and painted paintings. I felt excited to be in the place where Jesus was born one thousand nine hundred and seventy three years ago. For the first time in my life I had no doubt that Jesus had existed.

The next day, while walking around the Old City, we happened to meet Steve, a guy we knew from Nueiba. "What's happening?" I asked. "Where've you been?"

"I'm living here in Jerusalem now. Started reading the Bible."

"Any idea where I could find one?" I asked. "I've also been wanting to read it."

Steve told us about a place on the Mount of Olives where they gave them out for free.

We climbed up the steep narrow road flanked by high stone walls, and behind them ancient olive trees, tall straight cypresses, and numerous churches, and easily found the house Dave had described. A few hours later, my new Bible tucked in my backpack, Jacques and I were on our way back to Nueiba, having taken a bus to the outskirts of Jerusalem.

Outside of Bethlehem a few minutes after I stretched out my hand to hitchhike, an Arab driver stopped his van for us and a short distance farther on picked up two more hitchhikers.

"Where're you headed?" I asked as I slid over on the bench.

"Eilat," replied the guy who was obviously the spokesman. He had long blond hair, a reddish beard, cutoff jeans, and sandals held together by pieces of wire.

"We're working on the Moses movie in Eilat, but we were filming in Jericho for a few days," he said. In those days, many movies with biblical and Western themes were made in Eilat. "Here. Take this folder about the Bible, how to find a new life. I started to believe in Jesus last year."

"Amazing!" I told him. "I just got a Bible today and plan to read it when I get back to Nueiba."

"I'm John," he said. "When we have time off, I'll come down to Nueiba to visit you guys."

Back in Jacques's camp on the beach, I began reading my Bible, and I couldn't stop. I began reading Genesis—but the New Testament particularly interested me, because it had always been forbidden. So I quickly jumped to reading the Gospel of Matthew concurrently.

Right away I loved the way Jesus related to all kinds of people and how he always had the perfect answer for everyone. I couldn't understand why our people didn't believe in Him who was so good and kind. I began to realize, though, that it was the religious leaders of his day who opposed Jesus whereas the common people followed Him readily. I imagined He would have felt more at home in our camp under the palm trees than among the Pharisees in Jerusalem.

Day by day I was simply falling in love with Jesus. As a Jew, even a non-practicing one, the decision to follow Jesus wasn't easy. Many thoughts swirled through my head. What about my heritage? What will my parents think? And what about any future children? Would they still be Jewish? I thought that I would be the first Jew since the apostles to believe.

For years I had been searching for meaning in my life and wondering where I would find love. Now I realized that Jesus shows the character of God. In Him I saw goodness and love expressed in forgiveness, healing, compassion, and blessing.

I couldn't deny what I'd been reading and feeling. I understood now that though "many roads lead to Rome," not all ways lead to the truth. I read that Jesus Himself said, "I am the way, the truth and the life, and no man comes to the Father but through Me." In Jesus I had found the answer to my questions and my spiritual search. Although I was just at the beginning of my new journey and had no idea where it would take me, I knew I could trust in Jesus. Without any effort on my part, gradually old habits and lifestyles began falling away.

הפסוק

Back in Jerusalem six months later I met an older couple, Rina and Clifford, who invited young people to their apartment for Bible studies. There I found I wasn't alone—other Jews also believed in Jesus.

When Rina asked if I wanted to stay and help them, I gladly accepted although at first I couldn't figure them out. At retirement age, Rina and Clifford opened their house and lives to all who came by and didn't build boundaries around their personal lives as most people did. I asked myself if I could live like them when I reached their age and be so giving and accessible.

Rina told me about a young Dutchman who had been with them the previous fall, who after working in the Moses movie all winter in Eilat, would be coming back soon to Jerusalem. Maybe this was the guy I had met while hitchhiking?

A few days later I answered a knock on the door.

"Hi! Come in." I had been expecting him.

John just stared.

"Don't you remember? We met hitchhiking last Christmas."

John took off his small backpack as I went to bring him a glass of water. "I can't believe it," he said. "How'd you get here?"

I could tell he was thinking about how different I looked without my old Bedouin dress, my hair brushed, and wearing normal clothes.

I smiled. "A lot's changed. Sit down, drink, and I'll tell you about it."

John's arrival was like that of a son coming home for Rina and Clifford. With him there, everything seemed to go more smoothly. Life was exciting, and his enthusiasm was catching. Every place John went, whether shopping in West Jerusalem supermarkets, the Old City souk, or just walking around, he easily got into conversations about his faith and invited people over to Rina and Clifford's. I liked going around with him, and gradually our relationship began to shift as we found ourselves falling in love.

Eilat, Red sea.

3. The Blond Dutchman
(Go to Israel and Do Something Useful)

Like a magnet, John had felt the pull of the sea from a young age. Growing up in Noordwijk, a small town on the coast of Holland, and gazing over the turbulent, gray ocean gave John the desire to travel and experience what lay beyond the horizon. School never interested him particularly; he much preferred wandering around in the wide swath of sand dunes that protected his village from the North Sea.

During World War II, the Germans had built bunkers to defend conquered Holland from an Allied invasion. Although their parents warned them of the dangers, John and his friends liked to search the underground tunnels for old weapons and other military gear. At age twelve when all Dutch children were expected to decide what they wanted to be when they grew up and be placed in the appropriate high school, John had no idea what he wanted to do. Looking back, he wonders how a boy only twelve years old could be expected to choose his future.

In those days before backpacking was popular, John

concluded that the best way to travel would be to study cooking in a technical high school and then sign on with the Merchant Marine. He quickly understood that learning about wines and gourmet cooking wasn't for him, but he enjoyed studying languages. English, German, and French were all required subjects in addition to Dutch, and these came easily to John.

So, following his graduation at the age of eighteen, John sailed out of the Amsterdam harbor on the Oranjefontein, a half-passenger, half-cargo ship, on his way to South Africa. The excitement of crossing the equator for the first time more than made up for his violent attack of seasickness on the third day in the Gulf of Biscay. The ship's crew included men from many different countries, and John loved getting to know them and learning words in different languages: Portuguese from the Africans of the Cape Verde Islands, Spanish from the Atlantic coast Spaniards, and Chinese from the laundrymen. The Indonesians taught him to prepare their national food, *nasi goreng*, fried rice. Little did John know that *nasi* would become his specialty, the trademark dish he cooks for every special occasion.

In his two years at sea, John called in at ports in the Canary Islands, South Africa, Mozambique, the Caribbean Islands, Venezuela, and New York. Sometimes when the ship had several days in port, and the kitchen wasn't responsible for preparing food, John set out exploring, seeking contacts with local people.

In Lorenzo Markus, Mozambique, he took the ferry across the river and quickly found himself in the jungle. People in the small African villages gathered around the tall blond stranger with the friendly smile who readily traded his jeans for drums or just gave his clothes away.

In Caracas, Venezuela, John wandered around the slum areas that crept up the hills of the city. The contrast between the poor children wearing rags and the rich Americans on his ship who lived from one extravagant meal to the next, disturbed him. More and more, John was feeling the urge to do something to combat the injustice he saw in the world.

On board the Randfontein, John became friendly with Alex, the chief cook. A Jew from Amsterdam, Alex took a liking to his young helper.

"This life is nothing for you, John. There's no future here," he said, pouring himself a cup of tea from the pot that always sat on his work counter. Later John discovered that Alex's teapot was filled with sherry. "Go to Israel, to a kibbutz where young people from all over the world work together and do something useful." On one of Alex's voyages he had stopped in Israel but never saw more than the port city of Haifa.

John, nineteen years old at the time, didn't forget those words.

ט י ק פ ו ט

After two years in the Merchant Marine and two years in the Royal Dutch Marine Corps, John had enough of discipline and longed to be free, or at least what he thought was freedom. He returned to Noordwijk, but didn't plan to remain home for long.

"What do you think?" John asked his friend Paul. "I've gotta get out of here. Holland's not for me. We'll end up just like our parents., leading boring, materialistic lives." John saw all his friends marrying girls they met in discothèques and settling down in the village.

Paul nodded. "Even living on a houseboat in Amsterdam didn't work; all we got out of that was fleas."

"I want to go to Israel," said John. "I read *Exodus* by Leon Uris, and I hear you can always work as a kibbutz volunteer. "

"My friend drives a truck with fish to Marseilles every week," said Paul. "If he'd be willing to take us along, we could probably get a cheap boat from there to Israel."

And so in January of 1970 John and Paul arrived in Haifa on board the Delphi, an old Greek ship, via stops in Italy, Greece, and Cyprus. Docking in Haifa, they expected a warm, sunny climate but encountered the opposite—cold and rainy. Some girls they met on the boat told them they'd find better weather down south.

Heading to the Negev, they arrived in Kibbutz Hatzerim near Beersheba, and John found it to be everything Alex had described and more. John enjoyed the kibbutz life. After a few months he decided he wanted to learn Hebrew and stay for the rest of his life. In the hard physical labor of driving a tractor in the wheat fields of the Negev Desert, he finally found work that suited him.

Getting into the spirit of Israel, where history and the Bible are a national passion, John even fancied himself an amateur archaeologist. Another volunteer, Eli Brown, was also interested in archaeology and on Shabbat, their day off, he would escape to the adjacent desert. Borrowing a few shovels, he convinced John and Paul to join him. They would hike to an open area where Eli pointed out to John and Paul where to dig. John's new hobby didn't last long, however, because after some weeks he grew tired of being Eli's drudge and found other ways to spend Shabbat.

Fifteen years later, when driving through the Galilee, John would pass by an archaeological site he hadn't visited before and stop to look around. To his surprise, the head of the dig was his old friend Eli Brown. After finishing his doctorate in archaeology Eli had become a department head at the Rockefeller Museum in Jerusalem.

In the kibbutz, John thought he had found what he had been looking for: happiness, equality, and friendship. Nevertheless, after two years, John understood that a man's nature is the same in whatever type of community he lives. While in the kibbutz they claimed that everyone was equal, John could see that some people were clearly "more equal" than others.

Disappointed and disillusioned, John left the kibbutz and traveled farther south to Eilat, which had the reputation of being the end of the world or of a Wild West town. Eilat was settled by Israeli pioneers in the early 1950s, people who weren't afraid to live in a place where there was no air conditioning while the summer temperatures soared to 45 degrees Celsius (120 degrees Fahrenheit) and where water was delivered by truck from house to house. City planning was obviously never a priority in Eilat, and the town appeared to have grown up haphazardly on the barren brown hills which stretched down to the Gulf of Eilat, otherwise known as the Gulf of Aqaba.

An air of "live and let live" still prevailed, and John joined a group of hippies living in tents and shacks near the beach. He readily found casual work in Eilat. In the evenings around the campfire he spoke with his friends about different philosophies and religions. A number of them had been in India and had "seen the light." John, who had always wanted to go to Australia, decided to go overland via India where maybe he too would find answers to his questions.

John never forgot his conversation one night around the campfire with Howard, an older hippie who had been a professor in New York before he began to travel.

"John," he said, gripping John's shoulder and staring into his eyes, "Who am I? Tell me!" Stoned as usual, Howard apparently had smoked too much.

If Howard didn't know who he was, John wondered, how was he supposed to tell him?

On the day before Christmas in 1972, John hitchhiked from Eilat to Jerusalem. Leaving the sun behind, he became completely soaked in Jerusalem's pouring rain, and though he had always liked meandering the narrow streets and bazaars of the Old City, he suddenly wished he was still swimming in the Red Sea.

He remembered an Arab bakery near the Jaffa Gate where hippies liked to congregate. Opening the heavy wooden door and stepping down the stone steps, greeted by the smell of yeast bread and burning wood, John ducked inside the warm, vaulted space. While ordering egg pitas and the bakery's famous *za'atar*, a condiment made from dried herbs, salt, and sesame seeds, in the semi-darkness he spotted Danny, an American he knew from Eilat.

Danny greeted John with a wide smile on his face and light in his eyes. "Great running into you here. Guess what? I found it!"

"What'd you find?" John pulled up a stool and warmed his hands on a glass of sweet mint tea. He figured Danny must have found a better kind of hashish.

"I found Jesus." Danny pulled a Bible out of his backpack and opened it. "After all these years of traveling and reading different books I discovered the answer right here."

"If it makes you happy, then why not?"

"It's not like that. In the Bible it says that Jesus is the only way, the truth, and the life. Look what's written here: '*Seek first the kingdom of God and His righteousness and all these things will be added to you as well. Therefore do not worry about tomorrow, for tomorrow will worry about itself.*'"

"That's written in the Bible? I've been trying for years not to worry about the future, but it never works."

"I've got an extra Bible," Danny offered. "It's an old English translation, but it's yours if you want."

At the age of twenty-five John held a Bible for the first time. Reading it opened up a new world for him. His old friends in Holland thought he led an exciting life, doing whatever he wanted whenever he wanted, but to John life had become dull and even depressing. Now he began to feel a joy he had never experienced. He chose to follow Jesus and to get to know Him. As those around him saw the drastic change in his life, John shared with them what he had found.

הפסקה

The following summer, John went back to Holland, convinced his family and friends would be excited to hear the good news he had discovered in Israel. Most, however, thought he was on another of his "trips" and would soon get over it.

"I'm embarrassed when the neighbors see you always reading the Bible in our back yard," his mother told him. "Why don't you become a priest, and then it would be normal?"

A good Catholic never reads the Bible was the unspoken law in John's family.

Frustrated by their lack of interest, John returned to Israel, and soon after his arrival the Yom Kippur War broke out. Even as he heard fighter jets screaming in the skies above him, he had perfect peace, knowing that God had a plan for his life. He visited his former kibbutz, as well as hospitals where friends lay wounded, comforting them with the hope he'd found in Jesus. He loved to open the Bible and point out the verse, "You shall know the truth and the truth shall set you free."

John felt more at home in Israel than in Holland. Everything about it suited him—the people, culture, climate, and landscape. He liked the fact that it was a new country, not built up like Holland, and the possibilities seemed to be wide open. He knew, however, that as a non-Jew he would have trouble staying there permanently.

He prayed for God to bring him a Jewish wife, a believer like himself, so that they could immigrate together.

4. The House on Poor House Lane

"Why do you want to go to the United States?" the visa officer asked John.

"My girlfriend is waiting for me there," John answered, "and we plan to get married." He was sitting in the American Embassy in Amsterdam.

"In that case, I can't give you a tourist visa," the clerk announced. "You have to apply for a fiancé visa, but that takes months to receive. We're on the lookout for men who slip into our country on a tourist visa, marry American women, and after they receive their green card, quickly get divorced."

"That's not my idea at all. Judy and I met in Israel where we both also started to read the Bible and to believe in Jesus. I don't believe in doing anything dishonest."

"I'm a Christian myself," said the clerk, "so I'll give you some advice. Coming from Noordwijk, you don't belong to our embassy in Amsterdam, but to the office in Rotterdam. Go there and ask them for a tourist visa."

הַמִּדְרָשׁ

On December 31, 1974, I had flown back to the U.S., which I had left two years previously. Staying with my parents while working at a temporary job in a bank, I could tell my parents felt sorry for me because none of my high school friends had stayed around. They urged me to go out to places where young people congregated, but I wasn't interested. I worked, came home, read my Bible, and wrote letters to John.

While my parents couldn't deny that I was happier and more at peace than I'd been in years, they weren't pleased about my newfound faith in Jesus. After some phone calls and letters to friends, they decided I should talk to two people: the rabbi and a psychiatrist. I readily agreed to see our rabbi, figuring that having chosen this profession, he was obviously interested in the Bible and spiritual things, and therefore I could easily convince him from the Scriptures that Jesus was the Messiah. We had a friendly meeting but neither of us was persuaded to change viewpoints.

"I'm not going to the psychiatrist, though," I told my parents. "I'm not crazy."

Three months after I arrived home, John flew over, having successfully procured a two-week tourist visa. Since we didn't have any Christian friends in the area, we got married in the Rockville, Maryland courthouse with my parents and our house-keeper as witnesses. My mother had helped me pick out an apricot-colored dress in the nearby department store, and John had bought me a small bunch of flowers from a florist shop. The marriage license cost twelve dollars and fifty cents.

For twenty-five dollars we bought two simple gold wedding rings at a pawnshop in downtown Washington. The design was of secondary importance; but we made sure they weren't engraved with anyone else's name. The pawnbroker offered to upgrade them when our financial situation improved. After the wedding my cousin invited us to a Chinese restaurant. Young, in love with each other and with the Lord, we couldn't have been happier if we had married at the White House.

"Where do you think we should live?" John asked me after our wedding. "Which direction do you want to start out in?" My parents had surprised us with a wedding present of a little Toyota pick-up truck after they heard we were planning on hitchhiking.

"It's hard to say," I answered. Not counting my three years in Alaska, I hadn't lived in the U.S. for six years.

"Why don't we drive around and visit friends and see where we end up, which place looks like we could fit in and do something for the Lord?" John suggested.

"We could start off by going to Pennsylvania to visit that guy we met in Jerusalem," I said. "He says he lives in some kind of community with believers up there. From there we could drive over to Iowa City where my sister Amy lives. Sounds like a neat place, a university town."

"If we sleep with friends and in the back of our truck, it won't cost us much and when our money runs out we'll get jobs." John was thinking aloud. "I can do any kind of work, as long as it's not cooking. I've had enough of that."

"My sister Jane asked if she could ride along with us to Amy's house," I told John.

John readily agreed, never being one to turn someone down who needs a ride. "I know that most people wouldn't take their sister on their honeymoon, but if you don't mind, neither do I."

On the drive through Pennsylvania, we picked up an older man with shabby clothes who was hitchhiking. Having traveled that way ourselves for years, we couldn't pass him by; with only room for three of us in the front of our truck, he sat in the little cabin in the back. Every time we turned around, he was eating an apple from the crate we had just bought.

Neither Pennsylvania nor Iowa suited us, and we enjoyed being on the road. We knew someone in Miami so we headed south, thinking that Florida might remind us of Israel, but Miami was just another big city. Enoch, a friend from Israel, wrote us that he was going to be in Key West and suggested we meet there. A highway crossing over a series of bridges connects the mainland with Key West, the most southern spot in the U.S. and closer to Havana than to Miami.

Maybe it was the palm trees with coconuts falling onto the sidewalks, or the bikes and old houses, or the Sunset Pier where people gathered every evening to watch the sun go down; or maybe it was the fact that our money was nearly finished; but in Key West we finally found a place where we felt at home. We moved into a pleasant studio apartment—the first time either of us had ever paid rent.

After a month John said, "Jupe"—his nickname for me—"we've got to find someplace else. This seemed like a good deal when we rented it, but it's too small with all these other folks staying here." We were sitting on our front steps playing with Joshua, the one-year-old baby of our neighbors.

"Yeah," I agreed. "When we invite people over for Bible studies in the evening, I don't have the heart to tell them to leave." Many transients and free spirits arrived in Key West with no money and no place to stay. The police, however, seemed to know every comfortable and sheltering bush in town and then picked them up for loitering.

"On my way home from work today I saw a place for rent on Poor House Lane near the cemetery," John said. "There are just a few houses on the street but it's got a real mixture of people: black Bahamians, Cubans, and a guy with long hair named Lloyd lives upstairs. Plus there's a big yard with banana and papaya trees."

"Wow, sounds great! Could you tell how many bedrooms it has?"

"I looked in the window and could see two bedrooms, and though they don't have doors, it would be a whole lot better than what we have now."

Unlike me, John never worried; and problems seemed to get

sorted out quickly with him. We moved in a few days later, hanging sheets in the doorways.

We nailed a sign on our front porch saying, "Welcome! Bible Discussions" and it didn't take long for people to find us. The winter is the big season in Key West when "snowbirds" from northeastern U.S. and Canada flock south. In those days, among the snowbirds came hippies and travelers. Besides sleeping under bushes, some camped on the mosquito-infested nearby islands and scrounged around for food, while others worked in hotels, restaurants, and shops. In any case, being from out-of-town, they were happy to be invited to a home.

The meeting place for everyone was Mallory Square, or Sunset Pier. Jugglers, acrobats, the Iguana Man, fortune tellers, locals, and tourists broke into clapping each evening when the huge, orange sun disappeared into the ocean. We became part of the scene, giving out pamphlets, telling of our faith, and inviting people to our home for a meal and Bible study.

Finding work in Key West wasn't difficult. John began working at a dry dock, repairing a yacht, which led to a job as a carpenter's helper in an old wooden house. I worked as a waitress and then as a dental assistant, but after several months we felt I could best stay home and deal with all our guests.

Although I had never cooked much before, I found this to be a great learning opportunity. Everyone was hungry; some hadn't eaten a proper meal for days, and so they weren't picky. After dinner, John gave a Bible study about why we believed in Jesus and how to become His follower. The fact that he had no formal training didn't hinder John at all. The main thing was to share with others the exciting news we had found ourselves. If someone didn't have a place to stay, we invited them to stay with us. When the house was full, they could sleep under the banana trees. We felt like one big family.

Life was never dull; every day brought surprises. John walked into the bathroom one morning and a young man wrapped in a sort of sheet, who had showed up the previous night, looked down at the floor and tucked his hand into a fold in his covering.

"I just can't do it," he said. "I can't get rid of my toothbrush."

We discovered that he belonged to a strange cult who lived together in an avocado grove south of Miami.

"We have three commandments: no sex, no possessions, and no lying," he explained to John. "I'm okay with them all—except for my toothbrush."

John patted him on the shoulder and told him it was fine, he could brush his teeth. "Jesus came to set us free."

I would have been happy to stay in Key West forever. "We've got everything we want and need here," I said to John. "The easy-going lifestyle suits us. We're always meeting new people and have seen lives changed, even hard-core addicts. I didn't expect we'd become a marriage bureau, but that's been neat too. I'm so happy for Ciastko and Sessie."

I never imagined when I met Ciastko in Fairbanks that he would show up in Jerusalem, meet John and me there, begin to believe in Jesus, then meet Sessie, a young woman from New Jersey, in our home in Key West, and marry her.

"You know I always felt we'd go back to Israel and I never planned to stay in America," John reminded me. "That's what I told the official at the American embassy in Rotterdam, and I meant it. Everyone who wants, can get a Bible here."

I knew John was right, both about his planning on returning to Israel and that in Israel most people had never heard of Jesus or that you could be Jewish and believe in Jesus as the Messiah. So when Bob, a guy who had recently become a believer with us, offered to stay in our house and continue preparing meals and Bible studies, we knew it was time to go. We departed as we had come—in our Toyota pickup truck with a few possessions in the back. The rest of what we had accumulated, we left for Bob. We were on the road again, heading towards Israel.

5. Down the Gangplank

"It feels strange that we've been married a year and a half and I haven't met your parents," I said to John as we flew across the Atlantic.

"Don't worry. I told them about you when I was in Holland on the way to get married. They're not complicated, and I'm sure you'll get along." John rarely saw anything as a problem.

"At least I met your sister, Netty, when she came to visit us in Key West," I said. Maybe it would be okay after all.

"That was nice of Mom and Dad to let us paint their house and to pay us," I continued.

"Also your grandmother doing the same thing in Rhode Island," added John.

With the payment from both painting jobs we bought cheap tickets with Icelandic Airlines and shipped our Toyota from New York to Rotterdam.

After landing in Luxembourg, John began to teach me a few key Dutch phrases on the train to Leiden. I wanted to make a good impression on my new family, but I needn't have worried; they accepted me easily and warmly. The Dutch have a reputation of being open-minded, and I felt that I'd married into a particularly tolerant family. We moved into their attic and John began introducing me to his old friends and neighbors.

Although we didn't plan on staying in Holland, we didn't know how long the bureaucratic process of getting to Israel would take. Neither of us could envision ourselves in the straight, organized Dutch lifestyle, but in the meantime I spent time every day learning John's language and his culture.

Since I am Jewish, we had the possibility of going back to Israel as new immigrants, but we had both been moving around so much in the past years that we couldn't imagine putting down permanent roots. On the other hand, as immigrants we wouldn't have to get our visas renewed; we'd be able to legally work, and would get help in renting or buying an apartment. We went to the Jewish Agency in Amsterdam for information. The interview went well and the clerk assured us we would hear from them soon, yet doubts ran through my mind.

"We have to pray they accept our application," I said as we stepped out onto one of Amsterdam's busy streets. "They seemed friendly, but what if they find out about our past run-ins with the police in Israel?"

"Sure, they were friendly," John agreed. "How many people do you think they get here who want to immigrate? The Nazis killed ninety percent of Holland's Jews and of those who survived, most who wanted to go to Israel have left already."

"But what if it's written someplace that you were picked up by the police for giving out tracts at the Cave of the Machpela in Hebron?" I asked. "That's nearly as bad as the Wailing Wall."

"They picked me up there, too," John reminded me, ever optimistic. "But both times they let me go."

"Yeah, but my case is worse. You know the story." The police raided our camp in the middle of one night in Nueiba and found a hash pipe. I was taken to Eilat and when questioned if I ever smoked hashish, I admitted I had. Having begun to read the Bible, I believed I should tell the truth. I was sentenced to three months in jail, but when I appealed on the basis that I hadn't had a fair trial, the judge declared my case annulled. Yet, I feared the record might remain.

"Well, I've wanted to go back to Israel since the day I left," John said, "but at this point all we can do is trust God. And anyway, if Israel doesn't work out there's always Africa."

Africa? Moving to Israel was already a big step for me. "I'll admit I was used to living in America and it's hard for me to leave my family," I said. "But when we filled in those forms and they asked where we wanted to live and we wrote 'Eilat,' I really could picture us there again!"

Six weeks later we had our answer: we were accepted as new immigrants and an apartment was waiting for us in Eilat. The secretary at the Jewish Agency asked if she should order plane tickets for us, but we told her we'd be driving our Toyota pickup. She neglected to tell us that at that time there were no Toyotas in Israel due to the Arab boycott, an effort by Arab states to harm Israel's economy by refusing to do business with companies that traded with Israel. In fact, there were no Japanese cars there at all, and our Toyota became one of the first ones. Wherever we drove in Israel, people waved and honked as they recognized our red Toyota with the white cabin on the back.

After celebrating John's father's birthday in November and the Dutch holiday of *Sinterklaas* in the beginning of December, we were off. The drive to Athens took less than a week via Germany, Switzerland, Italy, and Yugoslavia. In Piraeus, the port of Athens, we boarded a car ferry to Haifa. We had hoped to sleep on deck, the cheapest way to travel, but in the winter they didn't sell those tickets, so I slept in a cabin with other women and John with other men.

Three days later we stood on the deck of the ship as we came into Haifa Bay, gazing at the city's white buildings edging up the slopes of Mount Carmel.

"Reminds me of the first time I docked here with Paul in 1970 on that crummy old ship, the Delphi. I heard it sank on the following voyage," said John. "We just have to pray they don't refuse us now, even though the Jewish Agency in Amsterdam approved our request. You never know." He didn't sound too worried.

We were home.

We drove off the gangplank in our Toyota and at passport control went straight to the line for new immigrants. There on the spot we received our Israeli identity cards as well as a letter to the housing authority in Eilat.

"Here you are!" Haim proudly announced, stepping over the threshold. Arriving in Eilat, we went immediately to the housing authority, and Haim took us to our assigned apartment. "One of the newest and best locations in Eilat. There are forty apartments in the building and you're among the first to move in."

"Wonderful!" John exclaimed with his usual enthusiasm. "Can you believe it, Jupe? Our own apartment!"

I didn't want to seem unappreciative, but I wasn't used to living on the third floor, up in the air and disconnected from the earth. At least from the bedrooms we had a partial view of the sea. Nobody asked me where I wanted to live. There wasn't even a balcony to step out on to feel the weather.

Soon we were left alone—new immigrants in our new apartment in our new hometown of Eilat. The few belongings we brought from Key West, mostly wedding presents from my parents' friends, together with some things we picked up in Holland, looked out-of-place, like seeing an old friend from one period in your life suddenly appear in a different time and place. They didn't look like much when we spread them around our apartment, because how much stuff can you put in the back of a small pick-up truck and still leave room to sleep? As for appliances, we had no refrigerator, stove, or washing machine, so after moving in, we went out to get something to eat.

I walked down Eilat's main street as if in a dream. How many years had passed? Was it only two? When I left Israel I was single; I came back married. I left as a tourist; I returned as a citizen.

We happened to meet Simon, a friend of John's with whom he had worked in the Moses movie. Simon was happy to see us and we him, all the more when he excitedly told us he was on his way to his brother's wedding and he'd like to invite us. Although we didn't exactly have our wedding clothes on, Eilat back then was very casual. That solved our problem about what to eat, because Israeli weddings are known for huge quantities of food.

The following day we went back to Haim. As new immigrants, we received two metal-framed beds, two mattresses, a table, two chairs, and a couple of plates. On the floor of our living room we spread out the red Persian carpet we had found in John's parents' attic. The mattresses served as sofas. We liked the idea of sitting on the floor, because then we wouldn't be short of seating for the many visitors we expected. Buying a stove and refrigerator were our top priority, but after purchasing them we realized the washing machine would have to wait until we had more money. Anyway, with just the two of us, I could wash by hand.

Eilat being a small town with only twenty-thousand inhabitants at the time, in days to come we met many old friends. I was encouraged, but not surprised, to see how many people John knew and how glad they all were to see him. But who would be my friends?

Being acquainted with Eilat made it easy for John to find employment, especially because he was ready to do anything. After being a kibbutz volunteer John had worked in Eilat to buy a ticket home and had held all kinds of jobs: mixing cement, cleaning the hold of a ship, toiling in the Timna copper mines, working in a fruit and vegetable store, and building roads. The Peace Café served as Eilat's labor exchange where contractors and anyone who needed laborers could find willing workers. Now back in Eilat, John joined the scene and soon had a number of steady jobs.

For me it was different; I first needed to learn Hebrew. I found it ironic that John, the non-Jew in our family, spoke Hebrew and I knew little. John's Hebrew, picked up in an *ulpan* (a Hebrew language school) on the kibbutz, had proved useful when clearing all the red tape and bureaucracy as new immigrants.

I signed up for evening classes in Eilat. "I'm so happy I could start ulpan right away," I reported to John after the first session. "I hate being in a country where I can't speak the language. I'm also meeting lots of nice people and making friends. We're all in the same boat."

"Soon you'll be speaking better than me!" John laughed.

"Good news," I announced a few weeks after arriving in Eilat. "We're expecting a baby!"

"Wow, God answers prayers!" John exclaimed. "We'll have a little *sabra* [a native-born Israeli]."

"I've already decided that I'll speak to him or her in English; I don't want him to hear his mother stuttering in broken Hebrew. But I'll need to learn Hebrew well enough to speak to his friends and to help him in school." In those days we didn't meet people speaking to children in languages other than Hebrew, unlike years later when it not only became acceptable but was seen as an advantage. But I also wanted my children to be able to communicate with their family in America.

I began dreaming of a little blond sabra who looked like John.

6. Melon Box Crib & Sandstorm Solutions

"I miss Nueiba," I said to John after we'd been back in Eilat for a month. "I wonder if it's still the same."

We were sitting in our usual spot on the beach after John came home from his job unloading crates at a vegetable store. Although later, after living in Eilat for years and getting used to the hot summers, I found January too cold for swimming, having just come from abroad I enjoyed our daily swim.

"I miss it too," John agreed. "I can easily take a couple of days off work, so what if we go down this weekend? It won't bother you, being pregnant?" John was always ready to pick up and go.

"I feel great. Anyway, an hour's drive is nothing."

In Nueiba we found the atmosphere hadn't changed in the two years we'd been gone. Lots of young people, Israelis as well as foreign travelers, were living on the beach in tents and improvised huts. We even ran into old friends.

Israel was popular in those days. Thousands of young people came every year to volunteer on kibbutzim, and many of them eventually made their way down to Nueiba. Easier to get to and much closer than India, the Sinai beaches had everything a backpacker could want: sun, dunes, coral reefs, other travelers, and Bedouins.

"Wow, a weekend was too short," I told John after we returned home and were unpacking the leftover food—half bags of rice, sugar, coffee, tea and more. "Now I remember why we liked it there so much." I had good memories of starting to read the Bible in Nueiba and of the time John and I had spent there together.

"I can't believe how open people were to hearing about the Bible," John said, holding the sheets and blankets out of the window and shaking the sand out. "We had more good talks there in one weekend than we have here in a month."

"I felt fine there," I said, "and it isn't so terribly hot yet like in the summer."

"I've got an idea." John was excited. "This ulpan of yours, are you learning much?"

"Not really. Twice a week for two hours isn't enough, and since I was in Israel for a year the first time, I know more than most of the class."

"So here's what we do. In the summer when it becomes unbearable in Eilat, say in another two months, we move up to a kibbutz and do an ulpan there. That's how I learned. You study four hours every day and work four hours. While you're working, you're also practicing your Hebrew."

"Makes sense," I agreed. "I'd be glad to get out of Eilat for a couple of months in the extreme heat. Being pregnant is like carrying a heater around inside of me."

"And in the meantime, we go back to live in Nueiba like before."

"Sounds great! But what about your job?"

"We have to come back to Eilat once a week anyway to get supplies of food and Bibles, so on that day I'll go back to my old job to earn money." John always had good ideas and a way of making things sound simple.

"When do you want to leave?" I was ready. Nueiba remained a kind of home for me, and I felt certain that living close to nature and other people would suit me more than being left alone when John went to work every day.

"How about tomorrow? You can tell your ulpan class tonight; I'll tell my boss in the morning; we'll shop and take off." John didn't waste time.

We were soon on our way to our new/old way of life. We easily found a spot under a group of palm trees not far from the sea. When we left Holland we had managed to squeeze into our car a big tent that friends had given us; John immediately set to work putting it together.

"*Balagan!*" ("Mess!") he muttered. "Maybe these poles and stakes are okay for grassy fields but they sure don't work on the rocks here. And their color codes make no sense."

Thankfully, we had a German engineering student with us who saw it as an outsized, three dimensional puzzle, a sort of Rubik's Cube, and took over for John. He also gave up on the color codes, but finally managed to erect the tent, which became our new home.

Our life fell into a simple rhythm, using the sun for keeping time. The day began by washing in the sea the dishes from the previous night. Bible reading followed a breakfast of oatmeal and tea. We spent much of the day sitting around, going to visit people in the neighboring tents, swimming, and just hanging out and interacting with people who lived with us or came by.

We prepared multiple pots of tea every day for our guests, making a new fire each time with twigs and driftwood we gathered. The smell of smoke permeated our clothes and hair. If our clothes needed washing, we waved them around in the sea.

Families from Moshav Neviot grew melons in the sand—a profitable business with the Sinai's enormous amount of sunshine. Exported to Europe, they reached the markets before those from any other place. Picking melons a few hours a day not only paid for our food and gas, but provided a healthy addition to our diet.

Wherever John was, people tended to gather around, and we soon had a small group of people staying with us in our tent. Not only could John speak many languages, but he showed people he was genuinely interested in them and willing to go out of his way to help. Whenever someone came with questions, John loved showing them answers in the Bible.

In the evening, after a dinner cooked over a campfire, we lay back and opened the Scriptures together. Candles and a kerosene lamp illuminated the pages. Though we didn't know the Bible well, we understood more than most of those around us and were excited and confident about what we knew.

"Let's open Chapter Three from the Gospel of John" is how John, with endless patience, often began his Bible studies. "'*You must be born again*.' What do you think this means?" Various people gave their opinions, and John explained that the writer wasn't talking about reincarnation.

"And now turn to the Tanach and read Isaiah Chapter Fifty-three," John continued. "Who do you think this is talking about? '*All we like sheep have gone astray, we've turned everyone to his own way, and the Lord has laid on him the iniquity of us all*.'"

A few suggestions followed. A young man who'd been to a yeshiva suggested that it was talking about the nation of Israel.

"But how can it be Israel?" John asked. "How has all our iniquity been laid on Israel? And can you really say about Israel that they've done no violence and there's no deceit in their mouth?"

"Are you sure this is in the Old Testament?" someone else asked.

"That's just the point!" John was animated. "A clear picture of the Messiah Jesus written seven hundred years before he was born!"

The message was simple and people kept coming.

By mid-April the heat drove most of the travelers away, and we drove north to Kibbutz Matzuba near the Lebanese border. We both enrolled in ulpan—John in the advanced class and I in the intermediate. John worked picking grapefruit until his supervisor discovered he was a cook and asked John to cater his son's bar mitzvah. The event was such a success that other requests followed and John spent more time in the kitchen than in the citrus groves. Because of my pregnancy I was assigned to the dining room, which suited me well because I could improve my Hebrew by speaking with the other women who worked there.

החופש

Six weeks before our baby was due we returned home to Eilat. Joshua was born in Yoseftal Hospital on a burning day in August nine months after we arrived in Israel.

"Josh seems to be happy wherever he is, as long as he's with us," John said, gazing at our month-old baby lying in his crib.

"True, but what are you getting at?" I asked.

"He doesn't seem to notice when he's at the beach in Eilat, and it was easy enough to take him down to Nueiba for the day when he was two weeks old."

I agreed. With a breastfeeding baby, it's not hard to move around. The fresh sea air even seemed to be calming for him."

"The three of us sleeping there in the back of our truck worked out okay, too," John said. "So here's what I'm thinking: why don't we move back to Nueiba?"

This time we built our own tent out of blankets and sheets. It even had bookshelves, a kitchen area, and a tarp floor I could sweep. On our weekly trips back to Eilat we bought thirty loaves of bread in addition to our own food. With supplies at the moshav's kiosk limited, bread straight from the bakery was popular with the beach people. Happy to supply a need and meet people at the same time, we went from tent to tent, palm tree to palm tree, selling bread and inviting people back to our camp for tea and Bible studies.

Living with a baby on the beach was also a way to meet people who often stopped to chat when they saw him lying in the diaper-lined melon crate that served as his crib. "Isn't it hard living with a baby here?" they asked. I didn't think so.

Unlike the isolation I felt in our apartment in Eilat, here I always had people to talk to and who wanted to hold baby Josh. The Bedouin women and girls who dropped by found a white baby fascinating, especially—for some reason—when they saw me nursing him the same way they did their own.

Apart from the scorching summers, the weather was generally pleasant, except during sandstorms. Most of the southern Sinai Peninsula is a rocky, mountainous desert, but south of Nueiba high dunes rise up so when the rare south wind blows, blinding, biting sandstorms ensue. Not only did the fine sand sting any exposed skin, it penetrated nostrils, eyes, ears, and mouths, not to mention ruining my housekeeping attempts.

We had a number of solutions. Sometimes I climbed in the back of our camper with little Josh and tried to remain there till it passed, though sandstorms could sometimes last for two or three days. Another possibility was to enter the sea. If I swam out far enough I could escape the sand barbs. But unfortunately I'd always have to come out and the sand would stick on me like sandpaper. Many beach people chose to either climb into their sleeping bags and stay put, or to walk around with a plastic bag over their head. Having had it drilled into me that I'd suffocate if I put a plastic bag over my head, I couldn't bring myself to try this, though I never heard about anyone smothered in Nueiba.

הַמִּקְדָשׁ

Sometimes we took long walks south in the direction of the Bedouin village of Mezeina to the "stone house," a unique structure standing alone unlike most Bedouin homes located in villages. Now abandoned, friends of ours had moved in. I enjoyed walking on the deserted beach and finding large conch shells. Or we went north on a shopping trip to the small store in Tarabin. We further supplemented our supplies when a Bedouin truck occasionally drove around selling small, sweet oranges from Gaza and whole wheat flour, important for the flat, unleavened pita we made every night. We strained the flour through a piece of tent screen, trying to remove the tiny bugs and worms.

"Don't worry," John said. "It's extra protein."

Many people wandered into our tent. One was David who lived as a hermit, not far from the stone house. Later he told us he had vowed not to talk, figuring he had nothing to say. Gaunt and long-haired, his diet consisted mainly of fish he caught, including some we had never seen eaten before. David, however, had to walk by our tent to fill his jerrycan with water from the moshav's shower facilities. Furthermore, he was impressed by the friendly people he met, who sold inexpensive bread and offered Bibles.

We'd invite David to our tent, and finally one day he took us up on the invitation. He sat quietly in the back, thankful to have a warm and filling meal, but not wanting to participate in the conversation or Bible studies. Gradually, however, our camp became his regular stop and his visits grew longer. The simple rice and vegetable stew John prepared was, for David, like eating in a three-star restaurant.

He began to open up but was convinced that, being Jewish, he couldn't believe in Jesus. John frequently went to visit him in his hut, and they began to read portions from the Bible together. From week to week we saw changes in David's life as he found in our tent a sense of community and purpose he'd never experienced before.

"I can't deny any more what I've been reading," David shared with John one day. He had gained weight, and a smile often lit his face. "I was worried that if I believed in Jesus I wouldn't be Jewish any more. But now I know He's real, and I actually feel more connected to my roots than ever."

David relocated to our tent and eventually moved back to Eilat with us, living in our apartment before going on to nursing school in Tel Aviv. He eventually married, had four children, and became the manager of a guest house in Jaffa and the leader of a local Messianic congregation.

Soldiers often came down to the Sinai on their leave. In
Nueiba they could throw off all constraints and feel as if they'd
traveled abroad.

"I really like these kids," John said to me. "I can identify with
them; they're looking for freedom and think they'll find it here.
But it worries me that hash is so easy to get and I hate seeing them
fall into that trap."

Gideon, one of the soldiers, used to come down every chance
he had and became a regular at our tent. In the beginning he
was quiet, because we didn't pay much attention to him or realize
he was so deeply involved with drugs. Yet slowly as he started to
believe in *Yeshua* (Jesus), we saw changes in his life. He became
more focused and friendly and loved playing with Joshua. After
his army service he came back to Eilat, found a job, and stayed
in our apartment. Later he moved back north, married, had two
children, and became the maintenance supervisor of a Messianic
congregation and guest house located on Mount Carmel.

חמשׁוּט

During the feasts of *Pesach* (Passover), *Rosh Hashanah* (Jewish
New Year), and *Sukkoth* (Feast of Tabernacles), Israeli families
flocked to the Sinai beaches and crammed into every available
space: wall-to-wall tents. We felt they were invading our territory,
but of course having no deed or contract for "our" spot on the
beach, our options were limited.

Young people also packed the beach for Nueiba's popular rock
festivals. On one occasion when we returned after being gone for
the summer, we found a concert underway. As we sought our
usual spot under "our" palm tree, a scruffy long-haired guy stood
with his arms out blocking the path, indicating his claim to those
few meters of sand.

"Hey, stop!" he yelled.

Pulling up next to him and hoping to negotiate, John suddenly recognized his old friend Cookie.

John jumped out of the car and gave Cookie a big bear hug.

"Hey what're you doing here?" they both asked at the same time. Having never met Cookie before, I was reminded of a friendly bear with a round belly, straggly beard, and broad smile.

John and Cookie had lived in the wadi in Eilat together where they partied and smoked hash before John started to believe in Jesus. Cookie had enjoyed coming to John's hut for his famous Dutch pancakes. At that time Cookie had already met some believers and, while he could concede that Jesus was the Jewish Messiah, his so-called faith hadn't gone deep enough to cause him to change his lifestyle.

After setting up camp together and making a pot of tea, John and Cookie had time to catch up. "I'm down for the festival; what about you?" Cookie asked.

"We were living under these palm trees till it got too hot," John said. "We've been up in Jerusalem for the summer. When did we last meet—that day in court?"

Whenever Cookie was in trouble, he sought out John until he got back on his feet and then continued on his way. In this case, he had asked John to go with him to court after being caught with drugs. They had prayed, and the judge had let Cookie go.

"That's it!" Cookie exclaimed. "You and God saved me."

When the festival ended a few days later, we resolved to keep in touch.

Around this time we also met Mike who spoke perfect Hebrew, French, Arabic, and English. He drifted around the country but liked to hang around our tent when he was in Nueiba. Mike, who had the knack for appearing just when we were starting to eat, learned enough of the Bible to approach groups of kibbutz volunteers who were camping, and quote a verse:

"*Give to him who asks of you,*" Mike would say as he begged for food.

Among the families who lived on the moshav, we counted some as our good friends. We worked in their melon fields, and they invited us to their homes. There were a few, though, who didn't like what we believed and felt we represented Jews who were betraying their heritage. One man even threatened to physically harm us. Knowing that he had a violent streak, and especially since we had a baby, we weren't willing to take any chances. So we moved to Dahab, another oasis south of Nueiba which was also a popular destination for travelers. The Bedouins in Dahab had built palm-frond huts that they rented out cheaply.

I loved living in the Sinai, close to nature and as part of a small community, but sometimes I asked myself how long we could continue like this. Was it good for Josh to be growing up in a tent on the beach? Should I be doing more to discipline him? By this time he was two years old and didn't have any regular friends except for the little Bedouin children. Having no other children to compare him with, I wondered if my little boy was hyperactive. He seemed to spend all his time running around and once he began to talk, he didn't stop!

A child psychologist from Jerusalem happened to be camping near us at the time. "Josh is simply a happy, bright child," she assured me. "He's a normal two-year-old."

In the summer, when the temperatures soared to 45 degrees Celsius, like most of the beach people we packed our bags and moved north.

7. Beginning and End of a Hostel
(Tomatoes? Is this All?)

"Do you have time now?" John eagerly asked Guy, having finished his bottle of grapefruit juice and standing up. As soon as Guy told him about his new lodgings, John—never one to waste time—was eager to check out the place.

Guy had arrived in Eilat and started to believe in Jesus together with John, and they had lived in neighboring huts in the wadi. The Eilat municipality tolerated this hippie shanty town for some years, but when Golda Meir made an official visit to Israel's southernmost city, the mayor decided it was time to clean up the eyesore of home-made shacks on the edge of town. When he ordered all the dwellings to be broken down and burnt, everyone except Guy left; until finally he moved into Rachamim's place.

The idea of renting Rachamim's house and turning it into a hostel immediately appealed to John. Eilat was a stopping point on the hippie trail from Europe to India; food was cheap; the weather was warm year-round; and though many people slept undisturbed on the beach, we figured that they might welcome a more comfortable alternative. At the time the only hostel in Eilat was the large International Youth Hostel which was expensive and impersonal.

"Will Rachamim be there?" John asked as they walked around the corner.

"Probably," answered Guy. "He doesn't live there but he stops by a lot."

John stepped in the metal front door and entered the house's large central room. "A bit run down." He gazed in all directions. "But wow, it's huge, especially compared to our apartment."

Rachamim had apparently planned on taking in boarders because he had already installed bunk beds, but at this point Guy was his only client. When the elderly man offered to rent to us for $250 a month, John didn't hesitate.

"It's yours now," he told John. "Do whatever you want with it."

"I'm sure if we open a hostel, Jupe," John said when he came home, "we can easily fill it up. What could go wrong? We know what travelers like and need."

"Yeah," I agreed. "I like living on the beach, but we can't stay there forever. I'd like friends for Josh besides the Bedouin kids. Did you know that Iris and Per, who used to live in Nueiba, are in Eilat now and have a boy Josh's age?"

"We could continue to go down to Dahab on weekends to bring supplies to our friends," John said, relishing the idea of having a reason to keep visiting the Sinai.

"This way we'll have two centers, three really, including our apartment," I added.

"Many travelers move back and forth between Eilat and the Sinai. So we can direct people to the hut in Dahab."

"So it's ours?"

"Yeah," John said. "That's what I like, *chick-chack* [quickly]."

הפסקה

Cookie resurfaced in our lives again just in time. Having been recently released from a mental hospital and looking for John to solve his latest problem, Cookie headed to Eilat. When he told us he had received a disability payment from the National Insurance Institute, John suggested he join us in our hostel.

"The way I see it," John told me, "we don't have much of a choice. We certainly don't have the spare cash to get started and though we don't need much, we need something. I know Cookie's a guy I can get along with."

It didn't take much work to get the house ready: a little paint on the walls, more beds, hosing down the mattresses, and airing them out, and soon we were up and running. Cookie slept in the small room which doubled as an office; and John, Josh and I slept at home but spent most of the day in the hostel.

We soon discovered that Cookie was still confused, unable to sit still, smoking three packs of cigarettes a day, and drawing weird pictures on the walls. When he tried to tell people about Jesus, he couldn't understand why he wasn't as successful as John. Not surprisingly, after a few months Cookie said he'd had enough and needed to get away. By then we were able to return his money, and he decided to go to the island of Patmos in Greece.

"I feel bad for him, Jupe," John said, "but I'm afraid there's nothing I can do. Cookie told me he thinks that on the island where the apostle John had his revelation, he'll find a cave and discover when Jesus will return."

A few months later we were surprised to find a letter from Cookie in our mailbox.

He wrote:

Dear John,

On the ferry to Patmos I met some believers who were on their way to a Bible school in Cyprus and they convinced me to go along with them. Being here I realized I knew a lot about God but never knew Him personally. So now

I've given myself fully to Jesus and my life has completely changed. I've even stopped smoking. And I won't be going by the name Cookie any more, but by my real name,

Israel.

Out of the envelope fell a photo of the new Cookie sitting at a desk with short hair and a tie.

Today Israel is married to Shlomit and has three sons. He led the work of starting a congregation in the north of Israel and wrote a study guide to the book of Hebrews, *Enter the Rest*.

Finding guests wasn't difficult. In the beginning we went out to the "highways and the byways," that is, to the beach and bus station, looking for people with backpacks. John often strode in to the hostel followed by a trail of backpackers.

I wanted to stay involved but wasn't sure how I could incorporate taking care of Josh into the hostel routine. We cooked our evening meal at the hostel, ate around a big table with the guests, and then opened the Bible together. Usually we had someone around who could play the guitar. By then, although Josh was sleepy, I didn't feel like going home and missing out on the after-dinner camaraderie.

"Just lay him in the back of the Toyota like in Nueiba," John suggested. "He's used to it."

"Nueiba was one thing, but in the car on the street?" I asked. "Is that safe?"

"Why not?" John answered. "Once he's asleep he never wakes up, and this is Israel—no one will bother him."

My problem was solved, so at the end of the evening we drove home, carried sleeping Josh up three flights of stairs, and laid him in his bed until morning.

One night when John didn't instantly fall asleep, he was in a reflective mood. "I was just reading in a book that young people seek three things: food, music, and fellowship. Without even trying, we've got all three."

"So many people these days come from broken homes or have

other issues," I added. "Few places offer of a sense of acceptance or belonging."

Operating the hostel came naturally to us. We did what we had been doing since we were married: invited people to share our lives. We didn't make a lot of rules and didn't even give our hostel a name. But it was obvious that young people responded when they experienced a community that lived out what they believed and accepted everyone, and we saw a number of people come to faith in Jesus.

With all our enthusiasm, however, we remained ignorant of a number of things. We never thought to draw up a written contract with Rachamim, to give receipts, or to pay taxes. Nor were we aware of the potential problems our openness could lead to.

"It's exciting that Sarit and Miri are coming around all the time for Bible studies." John settled himself in a chair at the long table in the hostel during one of our quiet moments.

"They're pretty young, in eleventh grade." I sat down across from him. "I wonder how much they really understand. Anyway, I like their enthusiasm."

John made himself a cup of instant coffee. "Yeah, last weekend with them in Dahab was fun. You could see they had a good time."

"And helped a lot with Josh too," I said, keeping an eye on him as he toddled around the big room. "Every time I turned around, one of them had him on her shoulders."

"I'm glad we went to their house and met Sarit's parents, though they didn't seem especially happy to get to know us," John remarked.

"Maybe they were having a hard day."

Not long after that, Sarit's parents went to the city hall and the high school to complain about us. "Our daughter received a New Testament from a young couple in town, and she's always hanging at their place," they charged.

Neither the mayor nor the principal took their accusation seriously, so they went to the rabbi.

"Don't worry," he assured the parents. "I know how to deal

with cases like this. We're a Jewish state, and I won't let this sect get away with polluting your daughter's mind and promoting another religion."

The rabbi had a clever plan: he went to Rachamim.

Rachamim liked John a lot, but he certainly didn't want to go to jail as the rabbi threatened.

With tears in his eyes he hugged John and told him we had to leave. John tried to gently explain that neither he nor we would ever go to jail; we weren't doing anything against the law.

"Israel is a free country and people are allowed to believe what they want," John told him.

But the rabbi had the last word.

Sitting alone in our apartment again, I told John, "It's been an amazing three months. We learned a lot." I wasn't used to cooking for just the three of us anymore.

"Yeah, maybe we'll have another hostel someday."

John, as usual, took the loss of the hostel in stride and set out immediately to find a job. I wondered what the future would bring. Maybe John having a regular job would bring stability into our lives. I liked the beach and hostel life, but sometimes I longed to have a real friend for an on-going relationship. It would be nice to get together with someone to share ideas and difficulties about child-rearing. I'd met with Iris a couple of times, but realized that just because she had a boy Josh's age, didn't automatically make us friends. I missed not only my parents, but also having older friends for role models and advisors.

John set out early the next morning for Timna Copper Mines, having heard they were hiring.

On the way a car picked him up and took him to the Eilot Regional Council's experimental station, forty kilometers north of Eilat.

"They seemed eager to hire me," John reported when he came home. "After I told them of my experience on the kibbutz, they didn't ask many questions. Maybe it had something to do with Vasily."

"Vasily?" I asked. "What are you talking about?"

"You remember him, the Polish guy who came on the boat with me from Athens and hangs around in Eilat. When I arrived at the farm I saw half the roof missing on the house where the workers stay. One of the scientists told me that Vasily had been working and sleeping out there, but when they had come to work that morning they had found him sitting in the tractor, asleep and drunk.

The front of the tractor was crashed into a pillar of the house. So they were looking for someone to take his place."

"Boy, I can imagine they'll be happy to have you there," I said.

הפסקה

"Moti asked me today to be field boss!" announced John, entering the door after work. "After only two months on the job, I've already been promoted."

"I'm not surprised," I said. "This job really suits you. It's an answer to prayer."

Since arriving in Israel, John had a special affection for the desert. The rocky mountains of Edom rose up dramatically toward the east, a backdrop that turned different shades of red and purple throughout the day. At dawn and dusk he saw desert foxes, porcupines, and gazelles. At the experimental station, he ran around all day barefoot in the sand, drove a tractor, picked vegetables, and enjoyed providing others with jobs too.

Whereas the agronomists with whom he worked did research to determine which crops could be profitably grown in the desert, John was in charge of the actual farming. Many of the experiments had to do with discovering how to produce tomatoes, melons, grapes, mangoes, and other vegetables and fruits using the salty water from the Arava's deep wells.

While the idea of a hostel didn't die completely, I became accustomed to our more structured way of life. Our second child, Racheli, was born, and Josh began nursery school. Maybe now that we were settled in Eilat, I'd find long-term friends. Sandra, Maria, Angela, Gaby, and Marieke—all of whom stayed with us for shorter or longer periods of time—were fine for a while, but I longed for a friend with whom we were already past that "let's get to know each other and see how we get on" phase. Someone to just hang out with together and who'd also be around in years to come, watching our children grow up together.

With no hostel anymore and no tent in the Sinai, all of our activities were centered around our apartment with two bedrooms on the third floor. We enjoyed having people stay with us: our way of life since we were married. After working in the hot sun for eight hours, John came home, took a short nap, and gave a Bible study after dinner.

"We have a great idea for you two this evening!" our friends announced to us one afternoon.

"What's that?" I asked, noticing the excitement in their eyes.

"Every evening we eat together and John gives us a Bible study," Gaby said.

"Right," I agreed. "So what are you saying?"

"So tonight…" Gaby eagerly explained, "you two take a few hours off and go out for a meal together! I'll babysit."

"What d'you mean?" I protested.

"We love being with you all," John added. "We don't need time alone."

But they gave us no choice.

Gaby had returned recently from Switzerland to help me as we awaited our third child, but she also had another reason to be back. Gaby wanted to spend time with Rami, a young Israeli man who had recently started to believe in Yeshua.

We had met Gaby for the first time in Dahab when she was on her way to India to find a guru. While living in one of the Bedouin huts, she walked by David and Sandra sitting next to the sea and overheard them speaking about God.

"Mind if I sit down?" she asked, already lowering herself onto the sand. "I heard you talking and I'm also interested in meditation and prayer, the way to get hold of a higher power. Some people call Him God, but for me the name doesn't matter."

"I understand, though we see things a bit differently from you," David said, excited to share the good news he had recently discovered. "We believe Jesus is the only way."

"Come back to our hut for tea and we can talk more," Sandra offered.

Gaby, a young woman with a round, European face and long blonde hair, began dropping by every evening for the Bible studies by candlelight. "It all makes sense," she admitted after a couple of weeks. "But how can I give up traveling when I've just started? I'm young and want to have a good time. I admire Jesus, but why would He be interested in me? You say He loves everyone and I read a verse like that in the Bible last night. I can understand He'd love nuns because they live straight lives, but I'm not that type."

"When you go to Eilat next week, you should visit John and Judy," Sandra suggested. "They can answer your questions."

"I don't want to bother them. They're probably busy with their kids and work."

"Not John and Judy," David said. "It seems the more people they have staying with them, the more they like it."

When I opened the door one afternoon and saw Gaby, I wasn't surprised because I never knew who would be standing in front of me.

"When I told David and Sandra I was coming to Eilat they suggested I stop by here," Gaby explained.

"Great!" I replied. "You probably need a place to stay." In the middle of cutting vegetables, I put down my knife and wiped my hands on the dress covering my big belly.

"Thanks!" Gaby answered. "Maybe for a day or two. I'm on my way to India."

"I know about that. I came to Israel on my way to India too," I said. "And I'm still here. Throw your bag in the corner. Wait a minute; Josh is waking up from his nap."

"Let me help with the salad," Gaby offered.

Gaby's day or two stretched into months. She quickly felt at home in the apartment on Yotam Road, happily sleeping on a mattress in the living room. Eager to learn more about God and His plan for her life, Gaby helped me towards the end of my second pregnancy. After John, David, Gideon, and others left for work in the morning and we finished cleaning the house, Gaby and I stopped for a coffee break and read the Bible together.

Although Gaby had no experience with children, she enjoyed playing with Josh and learned to hold and care for newborn Racheli. I was glad not only to have another set of hands around to help me balance the work with the children and all our guests, but also to have a friend living with us.

I saw Gaby becoming more at peace with herself, and her traveling plans disappeared like the Bedouin children who stopped by our tent—one minute they were squatting next to our campfire and when I glanced again, they were suddenly gone. A gifted guitarist, even Gaby's repertoire and music style changed.

When Racheli was six months old and Josh was four, we put our Toyota on the ferry to Greece and drove through Europe to John's family in Holland. Gaby came with us and we dropped her off at her parents in Switzerland.

"I guess this makes us matchmakers," John said to me after Gaby and Rami, the young Israeli believer, ended up getting married.

"Like in *Fiddler on the Roof*," I replied.

Today Gaby and Rami live in the Galilee and have four children. Gaby is an artist and musician, and Rami is a tour guide.

הפסקה

I didn't want to raise Joshua and Racheli stuck up in a box in the sky; they needed space and a garden to play in. After praying and looking for a couple of years, we finally found a house that met all our requirements: near the center of town, easy to find, four bedrooms, a large garden, and as a bonus—a breathtaking view of

the Red Sea and Mountains of Edom. I loved being able to spread
out and have two guest rooms.

Soon though, Moriah was born, and we were becoming
crowded again. We frequently woke in the morning to find someone sleeping on the old sofa on our front porch. Every Thursday
afternoon John brought home the local paper and opened it to the
real estate section.

"I know we have to be patient and one of these days we'll find
another hostel," John told me. In the short three months we had
Rachamim's house, we had seen the advantage in having another
building where our friends, friends of friends, and others could
stay.

John's back was hurting to the point that I had to put his shoes
on for him in the morning and help him into the truck. When I
urged him to get it checked, at first John hesitated.

"I like the job. I've worked at the farm now for five years and get
along with the guys. They know what I believe and respect me. Yet
sometimes I ask myself if God called me to Israel to pick tomatoes?
I can't help thinking that He has something more for us."

"I agree. Maybe we should pray more seriously for a hostel."

When John couldn't ignore the pain, he finally went to the
doctor and found he had two crushed discs in his lower back.
The doctor warned that if John didn't stop the heavy farm work
he'd need an operation. Since we believed that "all things work
together for good," as is written in the Bible, we trusted that God
had a purpose in this too.

At the farm they gave John a big farewell party, and the
government provided severance pay and workman's compensation. Entering a time of much needed rest, John was happy to
spend time with our sweet little Moriah and to give more attention to Josh and Racheli, who seemed to be growing up so quickly.
Though a few job offers came his way, nothing felt right.

"When we come home in August I'm sure something will turn
up," John assured me as we piled the three kids into our van on the
way to Ben Gurion Airport to visit our families.

8. Flee to the Refuge

Between Eilat's oppressive August (1984) heat and three energetic little kids who were delighted to be home again, unpacking our suitcases was barely underway. The phone rang.

"Hello," said an unfamiliar voice. "My name's Vera Kushnir. We don't know each other; but I'm here in Eilat with Dan of Bethel Hostel from Haifa. I'd like to meet at your home if you have time. I'm hoping you can help me."

"Wonder what she wants?" I asked John, holding Moriah in my arms. "This place is a mess, but she said she's here for just a short time." I handed Moriah to John while I tried to organize the house, throwing the toys into the playpen. "She sounded nice."

A few minutes later Vera and Dan stepped in the open door.

"Hey Dan!" John greeted him. "How're you doing?"

"I want you to meet my friend Vera."

"Sorry to bother you," Vera said looking around. "You look busy."

"We came back last night from the States," John said, "but we're glad you came. Have a seat and I'll bring you some drinks."

Vera, a neatly dressed middle-aged woman with a friendly smile, sat on the sofa opposite the vent of the desert cooler. Bypassing small talk, she began explaining the reason for her visit.

"I'm from Santa Barbara, California, though I was born in Russia," Vera began, quickly downing a glass of juice.

"Ah, that's the accent. No wonder I couldn't place it." For once, John was stumped.

"As you know, Dan has been managing the Bethel Hostel in Haifa. It's owned by my family and two years ago we purchased a building in Eilat. Noticing how many guests of ours came down here, we planned to start a second hostel but it hasn't gotten off the ground. A few couples have been willing to housesit, but we're looking for an Israeli couple who won't have to renew their visas all the time."

"So I suggested Vera get in touch with you," Dan added. "The place needs a lot of work, but I know you're looking for a hostel."

John leaned forward in his chair. "Wow, sounds interesting! How is it that you live in California and own a hostel in Haifa?"

"It's a long story, but I have time if you do." Vera helped herself to more juice.

"Sure, we have time." John rocked Moriah in her little hammock. "I haven't worked for nine months, since my back went out. Let's continue over lunch."

Vera told us that her grandfather, Leon Rosenberg, was born in the late 1800s into an orthodox Jewish family in Russia. An up-and-coming rabbinical student, he also studied secular subjects. One of his non-rabbinical teachers befriended him and after moving away, sent him a New Testament in Hebrew. The contents of the book were new to Leon, but his curiosity was aroused, and he decided to study it in depth.

After several years of struggles and questions, Leon concluded that Jesus was indeed the promised Messiah, and experienced a peace and freedom he had never known. Needless to say, his family and the Jewish community persecuted Leon greatly for his new convictions, especially as he actively shared his faith.

During the pogroms, World War I, and the Bolshevik Revolution, Leon, his wife, and all their family suffered immensely. Forced to move around continually, they eventually settled in Poland where they established an orphanage for Jewish children. Their greatest trial came during World War II when all the orphans and many of the Rosenbergs' family members were murdered by the Nazis.

After the war they, their children, and already-grown grandchildren immigrated to the United States and settled in California. Wanting to continue his work with Jewish orphans, Leon purchased two large, old buildings in Haifa for this purpose and had local directors to manage it. He called the home "Bethel," after the name of their orphanage in Poland.

In the 1970s when the orphans had grown up and many travelers were coming to Israel, they converted it into a hostel. In the meantime, Leon Rosenberg died, as well as the daughter who had continued with his work. Vera, his granddaughter, was currently directing the organization that ran both hostels.

"So that's why I'm here." Vera laid down her fork. "And I'm wondering, would you be interested in taking the place over?"

"Would we?!" John exclaimed. "Of course, we'll have to talk and pray about it, but when you hear our story, you'll realize how everything fits together. Jupe, can you come over with us now to look at it?"

"It's close by," Vera told us.

"Sure, let's go."

Later, after peeking into every corner of the building, John told Vera, "I'm sure we can make something out of this place. It's been our dream to open another hostel since we lost our first one, and I believe this is the answer to our prayers. We've been in Eilat for eight years trying to serve God as we feel Him leading us. I'll be honest with you, Vera. I've never worked for an organization or had anyone telling me how to go about my business. And I don't think that I could begin living like that now. Can you understand?"

"That's fine," Vera agreed. "Use the place as you see fit; I trust you. All I ask is that you send us a report a few times a year. Dan can come down if you need help."

A few days later Vera returned to California, and we finally had our hostel. John plunged into the work the way he jumps into the sea: as soon as we reach the beach, he's in the water. But I wondered what our life would look like now. What would my part be? I was occupied most of the day with our children and certainly couldn't put them to bed in the car anymore.

"Don't worry," John assured me. "This is what we've been waiting for. Everything will fall into place."

הַמִּקְדָּשׁ

"What shall we call it?" I asked John. "I've been thinking about ideas, but nothing comes to mind."

"Call what?" John answered. "The baby?"

"No! I'm talking about the hostel. We've got time before the baby's due, but the hostel needs a name. We're definitely not going to keep calling it 'Beit Chen.'"

Although it was unofficial and no sign had been posted, the hostel had previously been called Beit Chen, meaning "House of Grace."

"Yeah," agreed John. "The meaning is nice, but if you don't know about Hebrew pronunciation and just see the English writing, it looks like a Chinese restaurant."

"I was thinking about a name connected to Eilat. Maybe something about the desert."

"What about 'The Oasis Hostel'?" John suggested.

I wanted to be sure, like when choosing a baby's name. And with this hostel I was determined to do things right from the beginning.

After dropping Racheli off at her nursery school, I pushed Moriah in her stroller over to see if I could help John with the renovation. Suddenly my eyes fell on the bomb shelter directly in front of the gate. "Hey, look what's written," I said to John, pointing to the word stenciled in black a dozen times.

"*Miklat* [shelter]," answered John.

"So, what do you think? Good idea or not?"

At first John looked at me quizzically but then his face lit up. "Wow! Makes sense 'cause it's already there. 'Shelter, shelter, shelter …'" His gaze roamed over the structure. "So that's the name. I like the biblical meaning too."

In the Book of Numbers *miklat* is used for the cities of refuge, places where a person who killed someone accidentally could flee for protection and safety. We wanted our hostel to be a retreat for travelers from the cares of this world, a sanctuary where they could rest their souls as well as their bodies.

"We'll put the verse from Isaiah Chapter Four on our sign," John added, his mind racing ahead. "*It will be a shelter and shade from the heat of the day, and a refuge and hiding place from the storm and rain*," he quoted.

When I looked at the hostel property I saw a dump that would take weeks if not months to organize. I could hardly imagine how people had actually lived here, let alone renting out some of the rooms. The so-called "storage room," currently room eleven, was crammed from floor to ceiling with junk, including tables, chairs, an oven, fans, paint cans, and brushes. Half a dozen old refrigerators stood around in the garden, if you could call it that.

John didn't waste time looking or thinking and tossed nearly all the storage room's contents into the nearby dumpster. The refrigerators didn't last long either.

"There's no sitting or dining room," John said. "But our friend Yaakov came to visit yesterday and figured we could fill in the area by the entrance to create a raised sitting area or deck. It's a big job, but he's already begun."

Unfortunately, after digging up the tiles, Yaakov departed unexpectedly and left John to continue with the work.

"Never mind," John said. "It's just what we needed, and now

we've got an eating space with a view. David's offered to help build a *sukkah*."

"It's nice having him around, isn't it? Finally we have some friends in Eilat who look like they'll be staying. And friends for our kids."

David and Anneli, who had recently moved to Eilat, had two young children close in age to ours. A carpenter, David had renovated their old house, rented a shop, and begun his own business. On Saturday mornings they joined us to read the Bible and pray, and we celebrated holidays and our children's birthdays together. This is how the Eilat Congregation got started.

In the early days when John and I had gatherings in our tent in the Sinai, then in our house on Poor House Lane, and later in our apartment in Eilat, we never intended to begin a congregation or a church. We preferred the idea of maintaining an informal atmosphere without a religious institution.

Yet, as we were joined by David and Anneli and others who also put down roots in Eilat, we understood that we needed to have regular meetings and some kind of structure; and so the Eilat Congregation began. Today, with about eighty adults and children, we meet every Saturday morning for worship, Bible study and prayer, and we try to maintain the feeling of community by getting together throughout the week also.

David's offer to help build a sukkah (a temporary hut for use during Sukkoth) was gladly accepted by John, who found old palm trunks and managed to lash them to the top of our truck and transport them back to the Shelter. Set upright and used as crossbeams, they provided a frame on which to spread the palm branches. Not only did we now have a comfortable sitting area, but the sukkah reminded us of our hut in Dahab.

Coming home for lunch one afternoon not long after we took over, John had a big smile on his face, "Guess what, Jupe? I met Irma Walsh at the post office." Irma was a German Holocaust survivor who started to believe in Jesus after the war and lived for many years in Eilat.

"She's leaving next week for Beit Ebenezer in Haifa, the old-age home. She told me she wanted to donate her furniture to us, so I went right away and picked the things up. Wait till you see them."

"Amazing! Let's invite her for a farewell party and the sukkah's dedication," I suggested.

"Good idea. Tomorrow morning."

Stepping into the Shelter the following day, I said to John, "Wow! Everything fits perfectly. An interior designer couldn't have done better. The rug and sofa fill the room, and I love the Oriental style of the coffee table and light fixture."

Irma, a widow who had lived alone for many years, was visibly moved by the party and the attention.

הַמִּקְלָט

Now that we had given the hostel a name, a thorough cleaning, and furniture, we turned our focus to management. After our experience running our first hostel, we knew we had a lot to learn. Obviously we'd have to play by the rules this time: open a file with the tax office, write receipts, and get all the necessary permits. When we consulted a friend in Jerusalem he cautioned us that getting involved with the tax office would be the biggest mistake of our lives. "Once they have your name and particulars, you'll never be free of them the rest of your life," he warned. "Better not to start."

"I really respect this man," John told me. "He's been in business for years and I know it's good to take advice. Many people say that running a business in Israel is complicated with all the bureaucracy, taxes, and so on. But the way I see it, God gave us the Shelter, so we just have to go ahead with our plans and trust Him to work things out."

"So what do we have to do?" I asked.

"For one thing, we need a good accountant," answered John. "Or do you think you could keep the books?"

Although I did well in high school math, I saw an unbridgeable gap between getting good marks on my calculus exams and understanding the Israeli tax system.

"I'm sure a paid bookkeeper will save us money and keep us from making mistakes," I said.

"I noticed an accountant's office down the street. I'll stop in and talk to them tomorrow."

But how does a person actually run a hostel? The Shelter, with seven guest rooms and forty beds, was much larger than Rachamim's house. I didn't want John spending twenty-four hours a day there as my friend's husband did at their hostel, and I knew John didn't want that either. With Josh seven years old, Racheli four, Moriah one, and another baby on the way, I didn't have extra time to devote to hostel work. We clearly needed help and wanted to be prepared for our anticipated guests.

John's experience on the kibbutz showed him that in Israel much work could be done by volunteers. After the conclusion of the Six-Day War, the world's interest in Israel grew, and in the aftermath large numbers of volunteers arrived. Throughout the 1970s and into the '80s, thousands of young people, eager to experience communal living and to travel inexpensively, came to volunteer in one of the almost three-hundred kibbutzim.

Not only that, but we knew that since many young people wanted to stay longer and were looking for something to do, we would simply have to find the right ones for the Shelter. God had helped us in the past by sending nannies for our children, so we knew we could trust Him for hostel volunteers too.

John often went to the beaches where the hippies and travelers stayed, and on one of his visits he met Elke, a sixteen-year-old German girl. Lying alone on an old blanket in a makeshift tent, she looked too young to be there, like a plant stuck in the wrong kind of soil and pot.

"What are you doing here?" he asked her.

Elke coughed and tried to sit up, but she was weak from fever. "I ran away. My father was like a Nazi, a dictator in our home. I wanted to study, but he made me work in the family's shoe shop. One day when it became too much, I went to a travel agent and asked where I could go with the amount of money I had. She said, 'Eilat,' so here I am."

"You'd better come home with me," John said. "You're sick and can stay with us till you feel better. Do you like children? We've got three and another one on the way. But never mind, the main thing is that you get better."

I wasn't surprised when John brought Elke home; I was used to John's spontaneity and hospitality. Elke lay in bed for a couple of days, but as soon as she began to feel well again, she started playing with Josh, Racheli, and Moriah, and helping around the house.

"When did you speak to your parents last?" John asked her one evening after the children were asleep.

"They don't even know where I am."

"So that's what you do now—call your family," John told her.

Elke's parents, thankful to hear from their daughter, agreed that she should continue to stay with us. I enjoyed her company and assistance. Elke joined me in reading the Bible every morning and in a short time began to believe in Jesus. She returned to Germany six months later with a new hope and joy.

Our prayers for volunteers were quickly answered with Colleen and Mari. Colleen, a teenager with a cheerful disposition, had come to visit David and Anneli and was happy to lend a hand at the Shelter. Friends in Tel Aviv with whom she had worked at The Shelter Christian Hostel in Amsterdam told her to look us up when she came to Eilat.

We had heard about that Shelter a few years previously when one of the managers and his wife had stayed in our apartment. We knew it was an old building, formerly a school, in the red-light district of Amsterdam, and that it was large, with one hundred sixty beds. It was run along biblical principles, as was our goal for our Shelter. Although Amsterdam and Eilat didn't seem to have much in common, they were both stations on the hippie trail east and attracted the same kind of travelers.

"God's perfect timing!" I told John excitedly after Mari showed up at our house and we sat down to talk in our living room. "She'll be able to tell us how they do things in Amsterdam."

"What kind of rules do they have?" I asked Mari. "Do they have Bible studies or discussions? As a youth hostel, do they have age limits? And what was your job as a volunteer?"

I had lots of questions and Mari had answers. She explained that they had a midnight curfew to allow their guests a quiet night's sleep. That made sense to us because especially during the holidays, many young Israelis come to Eilat to party throughout the night and those weren't the guests we wanted to attract. We had already decided to adopt the policy of same-sex dormitories.

"They don't take guests above thirty-five years old," Mari informed us. "People older than that who stay in hostels can be strange."

John and I had met enough weirdos in our day to know that there is no cut-off age for weirdness, so that was a rule we decided to waive.

"One thing you need is a place for guests' valuables," Mari advised. "There'll always be thieves around."

That was easy for John. An old coffee table with a top that lifted open became our safe where guests could deposit their money, plane tickets, passports, and cameras. Thankfully, no crook ever discovered our unsafe safe. Nevertheless, a year later when a handyman was doing work for us, John commissioned a proper vault with a padlock.

John had spent hours and days getting things ready, immersing himself in making the Shelter livable as well as workable. "So now I'm just waiting for the registration and receipt books I ordered," he told me.

"And for guests," I added.

9. Sorry, We're Full

Eilat had plenty of backpackers, but how would we get them into the Shelter?

"Don't worry," John assured me. "You can't go wrong in Eilat. Our friends and friends of friends are already a good start. Wait till you see. I've ordered business cards with a map on the back."

I began carrying cards in my purse and often found guests while out doing errands or walking with the children. When I saw someone with a pack on their back I simply walked up and invited them to the hostel. But John with his outgoing personality was even more effective—as long as he stayed away from the bus station. He didn't need to venture there more than a couple of times to realize it was off limits. Since Eilat's early days, people used to rent out rooms in their homes by waiting on the platform for intercity buses to arrive and offering accommodation to the disembarking passengers. Unfortunately, after handing over their money in advance, the unsuspecting vacationer often found that the so-called hostel or apartment was nothing more than a mattress on the floor of a dingy room.

Most of the "bus station mafia," as we called them, didn't look like the most trustworthy individuals or speak much English, thus John with his blond hair and big smile had a tremendous advantage. Needless to say, they didn't appreciate John's incursion on their territory, so after being threatened a few times, he used different methods to find guests.

The story of Barbara, a Swiss kibbutz volunteer, was typical. When she announced she was going to Eilat, a friend recommended the Shelter saying, "It's got a great atmosphere and friendly people."

As Barbara and her friend Ruth stepped off the bus, one of the locals accosted them.

"We're looking for the Shelter Hostel," Barbara told him.

"I'm from the Shelter," he said, latching on to the girls. "I'll take you there."

Asking no further questions, Barbara and Ruth naively followed him.

Heading up the street he asked, "How long do you want to stay?"

"A week," Barbara answered.

He brought them to a dark apartment in an old section of town. "That'll be forty shekels a day or two-hundred-eighty shekels each for the week," he said. "You can pay me now."

With no further thought, Barbara and Ruth handed him the total sum.

When he left and they found themselves alone, Barbara and Ruth looked at one another. "Do you think this is really the Shelter? It doesn't seem like the place we heard about."

The following day while walking around town, they happened to see a building with a sign indicating "Shelter Hostel."

"Amazing!" Barbara said to Ruth. "I knew that wasn't the real Shelter. Let's go in."

A volunteer named Adriaan was on duty and welcomed them warmly, offering them some water. "Where are your backpacks?" he asked.

When he heard their story Adriaan was outraged. "Take me to that apartment," he told Barbara. "I'll get your money back and give you a place here."

"Are you sure?" Barbara asked. "That guy didn't look like someone you'd want to argue with." She could hardly believe that Adriaan, whom she'd met five minutes ago, was willing to take up their cause.

An hour later, however, Adriaan and the girls returned with smiles on their faces. "I just insisted he give them their money back and he did," he explained.

Visitors began to arrive, and though we didn't advertise or take reservations, we were usually full. Those who found the Shelter, recommended us to others, and we discovered that Eilat has no off season. Guests came to us year round—in the winter when it's cold, rainy, and snowy in Europe but beach weather in Eilat, and also in the summer when it's broiling in Eilat, but when most people take vacations.

"Maybe we should hang a sign on the front gate saying, 'Sorry, we're full,'" I suggested to John. "Like motels that write, 'No Vacancy.'"

"Yeah, that's an idea," John agreed at first, but then he thought further. "Nah, we won't do that. We can invite them to sleep outside and even if we're full there, it's good that people see our place. We can always give them a glass of cold water, invite them to stay another time, and offer a gospel tract. We don't want to send anyone away."

So that became our policy: invite everyone in, interact with as many people as possible, and allow even people who weren't staying at the Shelter to use our facilities. We set up a table near the office with a large water boiler and jars of instant coffee, tea bags, sugar, and creamer to add a welcoming atmosphere. In many ways, the Shelter was an extension of the lifestyle we'd begun in Key West and continued in our tent in the Sinai, in our first hostel, in our apartment, and house, with the emphasis on accepting everyone and creating a community.

In the 1980s Eilat began changing from a frontier and "anything goes" small town into a modern resort including luxury hotels and charter flights arriving directly from Europe. Yet with its proximity to Europe, reasonable prices, and opportunity to volunteer on a kibbutz, Israel still remained popular among travelers. We didn't realize at the time that we were riding a wave that would gradually taper off.

הפסקה

Coming home for lunch one day, John lay down on the couch and picked up the newspaper.

"I like it when you invite the volunteers over for lunch," I told him as I set the table. "I'd like to get over there more but I always seem to be busy. I cook plenty of food and it's fun to talk to them."

"You've gotta understand," John answered. "I'm with people from morning till night, and I'm glad to get away from them sometimes. Like today, you wouldn't believe what a busy day I had. By the way, Hani came by again for the Bible study. We had a good talk; and I suggested she move to the Shelter. You remember Hani—the Israeli girl with red, curly hair who stayed with us for a couple of days when she was sick but then went back to the beach. Maybe you want to come with me to visit her this afternoon?"

The Jordan Beach, so-called because of its proximity to the Jordanian border, where the travelers stayed, wasn't my favorite beach to go to with the children. On the one hand, I was glad they were growing up to be open to different types of people and to accept everyone, but I had misgivings about exposing them at a young age to hash smokers and drunks. When they were little, I figured they didn't understand, although they probably absorbed more than I imagined. But now Josh was old enough to see what was going on and these people definitely weren't my choice of role models for him. Or maybe seeing the messes they'd made of their lives would make our kids swear off drugs and alcohol forever?

One difficult part of taking the children to the beach was the nudity, and it wasn't confined to the hippie beach. Eilat, with its freewheeling atmosphere, allowed topless women on all the beaches. Most of the nudists came by charter flights from Sweden, Holland, and northern Europe, and local women, seemingly encouraged by the trend, joined in.

Didn't they understand? Even if in Europe they felt comfortable revealing themselves, Israel is part of the Middle East, and I felt sick seeing these women stretched out on a beach chair while a meter or two away a couple of men sat staring. John and I tried to avoid sitting near half-naked women, but sometimes they just plopped down next to us. What could we do? The beach was so much a part of our lives.

I hadn't had a chance to talk to Hani much until now, but she seemed like someone I'd like to get to know. After lunch we piled the children into the van and headed to the beach. Hani was happy to see us, and I could keep an eye on the children swimming and playing in the water while we sat under her lean-to, one of the dozen or more makeshift tents in Eilat's latest hippie colony. With little prompting, Hani began telling me her story.

"I was working in a hostel in Jerusalem and hanging around with people from different countries who played music on the streets. At the same time I was looking for God, for something spiritual in my life. Things should have been going okay for me, but I was fed up with the emptiness of life and had no power to stand up to things I knew were wrong, like sex, drugs, and cigarettes. A number of my friends suggested I come down here to Eilat."

I liked Hani's honesty and found her easy to talk to, and the gentle lapping of the Red Sea's waves provided relaxing background music. "So how'd you end up at the Shelter?" I asked.

"I met some believers in Jerusalem who told me about you, but when I got to Eilat, I decided first to go to my old friends on the beach and afterwards check out the Shelter," Hani continued.

"I got stuck here and didn't have the strength to pull away and go to the hostel—not until I got sick and needed a warm bed and rest. I liked the Bible studies; things made sense to me. But when I felt better I came back to the beach."

"I was a lot like you," I said. "Brought up Jewish, searching, living in the Sinai. But when I began to read the Bible, my life totally changed. Why not stay with us again? You could use a change in your life too."

Hani promised she'd consider my offer, but I had no idea which way she would choose—the hostel or the beach. Not long afterwards, however, Hani was celebrating New Year's Eve on the beach with friends. Later she explained to me that whereas the campfires, music, grass, and alcohol normally made her feel good, this time she felt empty. Stepping away from the crowd, she felt God telling her, "They laugh but it's counterfeit. I have joy that's not dependent on drugs or anything artificial."

That's when Hani decided that if Jesus was truly the Messiah, she'd follow Him whatever the cost. So the next day Hani returned to the Shelter and began reading the New Testament earnestly. In it she found the truth she was searching for and the power to stop her destructive behavior, and this time she didn't consider returning to the beach. Within three weeks she even stopped smoking. Hani fit in at the hostel like a child in her parents' house and ended up staying for six months and working on staff.

$$\boxed{\text{עשרים}}$$

Although much of our life revolved around the Shelter, we still had many people visiting and staying in our home. The nannies, or au pair girls, who lived with us, helped me through those busy years.

Gaby, then Elke, and others too, were like being able to double myself—one of us could take care of the children and the other attend to our guests. As a mother with four young children, I enjoyed having someone in the home to talk to and read the Bible with, and the children benefited from extra attention.

Elke was with us during a critical time—when Yonatan was born premature and lay in an incubator for six weeks. Spending hours every day at the hospital, I couldn't have managed without her.

When Elke finally went home to Germany, God brought Sisi, the fifteen-year-old daughter of friends. She was going through a difficult time and not managing in school, when her parents called and asked if she could stay with us. Since I neither knew Sisi personally nor had experience with teenagers, I was at first hesitant about her coming. But I needn't have worried; Sisi turned out to be a perfect match for our family, seeming to thrive on taking care of and playing with the children. I missed her when she left after half a year.

"Now what?" I asked John. "D'you think God will send someone else?" Between the children, our meetings, and guests, I felt like a juggler in a circus, trying to keep all the plates in the air.

"He always does," answered John. "You never know who will turn up. Anyway, it's not so bad to be alone with just the family for a time."

Anne walked up to the house not long afterwards. "Do you remember me?" she asked.

"Sure, you were here a year ago, from Canada, right?" I answered. "You shared a room with Gaby."

We hadn't kept in touch, but suddenly things came back to me. Anne had studied at Bible school in England with an Israeli couple. When she came to visit them in Jerusalem, they suggested she go down to Eilat, gave her our address, and she stayed for a few days.

That first time when Anne knocked on the door, it was Friday evening and we were preparing for our weekly gathering. Since moving to Eilat, we began inviting travelers, lonely, and single people to our home for a Shabbat dinner followed by singing and a short Bible reading. At first we used to sit around our table, but word spread, and we soon had to build benches to accommodate the dozens of people who came.

When Anne stepped in, we were setting up the big pots of soup and rice and beans on the table, stacking the plates and silverware, and cutting the challah, the braided Shabbat bread. I immediately put Anne to work. Later she told me she couldn't believe how quickly she was thrown into such a busy and chaotic setting.

Now Anne was back again but with a different story. She had returned to Israel to work on a kibbutz, but things had gone terribly wrong. "It's a big mess," Anne confessed when we found a few minutes to sit down quietly. "There's this guy, Eli."

John and I had been listening patiently, but now John took over. "Stay with us. Forget about the kibbutz and about Eli."

"I know I should," said Anne. "But he'll come after me."

"You're safe here and that's it," John told her. "You need to get back to reading the Bible and being with believers. Judy will love having you around."

John drove up to the kibbutz to pick up Anne's belongings and Anne moved in with us—perfect timing for me. She needed time to wean herself emotionally away from Eli, and slowly we saw her joy and self-confidence return. When she left after three months, we made plans for her to return after the summer to volunteer at the Shelter.

During Anne's year on staff she grew close to our family, to the point that when she began working as a teacher in Canada, she used her first vacation to visit Eilat. In the meantime, Herbby, a nuclear engineer from a small town in Alabama, was volunteering and when Anne returned to Ontario they decided to keep in touch. Their long-distance relationship flourished and when he finally visited Canada two years later, Herbby asked Anne to marry him.

Herbby and Anne moved to Eilat to help at the Shelter and lived here for fifteen years before relocating to Netanya, a city on the Mediterranean Sea, with their three children. John appreciated having Herbby as his assistant, and Anne became one of my best friends.

הַמִּדְבָּר

To celebrate our eleventh wedding anniversary in March of 1986 we decided to take a morning off and go hiking in the mountains outside Eilat. The quietness and simplicity of nature always helped us relax and see things in perspective. After two hours of strenuous walking we needed a rest, and reaching a peak, we leaned back on some rocks to admire the view and have a snack. The shining blue waters of the Gulf of Eilat spread out before us and the tawny Mountains of Edom, fuzzy and shimmering in the bright sunlight and dust, towered in the distance. Across the Gulf, like Eilat's twin, we could see the Jordanian city of Aqaba with its white buildings and green strip of palm trees along the seaside. From such a distance we couldn't distinguish the border fence, but the wide empty stretch of no-man's land marked the frontier between the two antagonistic states.

I took some dates and a couple of oranges and apples from my backpack. "It's good to be out, isn't it? I've been thinking, people say a business needs a couple of years to know if it's successful, but we're already full most of the time."

"Yeah," John answered. "It's just over a year and think of all the people we've met already."

"The hostel's becoming like a family."

Unfortunately it was the first hot day of the season, and we didn't know the area well. A couple of hours after we resumed walking, our water bottles were empty. Trekking through a deep wadi, we couldn't get a broad view of the landscape nor locate our position on the map. We were searching for a particular cleft in the canyon walls that would lead us out but weren't sure if we had already mistakenly passed it by or hadn't come to it yet.

Realizing we would soon become dehydrated, we decided to leave the marked trail and simply head in the direction we sensed was right. Thankfully we weren't far out of the way and soon came to the road where we stumbled upon some soldiers.

After drinking the water they gave us and sitting down for a few minutes, we quickly revived and began hitchhiking back to where we left our car.

"Next time I'll pay more attention to the map," I said.

"And we'll take extra water," John added.

John returned to the hostel work with a new burst of energy. "We should do this more often," he told me.

A couple of days later, John found a notice for a registered letter in our post office box. When he walked in the front door I noticed a tense expression on his face, and he didn't have the usual spring in his step.

"I've got a summons to appear in court," he announced.

10. Dutch Wall Climber, Russian Coffee Seller & Egyptian Doctor

"Just when everything seems to be going our way, I get this letter." John slumped down in his favorite chair. "Balagan!"

"Can you understand the legal language in Hebrew?" I asked.

"The municipality is charging me with operating a business without a license. The court date's set for two weeks from now," John told me, his eyes slowly skimming the document.

"We learned our lesson from the first hostel and can't take a chance on losing this one," I said. I knew that even if the story with Sarit's parents and the rabbi hadn't happened, we couldn't have continued the way we were going—not writing receipts or paying taxes. We had made mistakes, but believed God used the hostel for a time in our lives. I had thought that this time we were abiding by the law.

John explained that when John and Sven, who had been living in the hostel before us, had gone to the municipality to apply for a license, the clerk had sent them home saying that they would never get it because they weren't located in a commercial zone.

"So I guess now the authorities have caught up with us," John told me.

Vera Kushnir retained a lawyer named Meir for Bethel Hostel's legal needs, so John called him.

"Boy, am I glad Meir's coming with me," John told me when the set date arrived. "I know things are in God's hands, but it's not a nice feeling having to go to court."

"You don't think they could close us down, do you?" I asked as John left to pick up Meir at the airport and continue on to the hearing.

"Nah. But people tell me these things can drag on for years."

John had never been in court before, but talking to other people waiting outside helped him feel better. When his turn came, the judge's verdict was simple: pay a fine of two hundred shekels and go to the municipality to sort things out.

The following day, Meir went with John to the municipal engineer's office. In a country where personal connections are important, and new immigrants are therefore at a disadvantage, we were thankful Meir had friends in key positions.

John finally came home looking exhausted. He loved everything about the hostel—except the bureaucracy.

"Nu? What happened?"

"We need a *shimush horeg.*"

"What's that?"

"That means 'unusual usage.' They claim that hostels aren't allowed in our neighborhood—we're a residential, not a business zone—but that we can apply to be an exception. Meir told them that before Vera bought the hostel, it had been used to house hotel workers and that the Soldiers' Hostel and the Melony Hotel are close-by. But they didn't listen. Anyway, he's applying for the shimush horeg and hopefully they'll leave us alone for a while."

I couldn't believe we might have to close down just as we were getting started, and when exciting things were happening.

הַמִּקְלָט

Rob from Holland was typical of travellers who kept coming back to the hostel for years.

Having arrived in Israel to volunteer on a kibbutz and then being thrown out because of his drinking and drug use, Rob drifted down to Eilat. Sleeping on the beach was fine for a while, but then his friend told him about the Shelter. "Check it out. It's clean and cheap. Run by some friendly religious freaks, but anyone can stay. They won't bother you with their views if you're not interested."

Later Rob told me, "I couldn't explain the sparkle I felt at the Shelter. In some ways it was like other hostels, but it was also very different: having separate dorms for men and women, and the curfew. Of course I didn't attend Bible studies; I thought you believers were a bunch of weaklings."

Rob preferred hanging out with another group of hostel guests: guys who worked at construction sites. Every evening after cooking and eating a meal together, they headed for the Red Lion Pub known for hard-core drinking. Afterwards we found out that they would sneak beer into the Shelter against our rules, and that when they returned after the front gate was locked, they climbed over the wall.

"There's no way I can believe in God," Rob told John one afternoon in the sukkah. "All my life I've been an atheist."

"Why don't you at least try reading the Bible?" John suggested. "Give it a chance. That's how I started to believe."

Arriving home for lunch one afternoon, John told me, "Rob left. He's going to the University of Leiden to study political science. I hate to see him go." John had enjoyed talking with Rob, maybe because they came from the same part of Holland and Rob reminded John of himself before he started to believe.

On the other hand, I'd been feeling that Rob should get away; lately he was often drunk during the day as well as at night. We had seen before that when people start getting interested in the Bible, the inner conflict causes them to get worse before they get better. I was sure he'd be back.

"The student life at Dutch universities with all the drinking will be a mess for him," John said. "Remember how we were in Leiden on some holiday and saw students in boats on the canals drunk out of their minds?"

Months later I walked over to the Shelter, having managed to round up the kids, put their shoes on, and convince them to go for a walk. Each time I entered the gate, I often wondered if new people had arrived whom I didn't know. Not being there every day made me feel disconnected, as if I should know all the guests, whereas in fact many were strangers to me. So I was happy to see a familiar face.

"Hey, Rob! When did you get back?"

"I finished my first year of studies and decided I needed a long holiday. Travelling usually makes me feel better; I'm free when I'm on the road." We sat down together while the children had fun playing with pebbles.

"It used to be like that for me, too," I said. Although I knew that Rob had a severe drinking problem and could get violent when drunk, with his wide, friendly smile it was hard not to like him.

"But roaming around Europe didn't satisfy me and I decided to come back here. I arrived a couple of days ago," Rob informed me. "And you know what? This time it's different. Now I'm the one who wants to talk to the staff about God, and it makes sense to me. Herbby explained that first I have to believe in God and then my feelings will start to change, not the other way around."

A few days later John came home with the good news: Rob had decided to trust in Jesus. He soon stopped drinking, found an excellent job as a tour guide, and eventually met his future wife, at the Shelter.

When Dov, a Russian Israeli, showed up at the Shelter one day followed by his large dog, John felt instantly attracted to this young man with long dark hair and beard, ripped jeans, and who dragged himself along as if he'd just heard some terrible news.

"I'm a neighbor of Miki and Felix, and they suggested I come here," Dov introduced himself. Miki and Felix from Columbia were friends of ours.

"Great!" John responded. "Come in. You're welcome anytime. Let us know if we can help you."

Although Dov didn't stay long that first visit, he soon began to drop by daily.

Years later, after he had moved to the center of the country, Dov sat with me in the Shelter on one of his trips back to Eilat. In his slow and deliberate way he told me his story.

Dov emigrated from Lithuania with his parents and elder brother when he was twelve years old, a difficult age to be uprooted and have to adjust to a different culture. And although Dov's parents were Holocaust survivors and ardent Zionists, life in Israel wasn't easy for them. With his parents working long hours, Dov grew up on the street and slowly got drawn into a life of alcohol, hashish, and looking for fun. Studying and working didn't fit into his lifestyle.

After three years of army service, Dov came down to Eilat to join his brother who lived here. Since he didn't want a regular job, Dov bought a large thermos and sold coffee on the beach, moving between the sunbathers. Although his walking route took him by the Shelter, at first Dov wasn't interested in Miki and Felix's recommendation to stop by.

"I felt ashamed for some reason," Dov told me, "and didn't care to meet new people. Actually I didn't like people at all—just my few friends."

Dov had always hated gentiles and Christians. He quickly understood that John was passionate about the Bible, something else Dov hated. Yet, he was surprised to find himself liking John.

Dov felt peace when he stepped through the Shelter's gate and appreciated John giving him a new coffee thermos and letting him use the hostel's refrigerator.

"I did have my limits though; as soon as the Bible study began, I was gone. As a Jew, I couldn't imagine opening the Christian Bible. When once I found a Bible on the beach, I threw it in the garbage," Dov continued. "Then God did something amazing in my life. I picked up a modern version of the New Testament off a shelf in the hostel without realizing what book it was."

Once Dov started to read, he couldn't stop. He felt Jesus' words speaking to him personally, and for the first time in his life he felt loved, knowing that God was his Father.

"And that's how I started to believe in Yeshua," Dov concluded.

After years of being depressed, Dov experienced peace in his heart. His life began to change and old habits fell away. After a week he stopped smoking cigarettes, as well as hashish, and gave up drinking. He trimmed his hair and changed his clothing style.

"I've asked Dov to work on staff," John told me one evening when he came home from the evening Bible study. "He's at the hostel every day anyway. He can't get enough of the Bible!"

I liked Dov, and the children loved his dog. Having an Israeli in the hostel would be helpful. And Dov spoke Russian, too, though it was hardly needed at the time.

אמסקרט

Since the Sinai Peninsula had been given back to Egypt as part of Israel and Egypt's peace agreement, we regularly returned to visit our Bedouin friends. Especially in the first few years after the pact, the Bedouins suffered from a lack of income and many were destitute.

In a corner of the Shelter we had a "Bedouin box" where we stored used clothing that people gave us or that guests left behind. We periodically stuffed the box's contents into the back of our van to bring to the Sinai along with fresh milk products and vegetables, items that were in scarce supply there. We particularly tried to help our old friend Abdallah who, despite the severe diabetes that had left him with no feeling in his hands and no way to support himself, always received us warmly in his tiny lean-to.

With few worldly goods or even food, Abdallah shared with us whatever he had—sometimes simply peeling an orange and gracefully handing each person a couple of segments. He especially liked to serve the strong, sweet Bedouin tea. No matter how many times John tried to point out to him that for someone with diabetes, drinking a small glass of tea with three teaspoons of sugar was like taking poison, Abdallah didn't seem to understand; the tea was an important part of his culture and diet.

This time, however, John found Abdallah's condition had deteriorated drastically. Through a mixture of Abdallah's limited Hebrew, John's broken Arabic, and a lot of sign language, John understood that Abdallah needed an operation to amputate his fingers, rotting from gangrene. While they were sitting together, a heavyset man with a mustache, dressed in a clean white shirt and dark slacks, walked up and sat next to them on the ground.

"Dr. Alfred," said Abdallah, smiling and pointing his chin at his visitor.

Arriving home two days later, John threw his backpack on the floor and his clothes in the washing machine. Everything smelled like smoke. "I met an amazing guy," he told me. "You'll really like him, Jupe. Alfred's an Egyptian doctor who's in charge of Nueiba's medical clinic. We met when I was drinking tea with Abdallah."

After meeting Alfred in Abdallah's hut, John had gone over to his clinic. Something that he said, as well as his name, hinted to John that Alfred wasn't a Muslim, so John asked him directly, "Are you a Christian?"

"Sure, I'm a Christian," Alfred answered, inviting John to take a seat. "I was baptized in the Coptic Orthodox Church; I have the certificate, celebrate all the Christian festivals, and have a Bible at home."

"But do you live your life for Jesus?" John continued. "Are you born again?"

When he saw that Alfred didn't understand, John explained that he wasn't talking about possessing documents or being born into a Christian family, but having a living relationship with the Creator. "And can you tell me what's happening with Abdallah?" John asked.

Alfred told John how he regularly visited Abdallah to give him insulin injections, although, not having a proper blood glucose meter, he wasn't able to give him high doses for fear he'd fall into a coma. John was impressed by Alfred's care for Abdallah and also that he employed a number of Bedouins, because though the Bedouin were Egyptian citizens and also Muslims, most Egyptians disdained them and wouldn't give them permanent jobs.

"What made you come to Nueiba?" John asked Alfred. "The scenery and nature?"

Alfred explained that as a member of Egypt's Coptic Christian minority, he wasn't allowed to advance as a physician but was assigned to Nueiba, Egypt's boondocks. Rather than becoming bitter, Alfred developed a love for the Bedouin and even more surprisingly—since the average Egyptian still considered Israelis their enemy, notwithstanding the peace treaty—for Israel. Israelis, however, having developed an infatuation with the uncluttered, seemingly endless Sinai beaches, didn't let the new border stop them from returning to their favorite spots.

Through Alfred's encounters on the beach and in his medical clinic, he developed not only friendships with individual Israelis but also a deep admiration for the nation. This unfortunately proved to be his undoing, although Alfred would later say that God used these circumstances to lead him in unexpected ways.

"I'm glad to be home." John told me. "Next time you have to come with me. Hey kids! I brought you some presents." John pulled out of his bag some mango juice boxes and cookie packages with Arabic writing on them.

"The good news is that Alfred is taking care of Abdallah better than I could ever hope to. And also, though he was a nominal Christian and didn't know much about Jesus, now he wants to read the Bible," John said.

As John continued to travel to the Sinai his relationship with Alfred deepened, and he observed his new friend's growing love for Jesus. "I feel that by serving the Bedouin people, I'm serving God," Alfred told John.

Years later Alfred told me about the deep roots of his feelings for Israel. His mother had good contacts with the Jewish community in Alexandria and even as a young child Alfred had enjoyed hearing them singing. One of his mother's friends, a midwife whom he called "Mama Rebecca," suddenly disappeared one day when he was seven years old. When Alfred asked his mother why Mama Rebecca didn't come to his birthday party as usual, her answer shocked him. "She left Egypt." Only when he was older did Alfred learn that between the foundation of Israel in 1948 and the Six-Day War in 1967, due to confiscation of their assets, bombings, imprisonments, and torture, Egypt's ancient Jewish community almost completely disappeared.

When John and I heard in the news that a young Israeli woman was raped and murdered near Nueiba, we were shocked to think that this could happen in such a seemingly peaceful place, but at that time we didn't yet know of Alfred's link to the incident. Later he told us that when Israeli investigators found a body they were sure was the young Israeli, but which the Egyptians claimed was an old woman, he was called on to testify.

The Egyptians pressured Alfred to write their official version in his report, but he stated the truth. "The stupidity and corruption of the Egyptian police disgusted me," Alfred told me.

Not long afterwards a bus with German tourists overturned near Nueiba causing many deaths and injuries. Alfred, the attending doctor, chose to evacuate the wounded to the nearest hospital—Yoseftal in Eilat. The Egyptians took this as a blow to their honor, the second delivered by Alfred. For his career it was the final straw: he was never allowed to practice medicine in Egypt again.

Sent back home to Alexandria, Alfred attempted to contact the Israeli embassy in Cairo but was followed and threatened by Egyptian secret police. Desperate, he tried another tactic and turned to the Germans. After many clandestine visits, letters, and testimonies from others, Alfred finally received political asylum, the German government being deeply grateful for his life-saving decision.

When Alfred received his German passport after ten years, the first country he visited was Israel, and he returns every year speaking fluent Hebrew. When he retires as a doctor he hopes to spend part of his time in Eilat.

הפסקה

Although I didn't miss America, I felt the absence of my parents, sisters, nieces and nephews. I kept in touch as best as I could, mainly through letters and sending pictures, because phone calls were prohibitively expensive. Thankfully, though, a small community began to form in Eilat of people who believe that Jesus is the Messiah, from Jewish as well as Christian backgrounds, who didn't identify with any particular denomination but were united in our mutual faith and became one another's surrogate family.

My mother regularly sent carbon-copy letters to my sisters and me. "Guess what?" I said to John as I read her latest dispatch. "Mom and Dad want us to come to America this summer for a reunion. Think you can get away?" I wanted our children to know their families in Holland and America but couldn't see myself traveling without John as some women I knew did.

"Dov's doing really well at the hostel," John said. "I'm sure that if we have other good volunteers, he can manage. He's not an outgoing guy, but he's great at running the place. Let's pray about it, and I'll talk to him."

A friend of mine who also ran a hostel with her husband asked me how we could both go away at the same time. She wanted to know how the money that came in would be handled. She and her husband never took vacations together because they had no one they could trust.

Her questions made me thankful for our special, trustworthy friends. And anticipating being in the hostel business long-term, I knew that if we didn't take breaks we wouldn't survive.

11. Pee Mattresses, Snotty & Other Encounters

"This isn't bad, Jupe," John was lying on a mattress in front of our tent. A soot-blackened pot of sweet tea balanced on the fire next to him. "Instead of driving an hour or two to hang out on the beach, now we're only fifteen minutes from home."

Since the Sinai's return to Egypt in 1982 we needed passports to go to Nueiba and Dahab. But because Israel and Egypt both claimed Taba, this small sliver of territory near Eilat was still in Israel's possession. The issue was submitted to an international commission, and in 1988 they ruled in Egypt's favor. The following year Israel returned Taba to Egypt.

Until then, we usually went to the Taba beach on Shabbat with family and friends. And on the holidays when Israelis have long vacations, putting up our big tent there transported us back to the Sinai: the clear blue sea, palm trees, sandy beach, and stunning views of the Mountains of Edom. Only the Bedouins and endless beaches were missing.

Together with the thousands of Israelis who converged on

Taba during Pesach and Sukkoth and packed the area with tents, a group of hippies made the beach their home. Some of them lived there for years, supporting themselves from their savings or by taking odd jobs to postpone their return to cold Europe. Visas weren't a problem because Israel was lenient in those days.

With little to do all day, the beach people gladly welcomed John to sit with them, listening and asking questions, as he shared the good news that changed his life. When our tent was standing, he'd invite them over for a cup of tea or coffee, or homemade pitas and one-pot rice stew in the evening. He welcomed them to stop by the Shelter any time, but especially on Friday evenings for our Shabbat gathering, and many took him up on his offer.

For me, the tent in Taba meant getting away from the house and my usual routine. Our children enjoyed the freedom of playing in the sand and sea. I made sure they were water-safe by teaching them to swim at a young age. The colorful coral reefs a few meters offshore beckoned a dive. Putting on masks and snorkels, we felt we'd entered a magical, alternative world. The tent was also a time for fellowship and community because besides the hippies, we connected with families in neighboring tents, and friends from Eilat and the north of Israel visited us.

It was in Taba that John met Adriaan for the first time. Already in Israel for two years, Adriaan wasn't staying simply because he liked the weather or people, but out of necessity.

"My doctor recommended I come here," Adriaan told John over a cup of coffee at the hostel, having accepted John's invitation to stay there. Although from Holland, Adriaan had shaggy dark hair and tanned complexion, and was often mistaken for an Israeli.

Adriaan suffered from a severe form of psoriasis, a disease that resulted in scaly red and white patches on his skin. Various creams and even hospitalization didn't provide a cure, nor did the bottles of gin that Adriaan drank to fight the depression and poor self-image brought on by his condition. Finally a dermatologist suggested an alternative treatment: the Dead Sea, the lowest point on earth, and the world's most mineral-rich body of water. Lying in the high-oxygen and low ultraviolet air and bathing in the waters often healed sufferers.

Adriaan didn't need much persuasion; due to his disability he hadn't worked for years. He booked a plane ticket, and after landing in Ben Gurion Airport, took a bus to Kibbutz Ein Gedi on the shores of the Dead Sea where he began working as a volunteer. For Adriaan, the Dead Sea proved to be life-giving as his psoriasis slowly disappeared. Together with the unsightly and itching blotches, his other symptoms vanished too—the embarrassment, extreme self-consciousness, and social isolation. Furthermore, besides not needing gin anymore, Adriaan found new passions: reading the Bible and faith in Jesus.

When John met him in Taba, Adriaan was living and working at Yigal's Camping, a collection of simple huts built on a hillside outside of town.

Yigal, a one-armed war hero, aimed to create a laid-back atmosphere resembling what he had left behind in the Sinai. This suited Adriaan because, after all his years of alienation, he wasn't ready yet to fully integrate into society.

John invited Adriaan to the Shelter and he soon began dropping by every day. "My skin was clean and I wanted a change," Adriaan told John, "so I came to Eilat." He especially enjoyed the Bible studies but also the community. Later on, Adriaan came on board as a volunteer, and he and John called each other "First Mate" and "Captain." (Years later he would write me an email about his "highs and lows, successes and blows," and that he remembered asking himself: *How do we keep the ship sailing?*)

One day Adriaan brought John Zoetemelk back to the Shelter with him. A fellow Dutchman with unkempt hair and a wild look in his eyes, John talked nonstop and was always on the move.

"John, meet John," Adriaan introduced his friends.

(Although the Shelter is only a four-minute walk from our house, pushing a baby carriage or traipsing over with little children who stopped to pick up every stick and rock on the way, made me feel like I needed half a day for the trip to be worthwhile. Besides, it seemed like there was always something going on at home. But when Adriaan walked in with John, I happened to be sitting in the hostel's courtyard enjoying a visit with our volunteers.)

"John here is friends with Snotty," Adriaan added. "She and her boyfriend stay behind the Peace Café."

Snotty, a Jewish girl from London who was full of tattoos and piercings, used to come to our Friday evening Shabbat meetings.

"You mean on the pee mattresses?" my husband asked. The original Peace Café, once a place for travelers to hang out and listen to good music, had deteriorated through the years to become a den of hashish and grime. A person had to be desperate, broke, stoned, or all three, to crash on the stinking mattresses.

"I've had some good talks with Snotty," John said after we'd returned home. "Want to come over with me one of these days, Jupe?"

Visiting Snotty and the pee mattresses didn't sound like my first choice for an outing, so I said I'd think about it.

But John Zoetemelk soon began coming around to the Shelter. Attracted to the message of Jesus, John had one serious problem—his Israeli girlfriend was pulling him the other way. As John drew closer to Jesus, she could feel him growing colder to her and their drug world.

Finally John decided to break up with her and return to Holland, straight to a drug rehabilitation center. On our next trip to Holland we visited him there and were encouraged to see John growing in his new path of faith and freedom.

הפורים

Though not one of the feasts ordained in Leviticus Chapter Twenty-three, Purim is a popular holiday in Israel in which we celebrate the Jewish people's victory over wicked Haman. The scroll of Esther is read in synagogues, children dress in costumes, and we eat *hamantaschen* or "Haman's ears," a triangular-shaped cookie with a sweet filling. I had been busy for days sewing outfits for the children—a clown, a pirate, Little Red Riding Hood, and a Dutch girl—and after taking the traditional family picture, went with John to watch the school classes parading down the street.

Afterward, John went to the Shelter. He was sitting at a table near the entrance to the hostel, eating hamantaschen, when a neatly-dressed man walked in the gate. John sensed immediately that he wasn't seeking a place to stay.

"I'm looking for John Pex," he announced in Hebrew.

"That's me," John said.

He handed John a document ordering him to report to the police station. When John went there the following day, a police officer told John that if he didn't straighten out the problem with the license, the Shelter would be closed.

John looked upset when he came home.

"What happened?" I asked, putting on the kettle for a cup of tea.

"I know it's not as serious as that, but I'm reminded of the Purim story, when Haman conspired to destroy all the Jews," John answered.

We'd been open for two years now, much longer than our first hostel, but we couldn't help feeling there was a plot against us. We knew that other hostels didn't have the licensing problems that we had.

"I'm sure it's because of our faith," John said. "But if God wants us open, He'll work it out. And in the meantime, I'll go tomorrow to pay the fine and file the papers."

I was thankful that, like Mordechai and Esther, John didn't give up and wasn't intimidated. We could probably stay open a while longer.

הפקדש

Bronya and Ephraim showed up at the Shelter one day lugging

oversized suitcases. Elderly, wrinkled, and short, they weren't our usual hostel guests. Thankfully Dov was there to welcome them, as Ephraim, wearing a jaunty cap, managed to pant in Polish-accented Hebrew, "We ... need ... a ... room."

Dov, having glanced in the reservation book, informed them we were full. "But at least sit down, rest, and have a glass of water," he offered.

Ephraim couldn't explain who had directed them to the Shelter. He did tell us, however, that they had sold their apartment in Tel Aviv and needed a place to stay until they bought a home in Eilat.

"We only have one bed available in a girls' dorm," Dov told them. "But you can leave your suitcases in the shack while you look for another hostel."

When Ephraim saw the shack, which was our storage space for mattresses, luggage, and books, he decided he'd stay there while Bronya would take the last girls' bed. Dov called John with the odd request—no one had ever slept in the shack before—but before receiving an answer, Ephraim had already moved in, spreading out a bed for himself between their four huge suitcases.

As we slowly got to know Ephraim and Bronya they shared with us their story. Both Holocaust survivors, Bronya was the only one of her family to survive the Lodz Ghetto, and Ephraim had been a resistance fighter. They met after the war, married, and immigrated to Israel where they began a new life with Ephraim working as a tailor.

Even after they moved to their own apartment in Eilat, Bronya and Ephraim continued to be part of our family, becoming surrogate grandparents to our children. They celebrated holidays with us, such as Pesach, Holocaust Remembrance Day, and Hanukkah, when Bronya cooked for us the traditional latkes (fried potato pancakes served with sour cream and applesauce).

To our surprise Bronya and Ephraim came to the Bible studies and were unusually open to hearing about our faith. Most of our experience till then was with the traveler/hippie types, including young Israelis. When we did have opportunities to share with older Jewish people they unfortunately were often opposed to Jesus and the New Testament, arguing that Jesus was Christian and that the Christians had persecuted Jews.

Bronya told us how, as a child before the war, she would slip into Catholic churches and meditate, attracted by the person of Jesus. When John showed her prophecies about Jesus from the Tanach (Old Testament) about Jesus' birth in Bethlehem, His being born from a virgin, and eventually dying for the sins of all people, Bronya's affinity for Jesus turned into real faith.

The time came for us to leave for our biennial summer vacation in Holland and America. "We'll come with you!" Ephraim announced.

"I'm sorry, Ephraim," John explained in his best diplomatic manner. "You see, we stay with my parents in their small house. Don't worry—we'll be home before you know it."

After parting with kisses, hugs, and promises to see one another before too long back in Eilat, we were startled a few days after arriving in Holland to open John's parents' front door and see Ephraim and Bronya standing outside with their suitcases. "We missed you!" they said together.

John's parents were used to his friends showing up at their home. One time after a winter spent together on the kibbutz, before the volunteers parted ways they began talking about when they would ever see one another again. John suddenly had an idea. "Everyone's invited to my house in Holland this summer. We'll meet on the first of August at one o'clock on Platform One in the Central Train Station in Amsterdam."

To John's, and his parents', amazement, about twenty people turned up. John's mother and father, with their typical resilience, acted as if nothing was unusual when John entered the house like the Pied Piper leading his mixed group of friends, though his father later liked to tell the story of stepping over bodies on his way to work in the morning.

While touched that Ephraim and Bronya loved and missed us

so much, we knew we needed to find an immediate solution to their housing problem. A cup of Dutch coffee and a few phone calls later, we had our answer. Several months previously a Dutch Jewish family had stayed at the Shelter who, like us, believed in Jesus and who had told us about their many children and large house. Thankfully they were willing to host Ephraim and Bronya for as long as they wanted to stay.

Soon after coming home to Eilat, Ephraim was already planning his next trip. "I'm going to visit my cousin in Mexico City and afterwards go to San Francisco," he told us. "I haven't seen my cousin since we were youngsters, and I've always wanted to see San Francisco."

Nothing Bronya said could dissuade him. "He was never like this," Bronya said. "I don't know what's gotten into him. Suddenly picking up and leaving Tel Aviv and buying an apartment in Eilat. Then taking off for Holland, and now Mexico City. At least I have you."

During another round of hugs and good-byes, we never imagined this would be the last time we'd see Ephraim. A week later we received a phone call from his cousin. "Ephraim passed away last night. He had in inoperable tumor."

Suddenly Ephraim's bizarre behavior became clear: he knew he was going to die. He didn't tell anyone, but decided to live every day as if it was his last. John arranged for Ephraim's body to be flown back to Israel, and we attended his funeral in Tel Aviv. Soon afterwards, Bronya left Eilat. She died a few years later.

הסמוקרט

The summers when we didn't visit our families, we packed our van with our big Taba tent and camped next to the Sea of Galilee. Swimming, hiking, fishing, and campfires were a perfect break from the intensity of running the Shelter. Furthermore, John and I wanted to share our love for Israel's landscapes and history with our children. When our clothes were filthy and we had enough of the mosquitoes and biting ants, and the noisy Israelis camping next to us, we finished our vacation at Bethel Hostel in Haifa, now managed by Paul and Traci. We appreciated spending time with friends who understood the trials and triumphs of managing a hostel.

Home in Eilat, John went back and forth to the hostel several times a day, beginning by opening up at six thirty in the morning and ending by checking the reservation and receipt books after the children were in bed. But when we were away John realized there was nothing he could do, and just called every couple of days.

One summer Herbby managed the Shelter in place of John. John appreciated having Herbby on staff with his discernment and sense of humor.

After an afternoon spent floating on inner tubes down a tributary of the Jordan River, John found the campground's pay phone and rang the hostel.

Herbby answered.

"How're things going?" John asked.

"Great, except for Pascal. You know how he talks about wanting to be free? So today he opened all the gas cylinders."

"Balagan. But it's not the first time he's acted up. I'll be home tomorrow, and in the meantime try to calm him down."

John had had a run-in with Pascal from France a few weeks previously. Pascal and his desire for freedom reminded us of other guests, but he took it a few degrees further. One morning when John came to the Shelter, he found all the faucets running and the sewage holes open. As he ran from one to the other to close them, John suddenly looked up to see Pascal, whose long hair stuck out straight from his head, dancing naked on the roof of the girls' dorm, and flapping his arms like a bird.

Docile when John and Herbby coaxed him to the ground and brought him clothes, Pascal explained, "The water also needs to be free."

Even when guests have obvious problems, like Pascal, the staff often develops a bond and affection for them and is reluctant to have them leave. Having witnessed many instances of lives changed and people released from destructive habits, we continue to believe that a bit more time, good talks, Bible reading, prayer, and love will carry them through. But, sadly, none of this worked with Pascal.

Not long after we came home from our vacation, rested and ready to go again, we had some new excitement in the hostel: a movie, "Rambo in Afghanistan," starring Sylvester Stallone, was being filmed in Eilat and employed a number of our guests as extras. Sylvester himself was staying in one of the top hotels in town, located near the beach close to the Jordanian frontier. Early one morning, guards posted around the hotel spotted a thin, long-haired young man climbing over the barbed wire border fence. Although quickly perceiving that Sylvester wasn't in danger, they called the police, who apprehended Pascal. He gave a simple explanation: he didn't believe in borders and wanted to go to Jordan.

Needless to say, they deported Pascal, and later we heard the tragic news that, back in France, he committed suicide.

12. Elvis & Pilgrims

"I still can't figure out how someone from Ghana ended up in Eilat." We were pushing Josh back and forth between us in the water, our method to teach him to swim. "And then on a drilling platform as a cook."

Unlike some other people groups who came to Eilat, the Africans didn't arrive all at once, but rather came in as individuals spread out through a period of many years. When we first met Elvis, Josh was just three years old.

Our new friend worked on an oil platform that was normally positioned in the Gulf of Suez. Captured by Israel in 1967 and returned to Egypt in 1975, the Sinai's oil fields continued to serve as a major source of Israel's energy. At the moment, however, the rig was stationed in Eilat's port. Elvis had invited us to visit him at work and we looked forward to hearing his story.

Elvis's tour of the oil platform the following Saturday afternoon involved climbing ladders, walking over narrow bridges, and ended in his workplace: the kitchen. He invited us to sit on benches at long, plastic-covered tables and treated us to *hamin*, a heavy, thick stew consisting of grains, beans, potatoes, and meat, and left to cook for twelve hours on a hot plate to comply with the religious Jews' regulation against lighting a fire on the Sabbath.

How he came to Eilat wasn't the only question we had concerning Elvis. Meeting him opened to us a new world with a different set of characters. We had always felt comfortable interacting with backpackers and travelers, the mainstay of the Shelter's guests, because of our similar lifestyles. Whether they were from America or Australia, Sweden or Switzerland, England or places in between, we understood their mentality and background.

John related better than I did to drug addicts, homeless people, and alcoholics, and seemed to have endless patience with them. Yet even for me, seeing Dov, Rob, and others give up their addictions, start to believe, and turn their lives around, gave me hope for the next person we met on the beach or who entered our gate.

God, however, removed our feeling of adequacy when he brought us the Africans, a group of people with whom we had no experience and little in common. With John's heart for the underdog, needy, and stranger, it wasn't surprising that they found us, the only local community of people believing in Jesus; in a small town, word gets around. Yet we don't remember how or when we met Elvis, our first African contact and friend in Eilat.

"How'd you get here?" John asked Elvis over the meal. "And why Israel?"

"I came like most of the Ghanaians come. As a pilgrim."

"A pilgrim? What d'you mean?"

Elvis explained that while Ghana is mostly Christian, they have a significant Muslim population. With one of the five pillars of Islam being the pilgrimage to Mecca at least once in a lifetime, Ghana's government subsidizes the journey. To be fair, a trip to

Jerusalem is offered for Christian pilgrims. Many Ghanaians as well as Nigerians, who have the same option, take advantage of this offer, but upon completing their tour to the holy places, "jump ship" and stay on in Israel illegally to work.

Years later, John once stopped to talk with a bus carrying Nigerian pilgrims. Their pastor opened up to John, nearly crying, "I've lost almost all my group. We're only ten people left!"

Desperate to get to a Western country where they could earn and save money, coming on a pilgrimage to Israel was attractive. In an odd symbiosis, hotels, restaurants, and other employers in Eilat, with the tacit approval of the Israeli government, cooperated to allow the Africans to work.

The founders and early pioneers of Israel came with high ideals to settle the land of their forefathers. In Europe and in other countries where the Jews lived, they were prohibited from owning land and from working in most professions. In their nation-building quest, the new immigrants proudly elevated the work of a farmer and laborer. The kibbutzim thrived with these principles and the country was built up.

As the country modernized, however, fewer Israelis were willing to do those jobs which had once symbolized the "new Israeli," and preferred white-collar work; hence the need for others to work in agriculture and construction. During years of relative peace, Palestinians are a cheap and available source of labor, and they earn far more in Israel than in their under-developed economy. But at many times, due to suicide bombings and other terror attacks, Palestinians aren't allowed to enter Israel freely.

Eilat's economy had also changed through the years. Founded in 1949 on an empty stretch of land between the Red Sea and the mountains, the first settlers worked in the building of roads and apartment blocks as well as in the Timna Copper Mines and the port. Gradually, however, with 360 sunny days a year, beaches, coral reefs, and desert landscapes, Eilat gained popularity as a domestic and international vacation destination.

Hotels sprung up, and tourism became the mainstay of Eilat's economy.

But who would work as chambermaids and dishwashers? Israelis weren't willing to do these jobs anymore. The Africans stepped in like a gift to the hotels. With pressure from the hotel industry, the government turned a blind eye to the fact that the Ghanaians and Nigerians had overstayed their pilgrim visas. We needed them, they needed us, and everyone was happy—the hotel managers, the Africans, and presumably the hotel guests too.

Elvis, though not working in tourism, worked in the kitchen on the oil rig and came to our Erev Shabbat (Sabbath Eve) meetings at the Shelter for a couple of months.

"I love Elvis's songs," John said to me after one meeting when we had finally cleared away and washed all the dishes and dragged the furniture back to its place. "Reminds me of when I was in South Africa and Mozambique." John had a special place in his heart for Africans since his time in the Merchant Marine; he often said that if we weren't in Israel, he would choose Africa.

Elvis exited our lives as suddenly as he entered. We reckon that after being repaired, his oil platform was hauled back to the Sinai.

הקמיטו

Hammed, another one of the early Africans to join us, had a fine build and appeared to be a mixture of Arab and African.

"Where're you from?" John asked him. John always found this a good opening line and then could usually throw out a few phrases in a person's mother tongue.

"Timbuktu," answered Hammed. "I'm a Muslim but want to know more about Christianity."

After inviting him for a cup of tea, John explained that he wasn't promoting Christianity, but could tell him about Jesus and how to get a new life. Then he gave Hammed a French Bible. From then on, Hammed began coming regularly to our meetings.

"Wow!" I said to John later. "We've never had anyone from Mali here, let alone from Timbuktu."

Sitting on a chair near the door, one Shabbat morning he stood up in his place. "I have something to say," he announced in his quiet, humble manner and with a big smile on his face. "I want to tell you that I have decided to follow Jesus. I am no longer a Muslim." And he sat down. Not long afterwards he left Eilat.

הַמַּקֵּט

Following Elvis and Hammed, in the late 1980s more and more Africans began finding their way to our meetings, and the cultural differences came to the fore. Some stayed for an extended period, allowing us to develop friendships but also giving us a window into another lifestyle and manner of thinking.

Francis and Amelia, from Ghana, remained in Eilat for years and became part of our community. Energetic, friendly, and focused, this young couple had a goal—to make money and create a better life for themselves when they eventually returned to Ghana. While here, though, they were committed to our congregation and came to all our meetings, leading us in lively choruses accompanied by an African drum John had traded for a pair of blue jeans on one of his trips to Africa. Their songs, like "Great Change Since I Was Born," and "Lift Jesus Higher, Lower Satan Lower," were so simple and catchy that they quickly had everyone singing and clapping along.

Francis and Amelia began as the rest of their compatriots, working as cleaners in one of Eilat's large hotels. But being enterprising and motivated, they soon realized they could earn more by working independently; and they opened a private house-cleaning business. Giving good service for a reasonable price, they had more work than they could handle and continued this way for some years—saving money, sending part of their earnings home to their families in Ghana, and accumulating possessions.

"You mentioned your friends are coming from Holland soon," Francis approached John and me one Friday evening. "Do you think they could bring us a video camera?"

A video camera? We don't have one and we don't know anyone else who has one either. Where'd they get that idea?

"I'm not sure it's legal to bring something valuable into the country and then give it away," John replied, tactfully trying to evade the request. "Israel's pretty strict on importing luxury items."

"It shouldn't be a problem," said Francis. "I know someone else who got one that way, and I'll pay of course."

Our friends brought the camera for Francis, but I had to get used to their priorities being so different from ours, especially concerning material goods.

הַמִּקְלָט

Francis and Amelia introduced us to Jojo Jackson. Although many Ghanaians and Nigerians now came to our meetings, we developed a special relationship with Jojo. With his tall stature, good looks, and natural charisma, Jojo lit up any room he entered; while his bongo playing, ready laugh, and joyful singing added life to every occasion. He seemed to enjoy spending time with our family and often dropped by our house after work.

"Don't forget to invite Jojo to Herbby's birthday party," I reminded John. We find many occasions to celebrate in the Shelter: holidays, birthdays, farewell parties, and any other reason to bring people together; so with Herbby turning thirty, we decided to throw a big birthday bash.

When the day of Herbby's party arrived, Jojo and many others came to the festivities, which included music, food, a birthday cake with thirty candles, and funny hats. Eventually, after everyone had left, John and I had a few minutes for reflection, while the children were in good moods and continued to run around. We both agreed it had been a great party. Food, music, and fellowship—the usual Shelter elements—had come together to give everyone an enjoyable time, full of fun.

"Jojo's become a real friend, but there are still things I can't get used to with the Africans." John unwound the fire hose from its reel and began spraying the courtyard, his alternative to sweeping. Afterwards he grabbed a squeegee and swabbed all the water to the side. "Like why do they always come late?"

"Yes, they know our meetings start at ten o'clock on Shabbat, yet none of them ever show up before ten thirty or eleven." I hopped out of the way of the water stream.

"It's the old joke. Europeans have watches, but Africans have time."

"Case in point, when their church service lasts half a day it's not important to be there from the start."

The previous summer while staying at Beit Immanuel Guest House in Jaffa with our family, we were returning from the beach when we met a couple of Ghanaians we knew from Eilat.

"Come inside to our meeting," one said to us. "We're just beginning."

"Great!" John turned to us. "Come on, kids, let's go!"

"Are you sure?" I questioned. "Look at us—still in beach clothes and the kids are wiped out after all the sun and swimming."

"Oh Jupe, come on, don't be a spoilsport." John loved any time believers in Jesus got together. "We've got Africans coming to our meetings, so now we'll see what their meetings are like. We'll just slip in the back and leave when we want."

The children, though they were used to their abba's behavior and knew they had no choice, held back. Then John gripped the hands of Moriah and Yonatan and guided us into the meeting hall.

Suddenly all eyes were on our family—six white people in the midst of a couple hundred blacks. The preacher, standing in front of a microphone wearing a suit and tie, interrupted what he was saying and announced, "We are pleased to welcome Pastor John and Judy Pex with their children, all the way from Eilat. John and Judy, please come to the front."

To applause, John and I were ushered to seats of honor facing the congregation at a long table in the front. The children were then settled in chairs in the middle of the room. Most of the men wore suits and the women were arrayed in elaborate African outfits or fancy dresses that looked like something from another era.

So much for not being seen in our beach clothes and slipping out early!

This service didn't seem to have any specific beginning and I hoped not to stay till the end. People kept entering and others stood up and left. Various men came to the front with rousing messages from the Bible, interspersed with gospel songs and choruses, some of which we knew from Jojo and our Eilat friends. John, of course, was also one of the speakers.

Glancing at the children, I noticed they seemed to be getting into the mood, especially when food was passed around: trays of meat on skewers, plastic cups with soft drinks, potato chips, and other food we rarely ate at home.

Finally after a couple of hours, John succumbed to my gentle under-the-table kicks, stood up, thanked our African brothers and sisters, excused us, and we were free.

Stepping outside into the fresh air with a big smile on his face, John said, "See, Jupe, it wasn't so bad. Admit it, you enjoyed yourself. And don't we want the kids to be open to different cultures and experiences?"

הפסיקו

When we first moved to Eilat we simply opened the Bible and studied God's Word any time people showed up, usually every evening. Although now we were more organized and meeting every week in our living room on Shabbat morning, we tried to keep our original informal and family atmosphere. With that purpose, we gave people the opportunity to share what was on their mind and to ask for prayer.

One Saturday, Francis stood up and said, "Amelia and I have a problem and would appreciate your prayers. We've been here a couple of years and have our business, as you know. But now the Ministry of Interior is rounding up people who don't have a visa and deporting them. Would you please pray that we could stay?"

John and I were in a bind. How could we pray for or even encourage Francis and Amelia to stay when they were here illegally? We tried to understand and put ourselves in their place: desperate to earn a living, the sole breadwinners within their extended families, and with limited options open to them. On the other hand, could God bless them in this position? We didn't think so.

The Israeli government, which in the beginning overlooked the Africans with no work visas—largely due to the hotels' insistence that they were a source of cheap labor—eventually caved in to demands from another direction. Manpower agencies received permits to import workers that, unlike the Ghanaians and Nigerians who arrived here on their own, generated a lot of income. The hotel, construction, and agricultural workers paid high fees for the privilege of registering to work abroad, and various middlemen benefited, all the way up to government ministries.

Amelia and Francis eventually left and we heard they ended up in Japan selling paintings. But Jojo had another idea.

"My dream is to study Communications at Moody Bible School," Jojo confided in John. "That way I can serve God back home in Ghana. I just have to arrange for a visa to the U.S."

Though John and I saw the benefit of pursuing an education and taking biblical studies, we had never been to Bible school and didn't feel that we had missed out. We learned mostly through "on-the-job training." From our early days as new followers of Yeshua, we placed a priority on reading and studying the Bible, and through sharing and interacting with others we were forced to find answers and to delve deeper. In the Sinai we didn't have access to any study guides or commentaries, though later we enjoyed reading books and listening to tapes about the Bible.

Jojo, who definitely had a gift for communicating, chose a different path. And Moody had a good reputation. We began contacting friends in the United States. One family offered to sponsor Jojo, while other friends helped him with expenses.

After many preparations, Jojo flew to America. We kept in touch for a while, but eventually lost touch with him, though later we heard that Jojo didn't return to Ghana but married and remained in the United States.

הפסוק

When the government began deporting people who had no visas, the Africans were the first to go, being the most noticeable. Nevertheless, Ghanaians and Nigerians continued to arrive in Eilat. Even after the wave including Francis, Amelia, and Jojo were expelled, the Israeli government, without a clear policy on foreign workers, continued to allow others in. At one point many hundreds worked in Eilat's hotels, so many that they formed their own churches based on country, tribe, and denomination, and didn't come to our meetings any more.

We missed their singing and friendships but were glad they had their own fellowships. We realized they could better care for each other's needs, and there was no cultural gap to deal with.

That latter influx was also later rounded up and deported, this time to make way for new workers from India and Nepal. The policy, though seemingly irrational and arbitrary, often had to do with how many illegal workers there were. As long as the numbers remained low, the government ignored them, but when the foreigners' presence became more visible, the immigration police stepped in and kicked them out.

"I miss seeing the Africans on the street, and having them

come around," John said. "But we've learned a lot and I have the feeling we haven't seen the end yet."

"The children also grew through this," I added. In a natural way we were teaching our children tolerance and acceptance of the stranger. John often says that racism is one of the worst sins, having its root in pride. People think they are better than others, whether by nationality, color, religion, or language, whereas in God's eyes we are all equal. When we began the Shelter as a youth hostel for backpackers we never imagined the range of people groups who would come our way and broaden our horizons.

13. Next-Door Strangers

"Kaput! It's all kaput," Adel cried, nearly in tears. He had been sitting on a chair in the courtyard of the Shelter getting a haircut, a towel draped over his shoulders. An audience had gathered around to watch this momentous occasion, and with the hairdresser's pronouncement that she was done, Adel stood up. But when he looked in the bathroom mirror, Adel panicked. Having just returned from spending time in Germany, he burst out in the German language.

Adel, nicknamed "Tarzan" or "Goliath" by his friends, was colossal in all ways: his height, weight, breadth, smile, and shoulder-length hair. Somehow, though, he had decided he was ready for a new look. In the Shelter we loved Adel as he was, but perhaps he had realized he looked threatening to some people, combined with his Arab ethnicity, and that short hair might modify his image.

Eilat is a relatively new city, having come under Israeli control a year after the establishment of the State of Israel. At that time, in

1949, it was simply a British police station called Um Rash Rash, barely reachable by any means of transportation. The ancient history of Eilat reaches back to the Pharaohs with their Timna copper mines, King Solomon and his fleet of ships, the Greeks, Romans, and Byzantines. However, it was Lawrence of Arabia leading Bedouin warriors to battle, who conquered nearby Aqaba and helped bring the area under British control.

When the Israeli forces, traveling in two units for five days through the Negev Desert from Beersheba, reached Um Rash Rash, they found the police station abandoned; so they raised a hand-drawn flag, sent a telegram to headquarters, and claimed the territory for Israel. The 10th of March, or 11th of Adar according to the Hebrew calendar, is celebrated every year as both the day Eilat became part of the rest of Israel and as the official end of the War of Independence.

Although it took some years before civilians were willing to make the long journey south and settle in Eilat—a stunning location but with primitive living conditions—groups of immigrant families gradually agreed to live here. On the shores of the Red Sea, a small village sprung up which became a town in 1959.

Thus, unlike many other cities in Israel, Eilat has no old buildings, no churches, and no mosques. And whereas the Arab citizens of Israel number about twenty percent of the population, concentrated mostly in the cities of Jerusalem, Jaffa, Haifa, and Nazareth, as well as small towns and villages in the Galilee, Eilat has no native Arab residents.

Nevertheless, Arabs do live in Eilat, with many having moved here for the same reasons that Jewish Israelis do: for employment opportunities and a change in their lives. Some of those who come to Eilat have conflicts with their families and seek distance from the insular and conservative Arab society. Despite being only a five-hour ride from Tel Aviv, Israelis often consider Eilat the equivalent of a foreign land, or like Alaska or Hawaii for Americans.

Adel wasn't the first or only Arab who had stayed in the Shelter; we usually had three or four staying with us at any given time. As outsiders in Eilat they appreciated coming to the hostel where they felt welcome and accepted.

In theory we like the idea of having Arabs staying at the Shelter. Although we live in the same country, in practice most Arab and Jewish residents have little social contact. We are happy to be an exception to this practice and to be a place of reconciliation. Away from the restrictions of village life in the Galilee, many of our Arab guests have been open to the message of the gospel of Jesus. On the other hand, having Arabs as long-time guests tested us in ways we had never yet experienced.

המקדש

Hussam from Shaab, a village in the Galilee, came to the hostel because his friend Jamal was already staying with us. Unemployed and feeling restless, Hussam decided to take a vacation and visit his friend in Eilat. Tall, good-looking, and speaking Hebrew well, Hussam later told us that he immediately noticed the peaceful, friendly atmosphere at the Shelter.

Initially Hussam connected mainly with Hebrew speakers like Jack, who was staying at the Shelter for the summer with his wife and two boys with the intention of emigrating from America in the future. Within a month Hussam found a job and also began coming sporadically to the evening Bible studies. Although he wasn't a religious Muslim, Hussam's first reaction to the faith was that it absolutely wasn't for him. However, he asked many questions which John, Jack, Herbby, and others patiently answered.

One morning Hussam showed up early in the staff room. "I couldn't sleep last night," he said. "I bothered everyone in my room and kept getting up. My mind couldn't get quiet. I need to pray."

After looking into more Scriptures with Jack, Hussam decided he wanted to trust Jesus and that the Bible was truly God's Word, as opposed to the way he'd been brought up to believe in the Koran. Slowly we saw evidence of more peace and joy in Hussam's life; previously he'd always appeared to be nervous and jumpy.

Yet Hussam clearly struggled. He began coming to our services carrying his Bible, although we never saw him reading much on his own. Furthermore, his friend Jamal had already gone back to Shaab with the news that Hussam had become a Christian, creating a schism between Hussam and his family. He found it easiest never to mention his new faith when at home.

Later Hussam went through some difficult years after being diagnosed with cancer in his left femur. He had three operations in the center of the country but spent time recovering in Eilat. Volunteers from the Shelter visited him in the hospital and in his apartment when he came home—theoretically a good thing but at times complicated.

"Jupe, I had to tell the volunteer girls no more leg massages for Hussam," John announced when he came home for lunch one day. "It's getting ridiculous. I know he's a cancer survivor, but I've had enough of them sitting around in the sukkah like that, with that look in their eyes—on both sides."

"How'd the girls take it?"

"Well, you know how it is," John answered. "These girls can be so naïve. I don't know what it is about the Arab guys. Maybe you can tell me."

I couldn't explain it either, though we'd seen this phenomenon before. Perhaps girls, especially the Europeans, found the dark look exotic. In their villages, Muslim men were barely able to speak to women, so here they found freedom to do so. When they turned on their charm, some girls weren't able to resist.

John feels fatherly towards our volunteers and approached them as he would our daughters. He didn't spare words when warning them about the dangers of entering such relationships.

"It's happening again," John told me. "This time it's Jeannie. Gotta nip it in the bud, so I'll sit down with her today and have a talk."

When John found a quiet moment and place to talk, Jeannie argued that Hussam had become a believer in Jesus and that now they had the same faith.

"The differences in cultures are huge," John pointed out to her. "And besides, you have to give these guys time, to see how they continue in their faith."

Most of our girls listened to reason and understood that John had their best interests in mind, but unfortunately at least two women we know married Arabs and later divorced. Believers from Muslim backgrounds face tremendous stress and challenges, even more than those from Jewish backgrounds; village and family relationships are usually tight and controlling. Some of the so-called believers aren't able to withstand the pressure to fast during Ramadan, one of the five pillars of Islam.

When Hussam decided to attend Bible school in the United States, we helped by finding contacts for him, and with the paper-work. He didn't keep in touch with us as much as we would have liked during those years, though we heard from him occasionally. When he finally returned to Israel, he totally dropped out of our lives and we've been left to wonder what happened to him.

"It's a mystery," John said to me one day when Hussam came up in our conversation.

"For us," I agreed. "But, as Jack said, probably not for him."

Had we stretched our boundaries too far, not understanding enough about the issues facing Muslim-background believers? On the other hand, when we tried to get Hussam in touch with Arab believers in his area, other difficulties arose. We discovered that the Arab believers from a Christian background don't accept those who have come out of Islam; even *their* cultures are different.

"For whatever comfort it is," John said, "we're not alone. I read that a high percentage of new believers from a Muslim background actually turn back to Islam, even ten or more years later. It's sad."

Our friendship with Adel likewise brought challenges. Although a super-sized, strong welder, Adel had a soft side and loved to cook. His specialty was *makloubeh*, a traditional Arabic dish made with rice, chicken, and cauliflower. Arab hospitality is legendary; you can drop by their house any time and they'll cook a meal for you which you cannot refuse. Adel enjoyed preparing makloubeh for us on special occasions. After mixing the ingredients and a Middle-Eastern blend of spices together in a large pot, he turned it all upside-down onto a round table where we sat around scooping up bite-sized chunks with our hands along with pieces of pita.

I appreciated how Adel befriended our son Josh and took him to check his fish trap which lay on the sea bottom at one of the nearby beaches. What excitement for Josh to help pull up the trap and find fish swimming in it! And then to put old bread in, lower the trap back into the sea, and wait for the next catch. John had never been interested in fishing. When John's father took him fishing as a boy, he soon grew bored and began throwing rocks in the water until his father sent him home. Even beyond developing a fishing hobby, I was pleased that Josh was learning acceptance for the "other" in our society.

One evening John came back from the Shelter later than usual. Since I didn't get over to the Shelter much, I was surprised to hear John's story about a side of Adel's that I wasn't familiar with.

"What a balagan." John went straight to our room and lay down on the bed.

"What happened?" I asked.

"You remember I told you that Adel was building a deck for Avi? Well Avi wasn't paying Adel—the old problem—so Adel returned to Avi's house with an axe and chopped the deck to pieces. He was steaming when he came back to the Shelter."

I was glad I didn't see Adel in that state. I preferred to think of him with his arm around Josh's shoulders on the way to the beach, or with his wide smile after he flipped over his makloubeh like a magician and heard all the "wows" coming from the captivated and hungry spectators.

Like Hussam, Adel also professed to believe in Jesus and enthusiastically participated in our meetings while staying at the Shelter. Unfortunately when he finally left Eilat after a few years, he fell into depression. For a while he would call John with wild, paranoid stories, and John referred him to a physician near his home, but eventually even those phone calls stopped.

הפסקה

Ibrahim, from the Galilee village of Kabul, stayed in the hostel at the same time as Adel and had a similar story of not getting paid, but this time John was able to solve the problem in a unique way.

A friendly guy who also came sporadically to our Bible studies, Ibrahim worked with Shalom, a local roofer. Since we needed a new roof on our house, John decided to hire Shalom, not knowing at the time that Shalom wasn't the most upright citizen. Not only didn't he pay his workers, but he was a drinker and didn't pay taxes.

John reimbursed Shalom the usual way: part of the money upon beginning the project and the final amount upon finishing. When John heard that Ibrahim didn't receive his wages, he tried speaking to Shalom but to no avail. Herbby, who had taken a particular interest in Ibrahim, couldn't bear the injustice and went to Shalom's house a couple of times to reason with him, but was physically thrown out.

John and I could never understand how far some Israelis have fallen from God's laws in the Torah. To us the verse in Leviticus was clear: "You shall not oppress your neighbor or rob him. The wages of a hired servant shall not remain with you all night until the morning." Numerous other verses say the same. John realized he couldn't solve everyone's problems, but at least he wasn't going to let Shalom get away with his tricks and lies.

John finally gave Ibrahim the money he owed Shalom for finishing our roof. Shalom couldn't complain to any authorities that John hadn't paid him, because he was the one who was breaking the law by not paying his workers. Later we heard he ended up in prison.

Ibrahim told us a story about his village. "You know that we're supposed to make a pilgrimage to Mecca at least once in our lifetime. So a few years ago a man from our village got on one of the many buses that go there every year from Israel. At the end of the hajj he found a bus with 'Kabul' written on it, got on, and after two days when they finally stopped, he stepped out and looked around. 'Where are the olive trees?' he said to the man standing next to him. 'And it's too big to be Kabul.' This guy had ended up in Kabul, Afghanistan and it was an international affair to get him back to Israel again, but was he glad to be home!"

Sadly, Ibrahim eventually also disappeared from our lives.

הפסקה

Jeff was working with us on staff at the time, and I invited him over for lunch with John and me. After we ate, the kids went off to play and do their homework, and we were able to have a quiet conversation.

Jeff posed a question: "Why do you think the Arabs have such a hard time keeping the hostel's rules? I mean, it's not just once or twice; we're constantly after them."

"In a way it happens with many of our long-term guests," John mused. "They begin to feel at home, which is good, but it also brings problems."

"Did you know that some hostels limit how long people are allowed to stay?" I added. There's logic behind this rule. Some long-term guests become too confident, start to feel they're part of the staff, and then tell us what to do.

"Yeah," John agreed. "Balance is needed—like in everything."

I used to find it strange that people who stayed in Eilat for an extended time would choose to live at the Shelter rather than renting a room for themselves or a flat with friends. I asked myself if I'd want to sleep in a room with eight women, where new people are coming in every day, and I had no private space. Yet renting even a studio apartment requires payment in advance, plus at the hostel they don't have responsibilities—not even cleaning up after themselves if they so choose. And since some are thoughtless and irresponsible, the volunteers had recently put up a sign in the kitchen saying: "We're Not Your Mother, So Wash Your Own Dishes."

"I think one of the main attractions of staying long-term in the Shelter is always having someone to talk to," John said. "We see many young people adrift in life, with the sense of community and family disappearing. The hostel fills this need and provides them with a new family."

"But we're still left with the problem that our no-smoking rule doesn't seem to work for the Arabs," Jeff said. "Did John tell you what happened last night, Judy? We have this guy staying with us now, and I told him when he checked in that he's not allowed to smoke in the room. I was in the kitchen cleaning up after people who didn't wash their dishes when I smelled cigarette smoke. I knocked on his door and told him not to smoke. 'I'm not smoking,' he answered. Well, I knew that was a lie and ten minutes later I saw through his window that he was smoking. When someone defies the rules and also lies, our options are limited."

One of John's least enjoyable parts of managing the Shelter, besides dealing with bureaucracy, was telling people to leave, but sometimes it had to be done. What we couldn't understand, however, were those who refused to go.

"If I were in a place where they didn't want me and told me so, I'd get out of there," I remarked. "Are some people so lacking in self-esteem or sensitivity that they still want to stay?"

"Like Naghi and Tamir," John said. "I was beginning to think I'd have to close the hostel just to get rid of them."

Naghi, a Christian Arab from Jerusalem, and Tamir, a Jewish Israeli, showed up at the Shelter at the same time. We had met Tamir at the Shelter Hostel in Amsterdam on our recent trip to Holland. Tamir, introduced to us as a new believer, immediately struck up a conversation in Hebrew with John, happy to find someone who spoke his language. Although John always invited everyone he met to come to the Shelter, Tamir was one of the few who took him up on his offer when he returned to Israel a few months later.

Naghi was managing a restaurant on Coral Beach when some-one told him about us. Of the twenty percent Israeli Arab popula-tion, the Christians among them are a minority within a minority representing only about two percent, and most of them belong to the traditional churches: Greek Orthodox and Catholic. When he came the first time, Naghi told John that the system he grew up in didn't answer his spiritual needs, and so he was happy to find us. He liked the idea of following Jesus without religious rules and regulations.

The two men came from difficult backgrounds. Tamir had a terrible temper and hated his father. Naghi, a smooth talker, gave a good first impression, but later we discovered he was headstrong and estranged from his family. In the beginning we felt we could help these two young men as they seemed to be moving in the right direction—coming to Bible studies and fitting in with the staff.

We were happy to see them become friends with each other, too, because not only do we like seeing relationships formed between guests, but as Arab and Jewish Israelis they symbolized the reconciliation that is one of our core values. We had noticed that when Israeli Jews meet Arabs abroad, they often get along well. The Shelter's international atmosphere and clientele drew Naghi and Tamir to one another as they bonded in ways they weren't able to with our American or European guests.

But slowly the old story began repeating itself. Naghi and Tamir started feeling more familiar and confident, and together were a formidable bloc undermining the ambiance and unity in the hostel.

"These guys can't stand girls telling them what to do," John told me when he came home one evening, having found himself in a difficult position, caught between our guests and staff.

"It's like what happened with Adel and Michelle," I said. "I told her to get one of the guy volunteers to talk to Adel when he was acting up, but that went against her grain. Michelle insisted on stating her mind and Adel absolutely wouldn't listen."

"Yeah, so this time when the volunteer girls came crying to me because of Naghi and Tamir's harassment, I knew the guys had to go." The peace of mind and well-being of our staff always takes precedence. "But when I told Naghi and Tamir to find another place, they refused, claiming they didn't have money."

Something like this had never happened to us, and John said he was ready to shut down the Shelter.

"But what about our other long-term guests and policy of always being open?" I questioned. "You wouldn't really close, would you?"

Finally John came up with an original plan and gave Naghi and Tamir a proposal they couldn't refuse. "I'll pay your first month's rent," he told them.

They accepted and we never heard from them again. We were sad, not for the money, but that what began well with two young Israeli believers had ended like this. Yet we were thankful to have peace restored in the Shelter and to have learned valuable lessons, even at a high cost: one thousand dollars each.

"One thing I hope I'll remember next time," John told me after the whole incident was over. "Nip it in the bud. Don't let things fester. Take care of problems before they grow bigger."

Smoking in the rooms and abuse of authority were small difficulties, however, compared to what happened after George arrived.

14. Lebanese Fugitive & Jordanian Aristocrat

"A new guy came to the hostel today and guess where he's from?" John announced excitedly when he came home from his evening visit to the Shelter.

"I dunno," I said. "Just tell me."

"He's from a country from which we have never had a guest come before," John hinted and then answered, "Lebanon! I'm late because I was talking with him."

In 1982 Israel invaded South Lebanon in order to expel the Palestine Liberation Organization and remove Syria's influence on Lebanese politics. Together with the South Lebanese Army, a Christian militia, Israel established the Security Zone to protect northern Israel from attacks by the Hezbollah, a Shi'a Islamic militant group. Until Israel withdrew from this area in the year 2000, Lebanese Christians were allowed to enter Israel for work and medical care.

We had visited the Good Fence, the gateway between Israel and Lebanon, on a trip to the Galilee and seen the flow of

Lebanese across the border. Until we met George, however, we had never had a Lebanese in the Shelter because most workers remained in the north, closer to their homes.

Enthusiastic about another opportunity for bridge-building and reconciliation, we quickly embraced George in the Shelter community. His first priority was to find a job, so we directed him to a friend and member of our fellowship, Marvin, who had a small construction business. Messianic Jews from North America, Marvin, his wife Shirley, and teenage daughter, Anna, had recently moved to Eilat and were committed both to living in Israel and to our congregation.

Marvin had a project building stone walls at a new housing development and hired George to work for him. Like us, Marvin tried to make George feel welcome in Israel and used to invite him to his home on occasion. Even after George had been with us for a few weeks, we didn't know him well because he was a quiet person; but nothing prepared us for Marvin's early morning phone call.

"John, I need your help!" Marvin could barely get the words out. "It's Anna—George raped her!"

I couldn't hear what Marvin was saying, but I could see the shock and concern in John's face.

"I'm on my way," John said and threw down the phone.

He grabbed the car keys and as he ran out the door cried, "Pray! George raped Anna, and Marvin needs my help in trying to find him. Shirley's taking Anna to the hospital."

While Marvin went to the police, who set up roadblocks to prevent George from leaving Eilat, John began by going back to the hostel, where he'd last seen George. Others in the Shelter had seen him too, but no one had noticed anything suspicious. Not finding him there, John began driving around town, staring out the car's window in his search.

Someone at a convenience store in Marvin's neighborhood thought that a man matching George's description—dark complexion, Arab accent, wearing a cowboy hat—had purchased cigarettes from him; but apparently George had escaped Eilat before the roadblocks were set up, or he was in hiding.

Not only were we shaken by the fact that the daughter of our dear friends had been raped, but equally frightening was that the rapist had lived among us with none of us suspecting anything. Anna was a friend of Josh and Racheli's, and I realized that one of our children could have been the victim.

George had knocked on the door at Marvin's house after both he and Shirley had gone to work, and their young teenager Anna had innocently let him in. All of us were used to having open houses. Were we foolish or overly naïve?

The following day John was speaking on the phone to Paul from Bethel Hostel in Haifa. "How're things there?" Paul asked.

"You don't want to know," John answered. "Something terrible happened. A guy from Lebanon staying at the Shelter raped Anna yesterday morning in their home. He escaped and the police are still searching for him."

"What does he look like?"

"Dark skin, Arab, cowboy hat."

"Wait a minute!" Paul replied. "You won't believe it, but a guy like that checked in here last night, and he seems really nervous: eyes darting around, always looking over his shoulder."

"Call the police right away!" John told Paul. "And in the meantime, don't let him out of your sight."

An hour later Paul called to tell us that three police cars had surrounded Bethel and apprehended George. He didn't resist.

Several months later, in Beer Sheva, John was requested to testify at George's trial. The judge sentenced George to six years in prison and deportation from Israel when he finished his punishment. Shirley called me two weeks later to say that Anna wasn't pregnant—a small but important consolation.

On the one hand, everyone in our community resolved to be more careful about letting strangers into our homes and leaving our children alone, but on the other hand, we could see God's protecting hand on us up to this point. We suddenly became aware of our vulnerability.

המקלט

In 1994 Israel ratified the Peace Treaty with Jordan, and for the first time since the establishment of the State of Israel, citizens could freely travel back and forth between the countries. With our children, we were among the first Israelis to visit Jordan after the border crossing opened up, a ten-minute drive from our house. Having gazed across the Red Sea at the city of Aqaba from our living room window for thirteen years, we were eager to finally experience it. We weren't disappointed. Visiting Petra, the hidden, rose-red, Nabatean city, was an unforgettable experience, but just as thrilling was meeting ordinary Jordanians whom we found to be friendly and willing to talk to us.

Therefore when one of our guests walked in the front gate leading a young man with olive-colored skin, wavy black hair, and a mustache, whom he introduced as Mahmoud, a Bedouin from Jordan, we welcomed him warmly. Because of Mahmoud's limited English when he arrived, it took us time to piece together his story, but as always happens in the Shelter, a couple of our staff members took a particular liking to Mahmoud.

Actually Mahmoud's background and reason for coming to Israel weren't complicated: he had two wives already and was trying to save up money for a third. So he decided that he could make more money in Eilat than in Jordan and came across. Newly arrived and bewildered, Mahmoud was fortunate to meet one of our guests in the park near the Shelter, and find a warm place to stay.

Mahmoud found a job and settled into life in Eilat. In addition to a couple of our volunteers who spent time with Mahmoud, there was an elderly man in our congregation, Paul Fodor, a Holocaust survivor from Hungary, who "adopted" Mahmoud. As a result of having jumped off a train on the way to the Auschwitz concentration camp, Paul limped and walked with a cane, but with Mahmoud at the hostel, Paul made an effort to come by every day.

Gradually we noticed Mahmoud's English improving and that he was gaining a command of Hebrew too. But not only was he learning languages, Mahmoud was discovering the Bible. After Mahmoud came home from work in the evening, he could be seen poring over his Arabic Bible with Paul; a Muslim and Jew discussing God's Word in Hebrew! In between his meetings with Paul, Mahmoud constantly read the Bible on his own.

Els from Holland, a volunteer at the time, told me later, "I remember Mahmoud becoming a believer. One time when he was sick, he read the Bible all the way through in three days. And I'll never forget him giving the most courteous and magnificent testimony to a bunch of Dutch tourists—very kingly. I could imagine him addressing a bunch of sheiks, all dressed up to the nines, with gold daggers and fine robes. But they were Dutch aunties, with short hair, glasses, and white limbs, attired in bleak shorts and striped blouses."

After six months at the Shelter, Mahmoud approached John. "It's time for me to go home," he said. "My family needs me and I've earned enough. You'll come visit me, though, won't you?"

"Sure," John answered, and he meant it.

Mahmoud concluded his stay in the hostel by cooking a huge tray of makloubeh for his new friends, who felt like family now.

A few months after Mahmoud left, a Shelter guest who had befriended Mahmoud went to visit him in Jordan. "He's not living in his village near the Syrian border anymore," she told us when she returned. "They had a tragedy in their family and everyone had to pick up and move close to Amman. I have his phone number. He sends you special greetings."

Mahmoud's family had been attending a wedding, a typically huge affair that as part of the festivities included the traditional shooting of guns in the air. Mahmoud's nephew, thinking his gun's chamber was empty, pointed it at a friend's head—as a joke —and pulled the trigger. Shockingly, the gun was loaded and the young man died. The wedding's joy turned into chaos and anger.

The Bedouins still practice a system of blood revenge, so

suddenly Mahmoud's entire family wasn't safe and had to flee for their lives. They turned to Sheik Youssef, a Bedouin leader and senator in the Jordanian parliament to be their mediator. As the first step, Sheik Youssef relocated all the family to live under his protection on his large estate until both sides agreed on the amount of compensation.

"I think we should go to Mahmoud, Jupe," John told me after hearing the news. "It's not so far." John felt close to Mahmoud and wanted to support him.

Because the children were growing up and a volunteer could stay with them, I was freer to travel now. When John has an idea, he likes to implement it as soon as possible, so the next day we were on our way. We crossed the border, rented a car, and met Mahmoud in Amman.

After an emotional reunion, Mahmoud invited us to meet Sheik Youssef. "I told him you were coming," Mahmoud said. "He's planning a trip to Israel and thinks you can help him. By the way, you can stay in the house of my second wife, the Palestinian one; she's away visiting her family now."

First wife, second wife—it sounded complicated, but on this trip we had to let go of expectations and "just go with the flow," as John reminded me.

Mahmoud drove us through a guarded gate, and we were ushered into an elaborate reception hall reminiscent of something from *A Thousand and One Nights* or a biblical scene featuring King Solomon and his entourage. Sheik Youssef, with his bushy mustache, red-checkered keffiyeh, and wide black robe, sat in an imposing armchair at the end of the room next to a wood-burning stove. Chairs were lined up on both sides of the room with a dozen or more men, all in similar clothing, sitting in them. I quickly noted the absence of women.

Mahmoud, John, and I were invited to sit next to the sheik, and since he didn't speak English, one of his sons interpreted. Sheik Youssef asked questions, and we answered, instantly impressed by this intelligent, curious, open, and also imposing and authoritative man. First he wanted to hear about us—who we were and what we were doing in Israel. When the subject of our faith came up, he inquired how I, a Jew, could believe in Jesus. Though familiar with Jordanian Christians, a believing Jew was new for him. Simply, John explained our belief.

We happened to be in Jordan during Ramadan, the month that Muslims fast from food and water throughout the day, eating only after the sun-down. John pointed out that both Judaism and Islam emphasize a blood sacrifice: *Yom Kippur* (the Day of Atonement), and *Id-Al-Adha* (the Feast of Sacrifice), and that Jesus the Messiah was the ultimate and final sacrifice for everyone, whether Muslim, Jew, or Christian. The Sheik seemed to understand and listened attentively.

We went on to discuss his upcoming visit to Israel. Until the 1967 Six-Day War, before which Judea and Samaria (the Palestinian Territories) were under Jordanian control, Sheik Youssef used to travel to Jerusalem. He still had Bedouin friends near Beer Sheva and in the Galilee whom he knew from before 1948, the year Israel became a state and the region was divided.

"You must come visit us in Eilat," John insisted graciously, and then turned to the boy sitting next to me, a young teenager who looked out of place among the dignified guests.

"This is Fadi," the Sheik smiled, "my youngest son. I have twelve sons and eighteen daughters."

"Do you speak English, Fadi?" John asked. "How old are you?"

"I speak a little," he answered hesitantly and with a strong accent. "I'm fourteen."

"You speak very well, and you're just the age of our youngest son, Yonatan."

"Have you ever been to Aqaba?" John continued. "Do you like to swim? When you come to Eilat you can go snorkeling with Yonatan. You'll learn English from him, too."

Mahmoud nodded and smiled.

Several weeks later while we were sitting in our living room one evening the phone rang. John picked it up and heard an unfamiliar, accented voice on the other end. "Mister John, we're here!"

It took a second but John soon understood that the sheik's son was speaking. "Where are you? And who's with you?"

"I'm with my father, three mothers, and four brothers in three cars at the tourist center near the beach."

"Wait there and I'll come and bring you to my house," John answered him calmly and afterwards turned to me, "Fast! Call David and Jack and ask if they have blankets we can borrow. This is a lot of extra people to have sleeping here. Where'll we put them? Do I have to ask the sheik which wife he wants to sleep with tonight?"

One of the Bedouin's honor codes is hospitality; they are even mandated to provide for their enemies if necessary. Having been hosted by Bedouin in the Sinai we were familiar with this custom as well as another closely related virtue: generosity.

I enjoyed inviting people to our home and often entertained, but how could I hope to match the famous hospitality of the Bedouin? Furthermore, I knew that Arabs, and especially Bedouin, weren't interested in trying different kinds of food; they liked their own cuisine and seldom could be persuaded to taste anything else. We mostly ate vegetarian dishes, while for them a meal always included meat. I mentally crossed spaghetti and stir-fry, which normally worked well for feeding a lot of people, off my list of menu possibilities. Thankfully, when it comes to assembling a meal, John's experience as a chef comes to the fore. He has a way of throwing everything on the table, together with a big smile, and instantly creating a banquet.

Realizing there was no way I could compete, I chose to just be myself, including not dressing in long sleeves and a long skirt as I did in Jordan. We solved the sleeping issue by giving the sheik his own room and the three wives a room together, while the five sons slept on mattresses on the living room floor. The wives offered to cook a Jordanian lunch for us, rice and chicken, so that took care of the food problem.

In fact, their three days with us passed remarkably well, so well that a few months later we had another call from one of the sheik's sons. "Mister John. How are you? We'll be there tomorrow," he announced. "I'm coming with my brothers Ahmed and Fadi. My father wants Fadi to learn English, so he'll stay with you for six weeks."

From our short acquaintance with the sheik, we had learned you neither question nor argue with him. Even while they were staying in our house, every time the sheik stood up, if just to go to the bathroom, everyone else in the room rose to their feet until the sheik sat down again. So when the sheik said that Fadi was coming, we knew this was a certainty, even though our family would be gone most of that time visiting Holland and the States. Fadi would have to stay at the Shelter.

The sheik had impressed John and me as an unusually tolerant man who was open to the idea of co-existence with Israel. Although officially there was peace between the two countries, on a realistic level we had a long way to go, particularly among Jordanians. But for Sheik Youssef to send his youngest son to stay with people he hardly knew, who till a few months ago were considered his enemies, was beyond my imagination. I tried to picture myself sending Yonatan to their house for the summer.

The following day Fadi and two of his older brothers arrived as planned. Thankfully Jeff and Rick, our two volunteers, were willing to assume responsibility for Fadi, having been thrust into that position.

"Here's the money for Fadi while he's here," Ahmed said, handing a stack of bills to Jeff. "He's allowed to spend two hundred shekels a week. You give it to him." After spending a night at the hostel, the two brothers crossed back to Jordan.

Jeff soon discovered that serving as Fadi's bank wasn't as easy as Ahmed made it sound. Fadi clearly wasn't used to being on a budget, or at least to having two Western guys telling him how he could spend his money, and he had a fondness for pizza. But that wasn't the only challenge with Fadi, a teenager who was growing up as a spoiled prince. Fadi had never prepared food, washed dishes, laundered clothes, or made a bed. In the Bedouin patriarchal culture, the husband is the family boss and sisters serve their brothers.

On a later visit to the sheik's home, when Fadi was preparing to drive us back to Aqaba, one of his sisters was carefully packing Fadi's overnight bag, holding up clothing items for his approval and ironing the ones he selected.

As Fadi was adapting to a new way of life, Jeff and Rick were likewise adjusting to their new roommate. In their late thirties, which was older than most of our volunteers, they were the ages of Fadi's older brothers, and they took him into their care. Fortunately, Fadi was a friendly, well-mannered young man and a quick learner. His English improved effortlessly; day by day he spoke more fluently.

Like any teenager Fadi wanted to fit in, so after the first Friday evening when he stepped out of his room wearing his white jalabiya and red-checkered keffiyeh—having heard that it was our special Shabbat celebration—the following week he dressed in Western clothes. Fadi eagerly joined John and the staff when they gave out Bible portions and other literature on the beaches and building sites.

An area, however, where Fadi struggled was in his relations with the other Arabs staying with us. He felt superior to them, and they didn't appreciate that he was used to getting his own way.

"One day I decided to have a Bible study with the Arabs," Jeff told me later, laughing as he recalled that period in the hostel. "Hussam agreed to translate from English to Arabic, and we sat here in the staff room with Haled, Big Fadi and Little Fadi. Somehow Little Fadi got to arguing about something minor, and they nearly got into a fist fight. When I told Little Fadi to leave the room, he crawled back in through the window. That was my first and last attempt at an Arabic Bible study."

The young man with dark skin and an Afro whom we called Big Fadi, stayed with us for several months. From the Old City of Jerusalem, Fadi hated Israeli soldiers and used to throw stones at them after his friend was wounded in a skirmish. But staying at the Shelter softened and totally changed his attitude, especially as he read the Bible; and he loved David, our Jewish-American volunteer and a new immigrant.

David left for a while for army reserve duty. The evening he returned, walking into the hostel wearing his army uniform, with his gun slung over his shoulder, Big Fadi ran up to him and gave gun a hug. Those present who knew Big Fadi's background, will never forget the sight.

The day before Little Fadi's brothers returned from Jordan to take him home, he went on a shopping spree, buying presents for his family—not easy when you have three mothers, eighteen sisters, and eleven brothers. We returned from our vacation a few days before Fadi left, thankful that his stay with us had gone so smoothly. He proved to be an apt and eager student of English, going the following year to a summer camp in England and eventually attending and graduating from university there.

We maintained our relationship with Sheik Youssef and his family, visiting them numerous times, and they returned to visit us. And although we've had no other guests from Lebanon or Jordan, many Arabs from the Galilee stay at the hostel.

The cross-cultural issues of having next-door strangers living at the Shelter tested and tried us, though we have never had more than a few Arabs staying at a time. Meanwhile, storm clouds gathering from the direction of Iraq would upend daily life in Israel and also in the Shelter.

15. Scuds, Sirens & Sealed Rooms

To wear or not to wear a gas mask, to carry it around town or leave it at home, to show your toughness, or to be better safe than sorry—these questions confronted us for six weeks in 1991 during the First Gulf War.

"Things aren't looking good," John told me one day in early August 1990. Iraq had just bombed Kuwait City, launching the invasion. "It hasn't taken long for guests to stop coming."

In what should have been a time of maximum occupancy, the Shelter felt like a beach resort in the winter.

Tourists visit Eilat throughout the year, unlike some resorts which have high and low seasons. August though, and during the Jewish holidays in September and October is particularly busy, with people willing to brave the extreme heat during their vacation time.

"Yeah," I agreed. "If I were going to choose a holiday destination, I probably wouldn't go someplace being threatened with chemical warheads. Even Israelis aren't venturing far from home."

"I drove around town and didn't see any of the usual tourist buses," John said. "Not even crowds in front of the Underwater Observatory. At this rate there won't be anything happening at the Feasts either."

A hostel with no clients feels like a birthday party with no guests; and John worried that the volunteers, some of whom had come halfway across the world, wouldn't feel fulfilled. Moreover, we were expecting a group from the States during Sukkoth to help in our tent—to play music, help prepare meals, and interact with folks who drop by—and John was concerned they'd have nothing to do.

Living in Israel is like having your home in a bad neighborhood: one with many local bullies and gangs. Undoubtedly, if we had neighbors like Canada, Belgium, or Sweden, we would be living in peace. A glance at a world map shows Israel as a bull's-eye, situated on the land bridge between Europe, Africa, and Asia. Ever since ancient times we've been the focus of wars, and even when we didn't participate, opposing armies have swept through Israel on their way to fight one another.

In the biblical era, the Egyptians, Babylonians, Assyrians, and Persians warred with each other and with Israel; and closer by, the Philistines were a constant threat. During one of the rare periods of peace—the reigns of King David and his son, King Solomon—Israel's economy, politics, religion, and culture flourished as never before.

King Josiah, a king of Judah who lived around 600 B.C., was killed when he unwisely meddled in a war between Babylon and Egypt. Pharaoh Neco was leading his army through Israel, north to Carchemish on the Euphrates River to help the Assyrians in their battle against Babylon. King Josiah, rather than staying on the sidelines, apparently wanted to gain Babylon's favor by opposing their enemy, the Egyptians. Josiah mobilized to fight

Neco in the plains of Megiddo, or Armageddon. Sadly, entering into a war that wasn't his, led to Josiah's downfall and death.

More recently, but still over two thousand years ago, the story of Hanukkah begins with Israel caught between the two major Middle-Eastern powers of the day: the Seleucid Empire of Syria and the Ptolemaic Kingdom of Egypt. While the balance of power shifted back and forth between these realms, little Israel found itself trapped in the middle trying to maintain their autonomy and identity.

Similarly, the First Gulf War wasn't Israel's war at all, but began when Iraq invaded and annexed Kuwait in August 1990 because of disputes over oil fields and production. The coalition force authorized by the United Nations demanded Iraq's total pullout. Unfortunately for Israel, Iraq was a major supporter of Palestinian terrorist groups and made Israel's withdrawal from what they called "the occupied Palestinian territories" a condition for their retreat.

Less than a week after Iraq's invasion, the United States launched Operation Desert Shield and the first troops arrived in Saudi Arabia. Like it or not, Israel found itself a central player in a war between two Arab countries located one thousand kilometers away from us. We, as most Israelis, followed the news closely, particularly the negotiations between the United Nations, Iraq, and the United States, knowing that each decision could affect us personally. And though we soon experienced repercussions and major changes in our daily lives, in other ways, life continued as usual.

As we had expected, Sukkoth that year was the quietest and emptiest holiday we could remember. We even missed the traffic jams and the noisy, garbage-littered beaches. John ended up taking the American group on a trip to the Galilee.

Israel was in a difficult position, knowing we were a target, yet trying to keep in the background in order not to hinder the coalition's work. One of the big questions concerned whether to distribute gas masks to the civilian population. Both sides in the debate had valid arguments: on the one hand, the distribution could cause panic at home and make Iraq think we were planning to attack them; while on the other hand, in light of Iraq's threats, Israel didn't want to be caught unprepared. Furthermore, for a nation haunted by memories of the Nazi gas chambers, this issue was particularly sensitive. Eventually the Israeli government decided to start issuing gas masks to all citizens on October 1st.

הַמַּקֵּשׁ

"Did you see the kids' latest art projects?" I asked John as the children marched proudly in the front door after school, rectangular gas mask boxes slung over their shoulders. Joshua was thirteen, Racheli ten, Moriah seven, and Yonatan five.

"Well done!" John said admiringly. "I like the cat on Racheli's box and the butterfly on Moriah's. Where'd you get the ideas?"

"In art class they gave us all kinds of paper, glue, pens, and scissors to work with," Moriah explained, "and we've been watching television programs with suggestions for how to decorate your gas mask box."

"We're supposed to take them everywhere," Racheli added. "And when they look nice, there's a bigger chance we'll take them, and won't get them mixed up with our friends' boxes."

"Makes sense," I agreed.

For Leslie, a volunteer at the time, one of her sharpest memories is seeing the children on the streets with their gas masks, which symbolized for her how life went on and people adapted. What at first seemed odd, became part of their young lives.

Our staff faced challenges in trying to procure gas masks; the law wasn't clear concerning long-term tourists. Barbara, one of our volunteers, was refused when she went to the distribution center at the high school. Her boyfriend was in the Royal British Navy and had access to information about what might happen if a war broke out. He was worried for Barbara, but she found it difficult to follow the news and, in her ignorance, wasn't frightened.

Though she constantly wrote letters to her boyfriend, when Barbara read them through years later, she found enthusiastic and detailed descriptions of Shelter life, but no mention of the impending war—proof that except for the problem with the gas masks, Barbara was happily oblivious.

The first two times that Tom, another staff member, went to pick up a gas mask at the fire station, he was also rejected. But his persistence paid off when, on the third time, the young soldier on duty took him round to the back and handed him the prize—his own gas mask.

"I read in the paper that there are special masks for men with beards," I told John.

"I saw it too, but if you continued reading the article," John answered, "you'd see they only give them to religious Jewish men."

That didn't seem fair to me.

"They figure those guys are commanded to grow beards. And the rest of us aren't."

"The article says that if you don't have one of those special masks, you're supposed to shave your beard off," I added. "Did you think about that?"

"Are you kidding?" John laughed. "I haven't shaved for twenty years, so do you think I'd shave now?"

הפסקט

The pressure was ratcheted up on November 29th when the U.N. Security Council passed a resolution setting a deadline for Iraq to withdraw from Kuwait, before January 15, 1991, or face military action.

"I'm going to make our bedroom the sealed room," John announced one day. "It has to be airtight and have black plastic over the windows. I've already done it to one of the girls' dorm rooms at the hostel."

I tried to reason with John that I always sleep with a window open and don't close the curtains all the way so that I have air and light in my room.

"Sorry, but those are Home Command's orders." John said. "Every house needs a sealed room and our bedroom will work best. We've got to have water, canned goods, a telephone, and a TV or radio in it too."

John as usual didn't waste time. "Hold onto the plastic while I tape it to the window. I was lucky to get this tape. It's going fast and the stores are emptying out." We used a special type of gray plastic duct tape.

"But Abba!" Racheli, watching from the side, burst out with, "What about Peewee? They should have masks for dogs!"

"She's also part of our family," Moriah chimed in.

"Don't worry," John said. "If something happens and we have to go into this room, we'll take Peewee with us and she'll be fine."

"I wonder how they'll manage at the hostel," I said. "Everyone crowding into the girls' room together?"

"At this rate," John answered, "there won't be many guests left to crowd. I hope at least we'll still have some staff. Barbara was planning on leaving in December anyway, and Tom's getting phone calls from his family telling him to come home before the airports shut down and it's too late to escape."

"What about under the door? How do we close that off?"

"Wet towels," John answered.

"What did Alexis want when he called yesterday?" I asked. We hardly ever heard from Alexis, a colleague of Vera Kushnir from California. "You wouldn't believe it, Jupe. Alexis offered to send tickets to California for the whole family. He said we shouldn't endanger ourselves."

"So how'd you answer him?"

"I told him that as the leader of the flock, there's no way I'd leave the sheep here and run for safety. We'll trust God along with everyone else, and anyway, most people think Eilat's safe." John was looking beyond our immediate family and feeling responsible also for the hostel staff and the members of the Eilat Congregation.

"Let's hope so," I said. "But I agree—I wouldn't go either. Why do they think Eilat is safe, though?"

"Iraq's Scud missiles aren't accurate, to say the least. I read in the Jerusalem Post that a military expert called them 'Stone Age technology.' So even if Saddam aimed for Eilat, he risks hitting Aqaba instead, so he probably won't try."

On January 17th, U.S.-led Coalition warplanes attacked Baghdad and Kuwait, as well as other military targets in Iraq. In the middle of the night on January 18th, the ear-shattering rising-and-falling siren woke us up, our sign to enter our closed room and don gas masks.

"Peewee!" yelled Josh.

"Quick, get in here!" John ordered.

Turning on the TV we saw that the first barrage of eight Iraqi Scud missiles had landed in Tel Aviv and Haifa. After months of uncertainty and bluster, Saddam Hussein carried out his threat to attack the Jewish state. We crowded onto our double bed with the four children and the dog. "Next time I'm going to throw a couple of extra mattresses in here." John muttered.

A few minutes later our phone rang. John heard a muffled voice and recognized Jack, who recently immigrated with his family. "How am I supposed to breathe with this thing on? I'm suffocating!"

"Take the cover off the filter!"

"Oh, thanks!"

Unfortunately, the ritual of hearing the siren, entering the room, and putting on our gas masks became routine. Altogether thirty-nine missiles landed, mainly in Tel Aviv and Haifa. Apartments and other buildings sustained extensive damage and tragically, seventy-four people died as a consequence of Scud attacks: two in direct hits, four from suffocation in gas masks, and the rest from heart attacks.

With school canceled, the children stayed home and watched special programming on TV. All assemblies were forbidden, ruling out our Friday night meetings—the only time in the history of the Shelter that we stopped these gatherings. We enjoyed the novelty of having a quiet Shabbat dinner with the family, though one evening after I put the chicken in the oven and its aroma spread through the house, the siren went off and I feared the meat would burn or dry out.

After a week of sirens, the Home Front concluded it wasn't necessary that every Israeli enter their closed room each time a Scud was shot from Baghdad. In the few minutes between the launch and landing of the missile, they could estimate where it would land, so they divided the country into areas and immediately announced which ones were under attack. We used to hear the siren, turn on the TV, and expect to discover that Eilat was safe.

One time, however, we were shocked to hear the missile was aimed at the south.

"What!" I asked John. "Only us this time? How can that be?"

"They're obviously targeting the nuclear reactor in Dimona," he said. "And we're in that same area, even though it's two hours away."

הפסקֹו

Eilat residents could be divided into those who obeyed orders and carried their gas masks everywhere, and those who, after some time, realized that Eilat was the safest place in Israel and chose to leave their bulky boxes at home. Even finding ourselves at a friend's house when the siren went off could pose a moral dilemma. With a group at David's house one evening, all of us had masks except for Ruth.

"Here, take mine," offered John, the gentleman. The other men immediately attempted to give her theirs.

"That's okay," declined Ruth. "I never use one anyway."

We looked at each other questioningly, and all the men in the room felt obligated to prove their masculinity and didn't put theirs on either.

One volunteer, Tom, was jogging in the mountains one after-noon when he heard the siren. By this time, the war had been going on for a few weeks. Tom had missed his daily run, so now he allowed himself to grow complacent. He wasn't too relaxed, though, to sprint down to the Shelter and bang on the door for them to let him into the closed room. To his relief they opened for him, against orders. At that time we really believed that Saddam might attach chemical warheads to the Scuds.

Shira, a volunteer from the north of Israel, went home to her kibbutz when the war started. But after a few days, when John called and told her we missed and needed her and could she possibly return to the Shelter, she gladly came back. By this time she felt she belonged at the hostel, and Eilat was the safest place in the country.

In fact, whereas in the weeks leading up to the war, Eilat's hotels were empty, after the Scuds began falling, people who could afford it and even embassies relocated to Eilat, bringing to the city a mini-boom in tourism. The Shelter, however, didn't benefit; people who could afford to stop their lives and move to Eilat weren't our usual clientele.

At that time, we didn't have more than a dozen people a night staying at the hostel—a good thing, considering that all of them had to squeeze into one girls' dorm room with eight single beds. The guests and staff adjusted to the new reality of racing to the sealed room at all hours of the night and day, and they experienced a special time of bonding. One young man found it hard to refrain from smoking in the sealed room, though, and a couple of times the volunteers caught him trying to light up in the bathroom. Furthermore, having Adel in the sealed dorm was like enclosing a lion in a tiny cage; he paced up and down from one end of the small room to the other.

A German woman and her daughter stayed with us part of the time. The mother had managed to secure a gas mask for herself and a special children's model for her little girl with the encompassing hood. Unfortunately for everyone, the poor girl sounded like a miniature siren herself when she saw the adults sitting around her with those fearful-looking masks over their faces.

"We solved the problem by playing an elephant game with her," Herbby later told me. "We told her that we were in the jungle and were going to pretend we were elephants with long trunks. After that she was quiet."

Tom's ulpan class continued. Naturally the war was a frequent subject of their conversations and provided many opportunities for interesting discussions and new vocabulary words. In his best Hebrew, Tom attempted to express his qualms as well as his family's efforts to convince him to return to the United States.

"You're worried?" the teacher, a veteran Eilat resident asked. "But you've been telling the class about your faith in God. What about His protection?"

"Wow, that convicted me," Tom told us when he stopped by on his way back to the hostel from class. "Especially when I've been noticing the Israelis, even the secular ones, are so calm and not worried. It seems supernatural how God gives them peace."

Our friend Anne noticed the same thing about the Israelis. While on the one hand her sister and other family members were calling hysterically and crying, "Come home!" most Israelis seemed calm and collected. Nevertheless, seeing foreigners remaining in Israel continued to surprise them.

"What are you doing here?" a bank clerk asked Anne.

"What do you mean?"

"Most tourists have gone home. Aren't you leaving too?" he said.

Though at that time they had every reason to believe they might come under attack by various Arab armies and be gassed by chemicals, Anne and Herbby told the bank teller they knew their place was in Eilat.

Leslie's father called from America to tell her the whole family was worried, and that he had an escape route lined up for her. A doctor friend of his, of Egyptian origin, had family in Cairo who were willing to take Leslie in should things get tricky in Eilat.

We had a TV at the Shelter which we used exclusively for watching videos, having a movie night once a week. But during the war John told the staff they could watch the news. The Israeli news was only in Hebrew, but Jordan had a daily news program in English which became a lifeline for the staff. Unfortunately, though, the Jordanian news was slanted toward the Iraq perspective. And some of the guests and staff wanted to sit in front of the television all day. Debates ensued, and John had to step in and limit the amount of watching time.

Finally on February 28th, we heard the news we'd all been waiting for: six weeks after the ground campaign started, President Bush declared a cease-fire and held a peace conference. The Scud attacks halted and Israelis could finally go about their normal lives again. Significantly, the day of the war's end corresponded with Purim, the holiday from the book of Esther commemorating the Jews' victory over the wicked Haman who sought to destroy them. Purim's theme of joy, deliverance, and salvation matched our excitement of being liberated from Scuds, sirens, and sealed rooms.

One effect of the Gulf War that didn't end immediately was our reaction when we would hear loud noises. For months after the last nerve-wracking shriek of the rising and falling siren, when I heard the sound of a helicopter, motorcycle, or vacuum cleaner my heart would begin to pound and I needed a few minutes to calm down and remember that I didn't need to dart for the sealed room and slip on my gas mask.

The tourists didn't return to Eilat so quickly, but soon we weren't looking for tourists any more—we had other guests. And as we tried to resume our lives where we had left off before the war, other events on the world stage were having far-ranging influences on Israel and the Shelter.

16. The Russians Are Coming

"We have many Russians coming to our meetings lately," Olavi, the pastor of the Messianic congregation in Beer Sheva, told John over the phone, "but no one to translate. Do you think that Dov could come and help us?" The year was 1991 and Russian immigrants were just beginning to arrive in Israel.

"I'll drive up with Dov after our own meeting in the morning; we'll make it just in time. What time do you finish?"

"Don't worry. You can sleep at our house," Olavi offered.

When Dov and John entered the meeting room, they were disappointed to find few Russians in attendance.

"Never mind," John said to Dov when the service finished. "At least you had a couple of people to translate for. But only God knows why we made the long drive for these particular folks."

As they were drinking coffee and chatting with people, Olavi approached John. "Thanks for coming. Would you mind driving a family home? I think they live outside of town somewhere."

John happily agreed. He thought he knew Beer Sheva well,

having volunteered in nearby Kibbutz Hatzerim when he first
arrived in Israel. But when Alex, a new immigrant from Moscow,
directed him to his home, John couldn't believe what he was
seeing: a new neighborhood had sprung up on the edge of Beer
Sheva with thousands of white metal caravans or trailers, lined
up in rows.

"After coming off the plane, this is where they took us. It's
called Nahal Beka," Alex explained to Dov in Russian. "We're all
Russians here, except for the Ethiopians who live together in one
section. We don't have a lot of space, because each family gets only
half a caravan, but you'll stay for a cup of tea won't you?"

"First we'll give out the box of Russian Bibles we brought,"
John said. "You think anyone will be interested?"

A crowd instantly materialized when John opened the back
of our van. In minutes all the Bibles were gone, snatched up by
people fighting for them as if they were starving and John was
giving out precious loaves of bread.

The next morning after a delicious breakfast prepared by
Olavi's wife, John and Dov went back to Nahal Beka with boxes of
Russian Bibles that Olavi, who had access to Scriptures in many
languages, had given them. These Bibles were also grabbed out
of their hands.

When John returned home to Eilat he tried to explain to me
what had happened. "We're returning next week and I want you to
come with me," John said. "You have to see for yourself why I'll be
going up there so much. I've never seen anyone so hungry for the
Word of God as are these Russian Jews."

To people in the West, the Iron Curtain was a fact of life: the
physical and ideological boundary the Soviet Union had erected
to block off itself and its allies from contact with non-communist
areas. Except for a small group of Jews who were allowed to leave
in the 1970s, in which Dov's family was included, migration from
east to west was forbidden.

In 1989, this began to change as discontent intensified in
the Soviet Union. When the reform-minded Mikhail Gorbachev

154 COME, STAY, CELEBRATE!

launched a policy of *glasnost* (transparency) and liberalization, the small breach in the Curtain became impossible to close. In country after country in the communist bloc, protests were being held for the first time as people sought freedom. Citizens eventually overthrew their dictators and dismantled the Wall.

Suddenly the Jews, who had been shut up and separated from their heritage and culture for over seventy years, were free to leave. Israel was one country open to immigrants because according to The Law of Return, if a person could prove he was Jewish, was married to a Jew, or that at least one of his parents or grandparents was Jewish, he was eligible for citizenship. Long lines of people eager for the chance to escape oppression and move to the West formed in front of Israeli embassies in all countries of the former Soviet Union. Having some kind of Jewish affiliation suddenly became popular, and if a person didn't have a document to prove their Jewishness, they could buy one. The floodgates opened, and tens of thousands of immigrants arrived in Israel per month.

Although Israel had experienced large waves of immigration in the past, including an estimated six-hundred thousand Jews from Arab and Muslim countries such as Morocco, Iraq, Iran, Egypt, and Yemen from 1948 to 1972, the abruptness and extent of the Soviet influx was unprecedented. Between January 1989 and December 2002, over a million Russians arrived in Israel. (We often call all the immigrants from the former USSR "Russians," not differentiating between the various republics.)

Having our population suddenly increase by fifteen percent put a huge strain on Israel. Those who could, stayed with relatives or friends, but gradually the country began to fill up. As the immigrants continued to stream in, they had difficulty finding housing, and caravan sites were hastily set up. The media publicized telephone numbers to call in case anyone had a spare room to rent.

In Eilat we were following the current events and watching scenes on television of new immigrants arriving by boat and plane, but still the only Russians we knew were Dov and Vasily. In the beginning most didn't choose to come to Eilat. We couldn't identify a Russian's appearance or sound of their language.

The majority of the Jews in the Soviet Union had lived in large cities and were used to cultural events, which were highly subsidized and inexpensive under the communist system. In fact, the immigrant population included an unusually large percentage of musicians, as well as doctors, dentists, and engineers. Eilat wasn't attractive for lovers of theater, ballet, and symphony concerts. Nor did the climate resemble any area of Russia; minus forty degrees Celsius would have been more comfortable for them than Eilat's plus forty degrees.

John had befriended Vasily when they arrived together in Eilat in 1970. They had both lived in the wadi, worked in the same jobs, and found themselves on a ferry to Israel together in 1975 when John was returning from a summer in Holland. One of those people who didn't fit into any category with a Polish mother, Russian biological father, and Polish step-father, Vasily had a problem renewing his Russian passport. Discouraged, Vasily decided to take a rowboat and go to Jordan.

"I'm not sure what he thought he'd gain by that," John said as he was explaining Vasily's story to me later, "but in his mind it made sense."

"I was in jail for a month in Aqaba," Vasily told me as we sat in the courtyard of the Shelter drinking tea, "and they treated me pretty well. Good food and plenty of it. Afterwards I was in jail in Israel for a year for defecting to an enemy country."

Vasily came on and off to the hostel: on when he wasn't drinking and his mind was clear, off when he would get aggressively drunk or begin to act strangely and John had to tell him to stay away for a while. Vasily didn't identify or fit in with the new wave of immigrants and for some reason changed his name to Alex.

הַמִּקְדָּשׁ

Dov was our other Russian connection. After coming to the Shelter in 1985 and working with us for a year, he felt he should acquire a profession and took a chef's course. He still spent a lot of time at the hostel but was working in a restaurant when the Russian immigration began. Although his life had changed drastically since he began to believe in Jesus, Dov wasn't a person to share his faith with others. He had become more sociable, but Israelis seemed abrupt to Dov and unwilling to even consider Jesus, so he found it easier to bypass this subject.

Yet with the arrival of a million Russian immigrants, Dov's life took another radical shift. He became key not only in reaching out to Russians in Eilat, but throughout the country. In the right place at the right time, Dov and John made a perfect team.

"It began almost by accident," Dov explained years afterward. "I was walking down Eilat's main street when a couple stopped me. 'Where's the post office?' they asked. Maybe they could see my Russian face, and I for sure noticed theirs. Then I felt compelled to do and say something out of character for me. 'Maybe you'd like a Bible?' I asked them. 'You can come to the Shelter Hostel and we'll give you one.'"

"Well, they came and one thing led to another. This was the couple—you remember them I'm sure—who had a show with trained cats and dogs. John got excited and asked them to perform at the hostel. They not only happily accepted a Bible but in time they accepted Jesus into their hearts and became believers. We kept in touch for a long time. That's when I saw that God could use me. He gave me the courage to speak up about my faith. I got a bag and filled it up with Bibles and books and began going to the beach and talking to people. Around that time Olavi invited us to Beer Sheva to translate, and we discovered Nahal Beka and the caravan camps."

John quickly recognized that in Dov he had an ideal partner

to realize the spiritual potential of this *aliya* (immigration of Jews to Israel). Providentially, at that time Dov began to suffer severe back pain, and his doctor told him he'd have to stop working as a chef. With workman's compensation to support him, Dov began coming to the hostel every day.

"Come back on staff," John suggested to Dov. "We need you." All the rooms in the Shelter were full of Russians.

Dov didn't need convincing but began devoting all his time to helping the immigrants. Whereas before we didn't know what a Russian looked like, now we could recognize them on the street from a block away and grew used to the sounds of the Russian language. The Shelter turned into a center for Russians who needed help with bureaucratic matters and other challenges. They came to the hostel early in the morning, waiting for Dov to arrive.

Nowadays we find Russian speakers in all government and municipal offices, as well as in banks, health clinics, and hospitals; but at that time they were on their own to sort things out. Few spoke English; it hadn't been encouraged under the communists. For Dov—patient, kind, and sincere by nature—no request was too large or small: arranging welfare payments, registering a child for school, opening a bank account, or going to a doctor's appointment. He not only interpreted faithfully but mediated between the immigrant and the system.

In addition to Dov's social services, interpretation, and dealing with the Russians living at the Shelter, he and John drove to the caravan camp in Beer Sheva once a week and to other places with large Russian populations. Yanetz Publishing in Jerusalem began printing Russian Bibles and other literature which they gave out for free and John became one of their regulars. Before they left home, John and Dov would put together packets consisting of a Bible and several books or pamphlets, then when they arrived at their destination, they simply opened the back of our van and the free-for-all began.

John quickly learned a few key Russian phrases: "*pajalsta*

(please)," "*spasiba* (thank you)," "*bis platna* (for free)," "*padarak* (gift)," "*Biblia* (Bible)," "*kak dila?* (How are you?)," "*minya zovut John, kak tva zovut* (my name is John, what's your name?)," "*ochen kusna* (very tasty)," and more. When John rattled off these expressions in quick succession, some of the immigrants were convinced he knew Russian and were delighted to hear him speaking their language.

John liked telling the Russians, "Judy's from Ukraine." When they then smiled and looked at me as if they'd discovered a fellow countryman, or began speaking Russian to me, I quickly qualified his statement: "My grandfather was born in a small village near Kiev, but he came to the U.S. with his family when he was very young. They didn't speak Russian, but Yiddish, and later he only knew English." But my penchant for accuracy didn't stop John from repeating the same story to the next immigrant he met.

John tries to make each person he meets feel special, and one way he does this is by learning words in different languages and using them at every opportunity. Telling them I was from Ukraine was another means to connect. He sincerely made the Russians sense that they were his favorite people group—which they were at the time, because we hadn't yet encountered the Chinese, Romanians, and Sudanese. I sometimes cringe thinking that not everyone wants to hear John mangling a few sentences in their mother tongue, but in fact most people break into a smile and appreciate John's efforts.

I could understand John's excitement before each trip north. Since he became a follower of Jesus, John never tired of sharing his faith with others. From the beginning—maybe because he started to believe in Jesus here—Israelis had a special place in his heart. The fact that most of them had multiple layers of mis-understanding to be cleared away before they could seriously con-sider Jesus didn't deter John. He understood that history worked against their believing, but having seen enough Israelis start to believe through the years, he knew it wasn't impossible.

Though Paul the apostle says that gentile believers should "provoke [the Jews] to jealousy," sadly the opposite has usually happened. Christians have persecuted the Jews and even accused them of killing Christ—a terrible misunderstanding of the Scriptures and a monumental barrier preventing Jews from believing in Jesus. For two thousand years, the rabbis have been perfecting arguments about why Jesus couldn't be the Messiah, their case strengthened by Christians' shameful behavior toward Jews. Therefore today, for a Jewish person to believe in Jesus they first have to weed out the false information they've been taught.

But the Russians were different. Communism had nearly succeeded in its goal of wiping out religion. Karl Marx, whose economic theories led to the formation of the Soviet Union, wrote the frequently-quoted statement: "Religion is the opium of the people." And even though Marx, Trotsky, and other founders of the USSR were ethnically Jewish, they sought to uproot Judaism and Zionism, liquidating most Jewish organizations. The Russian Jews' identity was less about belief or faith and more to do with the persecution they faced when trying to advance in their workplace or get accepted into university.

As John spoke with the Russian immigrants he experienced something completely new. He was accustomed to offering New Testaments to Israelis who had likely never seen one before and who gladly accepted his gift. With the Russians, on the other hand, John just had to say "Biblia," and for most of them their joy knew no bounds. Old ladies fell on him with hugs and kisses. Sometimes in the people's eagerness to receive a Bible, John and Dov were nearly trampled.

Years later, as we reminisced about those times, John said, "There was such anticipation before we left home and as we drove up to the caravan sites and opened the back of the van. And the great thing was that ninety percent of the people we met took the literature."

"Only ninety percent?" I asked.

"Well, maybe ninety-nine percent."

The Russians didn't care that the Bibles we gave them included the New Testament. Most Israelis were suspicious to see a New Testament attached to the Bible they knew, and then assumed they couldn't trust the Old Testament in that edition. The Russians, on the other hand, were not prejudiced, making no distinction between Moses, David, and Jesus.

הפסוק

Although John had made sure I saw and understood what was happening in the caravan camps by taking me up there once in the beginning, I missed having John home for two days weekly. I was used to having him around and helping with the children, eating three meals a day as a family, and our evening ritual of reading stories and the Bible to the children.

"This is a once-in-a lifetime opportunity, Jupe. I've never seen anything like it—Jews, or any other people—who are so eager to get Bibles and so open to Yeshua. We have to ride the wave or the moment will pass. I'll call when I can and I'm sure you'll do fine without me." He was planning to leave early the next morning.

I was glad the Russians hadn't come when the kids were younger and I really needed John's help. When he was away on his trips, John was often so busy he didn't find time to phone till the night. Not only couldn't I call John in those days before cell phones, but sometimes he called me and our number would be busy.

"Who were you talking to?" John would ask me later when I finally picked up the phone. I could hear the annoyance in his voice. "Couldn't you tell that someone was calling and figure out it was me? Since early morning we were going from one camp to another, and when I finally had a spare moment and found a pay phone, you didn't pick up."

"Sorry, I'll try to pay attention next time. But I can't see who it is. Of course I'd answer if I knew it was you."

Caller I.D. hadn't been invented yet.

"We found a huge camp near Haifa and later went to the souk in Ma'alot. We set up a table near the entrance to the market and everyone's Russian there. You wouldn't believe the opportunities. So now I'm in Bethel. No matter how late we arrive, Traci always has something to eat for us and a good breakfast in the morning. Tonight we only arrived after nine 'cause of Adriaan."

"Adriaan?" I asked. "What happened?"

John often took volunteers with him on his Russian adventures. He needed extra hands and a strong back for lugging the boxes of Bibles and books, and he liked to give the young people opportunities to serve.

When they came home, Adriaan told me more about what had happened. "While we were giving out Bibles in a camp, a guy pointed his finger at me and insisted I come to his house. He wanted to talk and for more than an hour wouldn't let me leave. We drank tea together. In the meantime John and Dov were worried because they didn't know where I was, so they drove through half of the north of Israel looking for me. When I finally came out of the house they happened to be driving down the street and we found each other."

"I wasn't really worried," John said, "because Adriaan's traveled a lot and has been in Israel a long time. But I couldn't believe how he vanished. Anyway, he had a good talk."

הפסקה

For a few years most of the guests at the Shelter were Russians from the various former Soviet Republics, including Kazakhstan and Kirghistan, Armenia and Azerbaijan, Latvia and Lithuania, Uzbekistan and Ukraine, Belarus, and Moldova. We even had one Mountain Jew from the Caucasus. The Mountain Jews, a distinct minority of only several thousand, apparently left Iran twelve centuries ago. They speak a language that blends Persian and Hebrew in a way similar to how Yiddish combines German and Hebrew. The Mountain Jew was small of stature with a Middle-Eastern appearance, a ready smile, and simple demeanor. He came regularly to our Bible studies until he left Eilat for Ashkelon where he had relatives, and we lost track of him.

הַמִּקְדָּשׁ

Although for years the Russian immigrants held our attention, life went on and other travelers and long-term guests continued to stream into the Shelter.

Mike, whom we had first met in the Sinai, remained a presence in the Shelter for years. During one of his better times, he moved into the hostel and bicycled to work daily. Unfortunately, that period didn't last long, and Mike descended into the dark pit of mental illness and homelessness. We gave Mike, who lived on the flat rooftop of an office building near our house, innumerable blankets, clothes, and Bibles, and drove him endless times to the emergency room.

"Is he your husband?" the admitting nurse asked me once after Mike had begged me to take him. After so many years of friendship, we found it difficult to refuse Mike's requests.

Moshe, another young Israeli whom we met on the beach in Nueiba, supported himself by stealing backpacks. Continuing this pursuit on Eilat's beaches landed him in jail a number of times, but he liked us and we liked him. Moshe's lack of family support combined with his childlike manner motivated us to try to be his substitute family.

During one of Moshe's long-term stays at the Shelter, he became more and more agitated. John built a pen in a corner of the hostel for some baby rabbits that our children were raising, hoping that caring for them would be therapeutic for Moshe; although he loved them dearly, his mental state didn't improve.

We had just fallen asleep one night when the phone rang and John heard Adriaan's worried voice. "John, we've got to do something about Moshe. He's not sleeping and is pacing up and down in the courtyard talking to himself. And he's keeping all the guests awake."

"I could see this coming. If you leave now you can catch the midnight bus to Beer Sheva and take him to the mental hospital." John realized there was nothing more we could do and that Moshe needed professional help.

Thankfully Adriaan was someone who would go anywhere for anyone, including numerous trips to Egypt to encourage Dr. Alfred. He didn't hesitate to get ready quickly and Moshe didn't object. They arrived at three o'clock a.m. in Beer Sheva and went straight to the emergency admittance room of the mental hospital where a psychiatrist began questioning Moshe.

Adriaan remained present throughout the examination and at a certain point the doctor turned to him. "In the little Hebrew I know I told him about Moshe," Adriaan explained to us when he returned to Eilat the following day, "including that he believed in Yeshua."

"'No further questions. We close the case,'" Adriaan recollected the doctor saying. "Moshe was admitted immediately. But then for some reason he asked about me and when I told him I also believed in Yeshua, he wanted to take me too. I had to run away to catch the bus back to Eilat."

17. Seeking Culture, Finding Yeshua

"As Jews, we were in the midst of an exciting movement." Lena spoke rapidly in fluent Hebrew, her dark expressive eyes glowing as she remembered that decisive time in her life. "Finally, after years of being shut in, thanks to Gorbachev we were free to live wherever we wanted."

I rolled a large stone next to where Lena was sitting and leaned back. After a walk up the wadi and scrambling over boulders, I was ready for John's pita and a glass of sweet tea prepared on the open fire. When we get a chance, we like to escape to the mountains outside Eilat to experience the peace found in nature. And Lena, who often takes walks in the hills behind her house on the edge of town, was happy to join us on one of our outings. Since she first came to the Shelter after immigrating in 1992, I'd heard bits of her story, but took this opportunity to have her tell it from the beginning.

While still in the Ukraine, Lena had watched as people she knew began moving to Germany and Israel. "As more and more left, I also began to think about going. My brother was married and my father didn't want to leave, but I was ready for a new life. I never considered Germany; and getting to the States was complicated, so for me it was clear that my mother and I would go to Israel.

"We were completely secular; I wasn't seeking God, and all the synagogues were closed. I'd been to some churches, like a tourist visiting a museum. But around this time a friend invited me to come view *The Jesus Film*. I saw in the movie that Jesus and the disciples were Jewish like me. I could follow the message of Jesus' death and resurrection, but I didn't understand what I was supposed to do about it, and nothing changed for me even after I prayed at the end.

"Following our decision to immigrate we had to arrange our aliya papers in Moscow which was far from our home in Ukraine. After a busy time getting everything organized, we were finally invited to come to Odessa with all our belongings while we waited for our ship.

"When it finally came in, there were people on it who had emigrated and were already returning. 'You're making a mistake,' they told us. My mother was worried, but I told her everything would be fine.

"My father was crying when he stood on the pier to see us off. I felt that something huge was happening to us and that we didn't belong to the Soviet Union any more. Everyone was nice to us on board, and we had lectures about Israel and its history, sing-alongs, and career-related, informative sessions.

"On the morning of the fourth day as I stood on deck and Haifa came into view, I prayed spontaneously for the first time in my life. I had told my mother that we'd be fine, but before we left I'd been crying a lot thinking, 'I know what I'm leaving, but where am I going?'

"I prayed, 'God, this is your holy land. You gave us this oppor-tunity. We're two weak women, and my mother is a pensioner. Help us to survive.' Most people on the ship went to Haifa or Jerusalem."

"So why did you come to Eilat?" I placed a stick on the fire.

"When the Orthodox Jews on the ship heard we were going to Eilat they warned us against it, saying there was prostitution and other things like that here. But we had friends from home who had recently emigrated and had written to us, 'Eilat's nice. You can get an apartment here and find work. It's a pretty city with a beach and an easy winter. The only minus is that it's hot in the summer and far from the rest of the country. But come!'

"After five days staying with them we received an apartment around the corner from the Shelter, and Olga and Lydia were our neighbors—that's Olga who later married Dov. Not long after we arrived I met Dov on the beach giving out books. Although I'd prayed when I saw that Jesus movie, now I was cautious. In ulpan they had warned us not to take a Bible from anyone or we might get into trouble.

"Dov was nice, calm, and had a pleasant manner, but I told my mother it was forbidden. Dov said to us, 'I'm also a Jew,' and my mother said, 'I want the truth; I'll take the books.' She knew Olga and Lydia and that they came to the Shelter.

"At that time I had lots of conflicts with my mother; I wasn't a believer yet and wasn't respectful or humble. My mother was under stress and depressed because in Ukraine she'd had her apartment, work, and a *dacha* (the country home that many Russians maintain where they could escape the city, grow gardens, and collect mushrooms); here, she had nothing.

"But then my mother began going to the Shelter with Lydia and I saw changes in her and smiles on her face. She went for two or three months without me. I was afraid, but they kept inviting me, and finally I went to a Friday evening meeting. When I arrived, few people were there yet, so I sat in the back and can't explain the feeling I had: I felt free, good in my soul.

"Someone came in and I saw light in his eyes. 'Who's that?' I asked the person next to me. 'John, the manager of the hostel,' she answered. I could sense his open and friendly spirit. We sang some songs, John gave a message from the Bible, and then they served a meal. I didn't understand much in my head, but I rejoiced in my heart.

"I spoke to Dov afterward. 'Did you like it?' he asked. 'Yes!' I answered enthusiastically.

"So that became my life—working and going to the Shelter. I still had the same problems, but they weren't important any more. I truly felt born again. Sure, things were hard for us in the beginning: three times we were robbed; I worked hard as a chambermaid; we lacked money; I was stressed and ill with a neck infection and with nerves; my mother worked fourteen to sixteen hours a day in the laundry.

"On the other hand, life was easy because of the Shelter. I had a community where I was welcomed and wanted. In Ukraine I'd felt different, like a black bird among white ones. Here I could belong. I prayed to God, 'Show me the truth in your Bible.' And when I read the Old Testament, I saw Jesus everywhere, like in Isaiah Chapter Fifty-three and other places too. I read my Bible a lot."

הַמִּקְלָט

"Let's take a break now," John said. "Put the humus, salads, and pita on the blanket." The sun dipping behind the mountains gave a golden shine to the red and brown-hued rocks.

"Who wants Turkish coffee and who wants tea?" asked John when we'd finished dipping our bits of pita into the salads.

"I want to hear more from Lena," I said.

הַמִּקְלָט

"After a year I was baptized. This was a serious step for me, but I wanted to tie my life with His forever." Lena's countenance glowed.

As with most Jewish people who choose to follow Yeshua, Lena at first didn't think baptism was for her. But on further investigation and study she came to understand that it had a parallel in the *mikveh*, the bath used for ritual immersion in Judaism.

One of the obligatory regulations for an Orthodox conversion, the mikveh symbolizes purity, cleansing, and renewal from defilement. John the Baptist, who followed in the tradition of Old Testament prophets came proclaiming a baptism of repentance for the forgiveness of sins and baptizing all Judea and Jerusalem (see Mark 1:4). Not surprising then that Yeshua, raised a Jew and who lived among Jews, began his public ministry by being baptised in the Jordan River, and that His early followers, also Jews, were commanded to continue that identification. Baptism for us signifies identification with Yeshua and the beginning of a new life.

"What happened to your father after you left?" I asked Lena.

"My father had a good job. He wasn't an alcoholic, but at meetings with the directors he was expected to drink. His colleague, Vladimir, was a believer who had once given Abba a Bible.

An underground church met in Vladmir's home during the time it was dangerous, and some of his friends were in prison.

"When my father finally came to visit us, I couldn't wait to tell him the news. 'We go to meetings where they believe in Jesus.'

"'Why Jesus? Are they Christians?'

"'Many are Jews. Come see for yourself.'

"My father came along to the Shelter but soon had to return to his elderly parents in Ukraine. When I spoke to my brother on the phone he told me, 'Father doesn't watch TV any more. He reads books and isn't drinking like before.'

"The next time I spoke to my father his voice was trembling as he said, 'I went to talk with Vladimir, and he told me he's been praying twenty years for our family. He invited me to his church and I was baptized.'

"My father's eighty-four-year-old mother also started to believe. She was a judge, very successful and smart, and had been a member of the Communist Party. 'I can't go against the truth,' she said when asked how she could change her views.

"Three years later Father made aliya, and my aunt Bronya also started to believe, all thanks to the Shelter. I just thank God we came to Eilat and that He opened our hearts."

הפסקט

"So, remind me how you came to work at the Shelter," I requested.

"I was working long hours in a dental clinic," Lena answered. "There was a good atmosphere and everyone liked me, but I felt I was missing out on life. After Dov left Eilat I prayed that God would send someone to replace him in the work he was doing with the immigrants.

"One day when I was at the Shelter John said to me, 'We need you here.' That was around the time that Prime Minister Rabin was assassinated. I had been thinking about how short life is, so that gave me the push. I told the dentist I was leaving. I came on staff in November 1995."

I could imagine they wouldn't have wanted Lena to go. With her quick smile and friendly manner, she would add cheer and efficiency to any office.

"I knew little English when I began to work at the Shelter in November 1995. Sasha, who was also there, helped me learn. Even though the hostel was full of Russians, I needed English to answer the phone and talk to the other guests. I remember lots of people who were there, like Babushka Lena and how she used to make piroshki."

How could I forget Babushka ("Grandmother") Lena, the eighty-year-old grandmother who stayed at the Shelter for half a year, having moved in with all her possessions in shopping bags? Though we felt sorry for her to be in that position at her age, Babushka Lena carried herself with self respect and had a lovely smile and an open heart for God. She was too old to learn Hebrew, so John spoke to her in his limited Yiddish.

I couldn't forget her piroshki either. My parents used to visit us every year, and I was always looking for special experiences for them, wanting them to understand how we lived and to meet people with whom we were involved. Since they liked traditional Jewish food like chopped liver, chicken soup, and bagels and lox, I was sure they'd like Babushka's piroshki and invited her to prepare those at our house.

Mom had a pot of vegetable soup simmering on the stove when Babushka went to work. Though they couldn't communicate with each other, I sensed a bond between the cooks and was pleased to see things moving in the direction I had imagined: Dad and Mom hovering around and watching Babushka while she was pleased to be appreciated and able to contribute.

Babushka made the dough and set it aside. She cooked potatoes, mashed them, fried ground beef, and then mixed it with the potatoes. A homey smell of the beef and potatoes filled the house. Then she rolled out the dough, cut circles, filled them with the meat mixture, and folded and sealed the half moons. Now she was ready to fry her piroshki. Babushka used massive amounts of oil whereas Mom and Dad tried to avoid fried foods completely, careful of their cholesterol levels. I noticed their eyes widen as Lena emptied the bottle of oil in the frying pan, but I understood that my parents were trying to be open-minded and willing to make an exception, particularly with such a tantalizing aroma.

Babushka ceremoniously handed the first piroshok out of the skillet to Dad who wiped off the juice dripping down his chin. Mom received the second.

"Delicious!" Mom, a gourmet cook, declared.

"*Ochen kusna*," John interpreted.

When she was finished frying, for her grand finale, Babushka took the remaining oil in the pan and poured it into Mom's soup. Was this a Soviet thing—not wasting any ingredient? Mom and Dad turned pale. John and I looked at each other. This episode hadn't been part of my script.

הפסקה

"Don't you think we should be going?" John reminded Lena and me.

I was enjoying looking at the stars. With no moon, the Milky

Way was a bright swath across the sky and we saw satellites streaking from one side of the heavens to the other. "I think Lena just needs a couple more minutes to finish her story."

"I was remembering those Russian ballerinas," Lena said. "I met them on the beach promenade and invited them to the hostel. They looked like dancers—thin, tall, and straight-backed."

"Their legs reached up to their armpits," John recalled.

"In time they started to believe and stayed a year and a half in Eilat, coming to all our meetings when they didn't have shows. Do you remember when one of them came back to visit us two years ago with her husband and daughter?"

"She was still beautiful," I replied.

Since John loves the desert and likes to share his love with everyone, he naturally invited the ballerinas to come on a trip with us. The ballerinas gladly accepted our invitation, but when they showed up at the hostel, we saw they were totally unprepared.

"Didn't you tell them what to expect and how to dress?" I said on the side to John. "Have we ever taken anyone into the desert with high heels?"

"They won't need all that makeup either, but let's go or it will soon be too late. I thought I asked Lena to tell them, but I guess something got lost in translation."

Though we've taken hundreds of people on desert outings, the one with the ballerinas stands out. Their spiked heels snapped on rocks, their mascara and lipstick dripped in the heat, and when they asked for the bathroom, John pointed behind some rocks.

John stood up and began gathering the blankets, ice chest, metal pita plate, teapot, and other items and carrying them back to our van.

"I just want to say one more thing," Lena added. "I thank God every day. I was divorced, with medical problems, no hope and no joy until God found me. Now, even when I'm alone I'm never bored or lonely. I'm not jealous or disappointed—not in the congregation and not in God. So now I have no fear for the future but peace in my heart. God is my treasure."

הפושט

Many Russians have come and gone through the Shelter—too many to count. We still get piles of mail from banks and other institutions for people whom we don't remember, while other names bring back memories of stories or faces.

When they came as new immigrants, the Russians were eligible for rent subsidies, and many asked John to fill out their official contract. Afterward, besides receiving the stipend, they were registered as living at the Shelter and for some this remained their address long after they had moved on.

Sasha, from St. Petersburg, was similar to other drifters when we met him. He had the habit of coming by and then disappearing for weeks or months. Obviously something was pulling him to the hostel, while at the same time he couldn't commit himself to what he was hearing or decide if this was the direction he wanted to go. Nevertheless, John and Dov had endless patience for Sasha as they did for everyone, accepting him on his terms and in his time.

Blond, stocky, round-faced, and missing his front teeth as the result of a brawl, Sasha didn't look like a typical Jew. In fact, we found out later that he wasn't—he had forged papers in order to leave Russia and then planned to continue to another country. In Russia, Sasha had been a factory worker and teacher, but gradually his social drinking had turned into an addiction. He saw Israel as his opportunity to begin anew, his chance to come clean and live a normal life again. Unfortunately, after settling in Haifa he began to drink heavily again. And after a few years, for no clear reason he moved down to Eilat.

"We Russians all knew about the Shelter," Sasha told me years later while installing windows on our son Joshua's new house. He sat down with me during his coffee break. "We knew we could come on Friday night to fill our stomachs, and I liked the people I met there. They were different from the religious people I'd known, but I wasn't ready to change my behavior and quit drinking."

Sasha said that although he had heard the name Jesus Christ back in Russia, he had associated it with religion. In the Shelter he saw *The Jesus Film* and had read parts of the New Testament, but was torn because he was used to doing things his own way and wondered if Jesus could really forgive him. Though Sasha divided his time between living on the beach and at the Shelter, we weren't aware of the battle raging in his heart.

"At a certain point I told God that if He forgave me I'd serve Him all my life," Sasha continued. "But I didn't experience any change and things continued exactly the same for me until two months later. I remember the exact day and hour when suddenly I knew something had happened. I was filled with joy and began jumping, singing, dancing, and telling everyone about my new-found faith. I was free now, with no fear of death, and I've never looked back."

Sasha began to join John and Dov on their Bible expeditions to caravan camps in the north. He stayed with us in Eilat for another year and a half and then moved to Beer Sheva to help with the Chinese construction workers who had arrived in Israel. Later, after moving to Arad, he worked in a hotel on the Dead Sea and then started a business as a handyman.

Having a father who was a dentist, I was glad to see that Sasha had taken care of his teeth. For me, the change in his appearance symbolized his dramatic inward transformation.

הסלע

With the thousands of Russians living in Eilat, we tried to think of different ways to reach out to them and to make them feel welcome in Israel as well as at the Shelter. We were thankful that Dov and John could help them in practical matters, but they missed their cultural life. When Vera Kushnir—not only the owner of the hostel but a well-known Russian poet—visited, we organized a reading in the hostel. Even during the days when the Iron Curtain was firmly in place, Vera's poetry had been smuggled into the Soviet Union.

When we heard that Victor Klimenko, a well-loved Russian Christian singer, was coming to Israel, we arranged for him to come to Eilat. We sought an air-conditioned venue for his concert with comfortable seats, but were disappointed when the various community centers we approached turned us down.

"Never mind," John said. "We'll meet in the hostel and save money. It may not be as sophisticated a location, but at least whoever comes will learn about the Shelter."

We spread the word among the immigrants and on the designated evening John and I sat in the back enjoying watching the hostel courtyard fill up. Although I didn't understand the words, I appreciated the beautiful melodies and depth of feeling in Victor's songs and could recognize a few words such as *Bog* (God), *Isus Kristus* (Jesus Christ), and *lubov* (love). Between the songs, Victor—trim and handsome with thick, light-brown hair and a mustache—shared about his family, his many disappointments, and his search for truth. As we observed people following his every word, we were curious to know the content, so Dov interpreted into Hebrew for John and me.

"Now I want to tell you about a Jew who saved me and changed my life: the Lord Jesus Christ." Victor, with a wide, friendly smile, leaned forward and gazed intently at his audience. After explaining in a basic way who Jesus was and about the sacrifice He made on behalf of all mankind, Victor asked those who were ready to believe in Jesus to raise their hand.

I saw a middle-aged woman sitting on the side quickly lift her hand. "Anyone who raised their hand can come talk to me, Dov, John, or Judy, and we'd like to help you and answer your questions," Victor concluded.

"My name is Beate," the woman later introduced herself to me. "I didn't know what to expect when I came this evening. My neighbor invited me and when I left home I was sad, but now I feel different. When Victor asked if anyone wanted to believe, I felt as if someone was lifting my hand for me. I have a smile on my face for the first time since I can remember. My situation at home is very difficult. I'd like to come back and talk more if you have time."

"Gladly," I answered, never imagining that Beate would become one of our best and most faithful friends and a babushka to everyone in the Shelter. Few people who meet her forget Beate's wide smile and enveloping hugs. However, the joy and love that radiated from Beate weren't always her portion.

Years later, having heard pieces of Beate's story I wanted to understand it better, so I visited her home, a studio apartment in a building for senior citizens. When she opened her front door with the plaque on it, "*Welcome to God's House*," and ushered me inside, I instantly felt comfortable and enfolded in her affection.

"Tea or coffee?" Beate asked. "And I made the white cheese spread with garlic and carrots that you like, and a cake." Her little dog jumped into her lap.

Beate was born into a typical Soviet Jewish family in Odessa, Ukraine where they didn't believe in God and only managed to hold onto a few Jewish traditions. In school she learned that there is no God and in university took the required course, "Basics of Scientific Atheism," which she later went on to teach.

"About the time that I was teaching atheism, my oldest brother announced to our family that he had become a believer in Jesus Christ and was baptized in the Russian Orthodox Church. Our mother was terribly upset by this betrayal, but I became curious. After talking to him for hours about religion, faith, and church rituals, and finally visiting his church, I too was eventually baptized there. But my life didn't change and my heart remained empty."

In June 1991 Beate immigrated to Israel with her daughter and grandson. "We left because of anti-Semitism and because we saw no future there anymore," Beate said. "My daughter wanted to come because friends of hers had already made aliya.

"'Mother, we must go to Israel,' she told me.

"'I'm afraid,' I replied.

"'I'm afraid to stay here,' she said.

"There was a lot of bureaucracy and paperwork, including getting permission from the KGB and traveling to Moscow, but finally we were approved. We took a bus from Odessa to Bucharest where we got on an El Al airplane. We chose Eilat because we had friends here."

A few days after settling in Eilat, Beate met Dov. He told her of his faith in Yeshua and invited Beate to the Shelter. "You'll meet other Jewish believers there," Dov said.

"That's not for me. I belong to the Orthodox Church," Beate replied to Dov. In her mind the case was settled and three years passed before she was willing to visit the Shelter for Victor Klimenko's concert.

"Those were three years of confusion, disappointment, hurt, and heartache," Beate summarized. "I walked around bent over, looking at the ground. I was like a withered flower until I received the spiritual water and straightened up.

"As immigrants we received one apartment for me, my daughter, and grandson, but we couldn't live like that; my daughter and I didn't get along. A few months after arriving in Israel I met an Israeli man who asked me to marry him. Even though we didn't have a common language, I agreed and we signed a contract with a lawyer.

"It didn't work at all; I was crying and complaining all the time. But the good thing is that I mastered Hebrew quickly, unlike most immigrants my age who never learn. With so many immigrants from the former Soviet Union, they get along with only speaking Russian, but that's not good. As a professor of literature I knew English when I came; and already speaking one foreign language helped me to learn another.

"Though I was unhappy in my personal life, I was angry when other immigrants complained about Israel, saying, 'They owe us this or that'. 'No.' I'd say. 'We are the ones who owe this country.'"

After the concert, Beate's life changed radically. Though on the outside her circumstances remained the same, on the inside her unhappiness was replaced by contentment and even delight.

A neighbor noticed and asked why she was always joyful and smiling.

Beate longed to read the Bible in order to get to know God, and whereas when she had tried to read it after joining the Ortho-dox Church and found it confusing, now she felt God's Word opening up to her in a way she had never imagined.

"Because God gave me the gift of Hebrew, I believed I could use it for Him," Beate said. "I began going every day with other immigrants to interpret and help them at the bank, hospital, Ministry of Interior, and other offices. When they thank me I tell them I'm just a small channel. God gave me a desire to share with others the salvation He gave me. I love to go to the beach in the morning to swim, so I stop at the Shelter to pick up books to give to people I meet.

"When I open my eyes in the morning I have a whole list of people I pray for. I thank God for my memory, my brain, and more. I pray that as I get older He'll give me strength and understanding, and that I won't be a burden to others. I'm so happy here in Israel. I love the people, the language, and the country. I'm glad when I'm outside of Israel and I hear Hebrew spoken."

John would be expecting me for lunch.

"Take the leftover cheese spread and cake to John." Beate wrapped them up and walked me to the door, giving me a final kiss and hug.

הפרקט

With the growing group of Russian speakers, Dov began a weekly Bible study and our house seemed the logical place to meet. It was more private than the sukkah in the Shelter, and the home atmosphere was conducive to the dynamics of a small group.

In the Middle East people tend to show up late for everything, but with the Russians we had the opposite problem—they came early. Every week I found myself in a race against the clock to finish our dinner so that the children could clear out and go to their rooms. Complicating matters was John's boundless hospitality. When the Russians showed up a half hour early and sat talking on our porch waiting for the meeting to begin, John inevitably invited them in.

"Come in!" he'd say. "It's hot (or cold) outside. Sit and join us."

I shuddered inwardly because this slowed down our evening routine by diverting John's and my attention away from the children. Sometimes our guests attempted to resist John's offer, though refusing John is almost as difficult as declining Arabs. I did my best to overcome my initial reaction by reasoning that our Russian friends undoubtedly appreciated being welcomed into our home and that the children were receiving a lesson in hospitality.

The Russian Bible study in our living room was also a test for our teenagers in being open about their faith. Our family was already different from the families of their friends—peanut butter along with hummus on our table; we spoke English mixed with Hebrew; and a constant stream of guests flowed through our home. Moreover, the fact that we were believers in Yeshua was even less common and accepted in Israel twenty-five or thirty years ago than it is today. Our children's close friends knew we were Messianic Jews but other acquaintances usually didn't. Bursting into the living room while the Russians were singing, praying, or reading their Bibles introduced them to our faith, whether intentionally or not.

הפסקה

Besides the deep friendships and the Russian Bible study that continues to this day, Dov and Olga's wedding was another outcome of the Russian immigration. We were thrilled when Dov, who seemed to be a confirmed bachelor, began to take an interest in Olga, a new believer who faithfully joined all our meetings. Even more exciting, they announced their intention to marry.

"We'll first have a ceremony for the family under the *huppa* [wedding canopy] with a rabbi in Tel Aviv," Dov announced, "but we want to have the real celebration at the Shelter with our spiritual family and friends."

Some organizations ask their staff not to begin relationships with the opposite sex so that they won't be distracted from their work, however this rule never fit in with the spirit of the Shelter, perhaps a consequence from our old lifestyle of keeping rules to a minimum. But furthermore, in Israel they take the command to "be fruitful and multiply" seriously, and the calling of match-maker is an old and respected Jewish profession. We're thankful for the many couples who have met at the hostel and for their children who feel like grandchildren to us.

The Russian immigration changed the face of Israel mostly in positive ways: new orchestras and music schools founded, doctors and nurses added to the workforce, and colleges established. On the downside, until this point Israel hadn't suffered from the blight of alcoholism. Whereas Jews commonly drink wine on Shabbat, the culture of beer and hard liquor was mostly unknown until the Russians arrived. They were used to drinking vodka, and the move to another country created stress and exacerbated the problem. And perhaps the Russian immigration simply coincided with the time that Israelis were ready to embrace a drinking lifestyle.

When the Russian immigrants arrived we never anticipated the changes they would bring, not only to Israel but to our lives and to the Shelter. And that, over twenty years later, some would be our best friends, having bridged background, cultural, and language differences. The Shelter has never been the same.

The arrival of over a million Russians caused a building boom; families couldn't continue to live in caravans, so houses had to be built. With a shortage of Israeli construction workers, a radical solution was implemented: the importation of Romanian builders. The Shelter was on the threshold of a fresh set of faces, language, and people group.

18. God Exists In Romania

"John, come quick!" I was standing on the front deck in the Shelter on a usual Friday evening in 1993. "What in the world is Larry doing with fifty guys following him?"

Although many people were already seated, a few minutes remained before the meeting would begin, so I was enjoying the view over the Red Sea, the waters crimson at sunset, while John was sitting in his favorite chair in the corner of the sukkah, talking to guests.

The white plastic chairs were set in rows. John had cooked the meal at our house in the morning—restaurant-sized pots of soup, rice, beans, and cabbage salad—and transported them to the hostel in the back of our van, driving slowly so the soup wouldn't spill. Last minute preparations had included arranging English, Arabic, and Russian literature on the book table and choosing Hebrew and English song transparencies from the overhead projector's binder.

Although every week was different, and we never knew who

or how many people would show up, I didn't expect that this Friday would radically change the focus of our ministry for years to come.

John jumped up from his seat and rushed out the front gate to meet Larry, a Scottish man from our congregation, who gave John a sheepish smile, obviously also unable to believe what was happening.

"There's a small grocery store opposite our apartment," Larry explained quickly. "I saw half a dozen guys hanging around and walked over to talk to them. None spoke English but when I heard the word "Romania" and saw their hand gestures for building, I understood they're Romanian construction workers. They weren't doing anything so I invited them to our meeting, and they invited their friends. I hope it's okay."

"Wow, Romanians!" John smiled. "We don't have Bibles in Romanian, but of course they're welcome. Come in!"

הפסקט

Before the Gulf War, the Friday meeting had been held at our home, having begun as a small gathering to give travelers, single people, and newcomers a place to celebrate the Shabbat. Word of a free meal spread, especially among the hippies and beach people, and gradually the function grew in size to the point where we had to sit in rows on homemade wooden benches instead of around our table. I turned the menu into vegetarian instead of the traditional roast chicken, and stopped baking one challah bread but bought a number instead. We learned to put away the fruit or other food that was sitting on counters, as well as personal items laying around the living room and bathroom, having discovered from experience that anything left in sight might be picked up, used, or taken by our motley company of guests.

One man who had come up from the beach was helping himself to a frozen chicken from our freezer when we noticed him. I didn't appreciate people using our tooth- or hairbrushes either. And one Friday evening after John and I had retreated to our bedroom, having finally washed and organized everything, we heard water running in the bathroom.

"Strange," John said. "The kids are in bed; the front door is locked; so where's that sound of water coming from?"

John opened the bathroom door and found a tall man with long hair lying in the full bathtub.

"What are you doing here?" I heard John yell.

"There's no more hot water."

"No wonder. You used it up."

So the man stood up, climbed out of the bath, put his dirty clothes back on his wet body, and walked out the door.

John came back to bed. "He must have been stoned."

When we started again after the Gulf War, during which time all assemblies had been banned, we debated moving the meeting to the Shelter. On the one hand, we felt we had more control in our home and didn't want to subject the hostel guests to prowling or stealing by some of the strange folks who came by.

On the other hand, the hostel courtyard was larger than our living room, and although we hadn't had complaints from our neighbors—a miracle considering all the people and noise every week—we thought it wise to give them a break.

Furthermore, I felt the children were at the ages where they needed more privacy and personal space. They had always dealt well with the meetings, but life would be simpler if they didn't have to put away all their stuff every week and explain to school friends what we were doing.

Once we decided to give the hostel a try, we soon discovered the advantages as the volunteers became more involved and took on responsibilities. We stationed one of them near the gate to keep an eye on who entered and to be sure that no one slipped into the guests' rooms. Space, therefore, wasn't a problem by the time the Romanians showed up.

הַמִּקְלָט

"*Dobre vecher* (good evening)," John began speaking to the Romanians in Russian. He reasoned that as part of the Soviet axis they surely spoke Russian.

Blank looks.

"*Bienvenu!*" John tried French—Romanian is a Romance language, so the word for welcome was probably similar.

No recognition.

"*Bienvenida!*" Spanish is perhaps closer to Romanian than French, so surely they will get the gist of what he's trying to say. Still nothing, so he continued smiling and motioned for them to sit down.

After getting to know them better, we learned that few Romanians speak any language other than their own. Their ears were so unaccustomed to other sounds, that even if we said something that was close to a Romanian word, they didn't understand. Yet despite the language divide, the Romanians continued to return every week, evidently thankful to have a place to go on Friday evening where they felt accepted and to get away from the cramped, rundown hostels where the building contractors housed them.

John quickly learned a few key expressions: "*Ce faci?* (How are you?)," which is answered by "*face bine* (doing well)." "*Collega Romania* (Romanian friend)" was useful because if he was driving around and saw some Romanians at a building site, he would call out these words to get their attention and invite them to the Shelter. Then he would say to them, "*vineryi apte i jumatate* (seven-thirty Friday)," and ended always with "*la revedere* (good-bye)."

As had been our experience with the Russians, though previously we didn't know what a typical Romanian looked like or

recognize their language, we soon identified the Romanian construction workers by their usually short, stocky build and swarthy
coloring. Moreover, many had a sadness about them and could
be seen in town after work hanging around bars and shops that
sold cheap alcohol.

Clearly, however, we needed an interpreter. We thanked God
when Petre appeared, speaking nearly fluent English, and John
quickly enlisted him. We hesitated to have someone with no biblical knowledge interpreting a Scriptural message, but didn't see an
alternative solution.

"I've never done this, but I've decided to pay Petre twenty-five
shekels each week to be sure he comes," John reasoned. "At least
the men will understand the message instead of sitting here like
dummies."

But, unfortunately, after a couple weeks we discovered a more
serious problem: Petre was coming to the Friday meetings drunk.
Although he still managed to more or less do the job, we certainly
weren't willing to have Petre stand up in front of the men swaying,
trying to keep his balance, and stinking of alcohol.

John told Petre we didn't need his assistance any more, and
we found ourselves back where we began. We couldn't believe that
God had brought these men to us with no way to communicate.

A couple of weeks later we walked into the house after the
meeting, exhausted as usual after having interacted with many
people, John having given the Bible message, and me having led
the music. Suddenly I had an idea.

"Do you remember how I told you I met Hanna who just
moved to Eilat, a single mother with four young children? Her
neighbor in Tel Aviv had told her to look us up, and guess where
she was born?"

"Romania?"

"Exactly! Hanna came to Israel when she was twelve so she
speaks both Romanian and Hebrew. The only problem is that she's
terribly shy. She even has trouble looking at you when she talks and
her bangs cover her eyes. Not to mention those four little kids."

"Never mind," said John. "I'm sure she's our answer. Give her a call tomorrow, okay?"

When Hanna came to the Shelter on Friday, after a short exchange of words and encouragement, John stationed her facing the fifty Romanian men. Although she didn't have John's loud voice or Dov's confidence, the message came across. Keeping Hanna's children busy, including the four-month-old baby, wasn't easy, however, and Hanna kept turning around whenever she heard a peep from the baby. So we were glad when she began coming without them, feeling sure she had found a babysitter.

With her introverted personality, and as a woman among male construction workers, we hadn't expected more from Hanna than translation on Friday evenings. But as time went on we were happy to observe Hanna not only interpretting John's messages, but beginning to connect with the men. I could imagine how the workers were thankful for the opportunity to speak to someone local.

Through Hanna we also were able to learn the backgrounds of our new Romanian friends. I wondered if the heavy spirit I sensed in them came from having lived for over forty years in the Soviet Bloc and nearly twenty-five years under the totalitarian regime of Nicolae Ceausescu whose combination of communist policies, austerity program, and enforced police state had caused widespread poverty and deaths.

John and I remembered watching television in December 1989 when a demonstration broke out in the city of Timisoara. A crowd had gathered around the Romanian Orthodox Cathedral in response to the government's attempt to evict a pastor who had opposed the regime. We had followed the news daily as the turmoil grew and spread to other cities. Nine days later both Ceausescu and his wife were tried and promptly executed.

So we were excited to meet a worker from Timisoara to whom Hanna introduced us, and who was reportedly a Christian. "Wow! Were you at the demonstration?" John asked.

"Sure. But it wasn't easy to be a follower of Jesus in those days."

He told us how his friends had been imprisoned, tortured, deported, and killed for speaking about Jesus, and that because the government didn't allow them to be imported or printed, almost no one had a Bible. Nevertheless, he and others had managed to quietly practice their faith. When the protest began, they congregated in the square in front of the church and at one point all began shouting, "*Exista Domnezeu!* (God exists!)."

"That's when hope came into our lives."

Unfortunately, after several weeks of Hanna's translating, we realized that she was simply locking her front door and leaving her children alone. What should we do? We couldn't continue to have Hanna coming to our meetings while expecting her children to fend for themselves, but we were sorry to lose her so quickly. And how would I tell Hanna without offending her?

"Hanna," I tried to explain, "we're thankful to have you translate and don't know what we'd do without you. But we didn't mean for you to leave your children by themselves. They're too young."

"They're used to it," Hanna said. "The oldest takes care of the younger ones." From what I had learned about Hanna, she had herself grown up in a dysfunctional home and lacked basic parenting skills.

"But she's only eight. Let's think, and we'll come up with a better idea."

When my friend Alison heard about our dilemma, she offered to babysit for Hanna. Besides loving children, Alison saw this as an act of service. I hoped that not only would it allow Hanna to continue interpreting, but that this would teach her about being a responsible parent and that Alison's dedication to this family would bring long-term positive consequences.

הפסקה

Finding Bibles for the Romanians became a priority. Most of the Romanian workers were unbelievers and scripturally ignorant, thanks to Ceausescu's efforts to wipe out religion and replace it with Communism and his personality cult. Since both John and I became followers of Yeshua through reading God's Word, we have always put an emphasis on the importance of the Scriptures.

On John and Dov's still-frequent travels to the north to meet Russian immigrants, they stopped in Beer Sheva where our friend Olavi had a Bible storage depot. His father had begun printing and importing Bibles after he arrived in Israel from Finland in 1947, and Olavi continued the work. While loading boxes of Russian Bibles into our van during one of their visits, John noticed some old, dusty crates far back in the corner. Checking them out, he realized he had discovered a gold mine: Romanian Bibles and books including *Peace with God* by Billy Graham and titles by Richard Wurmbrand, a Romanian-Jewish believer in Jesus who had been imprisoned and tortured for his faith, and after his release had written many books.

Under Ceausescu's predecessor, over one-hundred thousand Romanian Jews had immigrated to Israel, ransomed by the Israeli government for up to three-thousand dollars a head plus agricultural products and political influence. Ceausescu continued the practice by "selling" over forty-thousand more Jews. Aware of this phenomenon, Olavi and his father had the foresight to secure Romanian Bibles for the sizable community settling in Beer Sheva, though apparently they had overestimated the demand. Now we had enough Bibles for the Romanians coming to the Shelter and also to give away. Olavi's Bible stash didn't last forever, though, and soon John began seeking other sources.

On one of his trips to Jerusalem, John stopped by Victor Smadja's Yanetz Publishing. "What do you think about printing Romanian Bibles for the construction workers?" John suggested. "These guys are similar to the Russians in that most don't know anything about the Bible and have no faith in God. But with this background, they are open to believe."

Victor didn't take long to answer. He explained to John that since he and his wife emigrated in 1955 from Tunisia they had been committed to supporting the local assemblies. Through

Yanetz Publishing they are able to provide Scriptures and other literature in the languages spoken in Israel. "That's the reason why when the Russian Jews arrived, I immediately saw the need to print Bibles for them." Victor felt that God hadn't called him to minister to the foreign workers, because others around the world were printing Scriptures and books in their languages.

Obviously John couldn't argue with Victor's personal conviction, and we appreciated his help in supplying Hebrew, Arabic, and Russian material. A few weeks later, however, when John was again at Yanetz, Victor opened the conversation by telling John that after their previous talk he couldn't stop thinking about John's request for Romanian Bibles.

"The verse from the Gospel of John Chapter Ten came to me. '*And other sheep I have which are not of this fold; them also I must bring, and they will hear my voice; and there will be one flock and one shepherd.*' I was convicted. So, what should I print and how many?"

"Since Christmas is coming," John answered, "what if we start with five thousand copies of the Gospel of Luke? They'll be easy to give out, because the story of Jesus' birth will speak to them in this season."

The Gospels of Luke turned out to be so popular that Victor went on to print *Peace with God* and *The Secret of Happiness* by Billy Graham as well as further editions of Luke's Gospel.

Simultaneously, in Beer Sheva, Olavi continued his importing of Romanian Bibles.

Later we read verses from Isaiah Chapter Sixty-one that spoke to us about the arrival of foreign workers. "They will rebuild the ancient ruins and restore the places long devastated; they will renew the ruined cities that have been devastated for generations. Aliens will shepherd your flocks; foreigners will work your fields and vineyards (NIV)."

"I'm not saying that Isaiah was prophesying two-thousand seven-hundred years ago about the foreign workers in Israel today, but this verse does describe what we see happening," John explained. "The Romanians are building, and Thai workers are farming."

Hard-working and not demanding high wages, the Romanian construction workers proved a success. By 1997, sixty thousand were already working in Israel, having entered through the auspices of the Contractors' Association. Many went on to desert the contractor to whom they were assigned in a modern form of bonded or indentured labor, and although some of the workers stayed in Israel longer than their two-year permit, most returned home eventually.

Groups of Romanian construction workers remained a presence in Israel for years and thanks to Hanna's faithful interpreting, showed up every week for our Friday meetings. The Africans' culture and mentality were unlike ours, but at least we could speak English with them. With the Israeli Arabs we could speak Hebrew. Some of the Russians spoke English and the younger ones were learning Hebrew. But we never had a common language with the Romanians, which made it difficult to develop meaningful relationships with them. Nevertheless, several individuals stand out in our memory.

A small gathering of Romanian believers in Jesus began to meet weekly in the sukkah with more than twenty coming at the peak. A few had arrived in Israel already believing and others took the step of faith here. Making a public declaration of their faith, they chose to be baptized in the Red Sea, and in connection with their immersion, they shared testimonies of how their lives had changed. They spoke about no longer spending their free time sitting on old chairs and crates drinking beer outside the local mini-market and how they had found a higher purpose in life than working, eating, drinking, and sleeping.

Although we couldn't understand the words, everyone was moved to hear the Romanians' enthusiastic singing. Often accompanied by the accordion, Romanian music sounded to me like a combination of gypsy and folk styles, both melancholy and melodic. When the men sang on Friday evenings, their voices carried over the whole neighborhood. We never tired of hearing our favorite, a stirring hymn with nearly the same tune as Israel's national anthem, "Hatikva." Samuel Cohen, the composer of the anthem, in fact acknowledged that he derived inspiration for the melody from a song he had heard in Romania.

Costa emerged as a leader among the believers. A grave, no-nonsense man, with short graying hair and small stature, he took his position as Bible teacher seriously. For Costa, a T-shirt wasn't suitable attire to preach in. He always appeared wearing a clean pair of slacks and button-down shirt. Standing up to speak, Costa never cracked a smile, and though none of us could understand his language, we were sure he didn't believe in using jokes or funny stories to illustrate his point. In fact, even when the number of Romanian workers was drastically reduced, Costa remained faithful, coming to the Shelter on Tuesday evening in his preaching clothes, and standing up in the sukkah to deliver his sermon—even when there were only two men in his assembly.

When Ariton began coming to the meetings, he seemed different than the other Romanians. Tall, with a charismatic personality and wide smile, he not only had learned some Hebrew but was an amazing guitar player. Before long Tony, as he liked to be called, became everyone's friend.

"Tony really contributes to the music, doesn't he?" John was stacking up the white plastic chairs one Shabbat morning after the meeting in our house. "Also on Friday evenings when he plays, especially that song 'Viva Isus.' I've wanted to plaster our outside wall, so I asked Tony to do it, and he said he knows where we can get materials. I'll pay him, of course, and I'm glad to have someone I trust."

"Did you hear what Mike said?" I asked. "You know, that Russian guy with the son."

"What'd he say? About what?"

"He said he doesn't trust Tony, because he's a gypsy."

"What d'you mean 'because he's a gypsy'? What's wrong with gypsies? Mike's prejudiced like lots of people: Jews, gypsies, blacks, Arabs, everyone's against the other. People are always picking on the new guy on the block. Once it was the Ashkenazi Jews against the Moroccans, and when the Russians came, the Moroccans turned on them. And now the Russians are biased against the Romanians. But God hates prejudice and so do I."

Tony continued to work his way into all our hearts, so when he asked John before the service one Saturday morning if he could share something about his family, everyone heard him gladly. Tony explained how his daughter was seriously ill and the only hope was a difficult and expensive operation which couldn't be done in Romania. "Would you please pray for her?" he asked.

Not only were we happy to pray for Tony's daughter, but many from our fellowship asked him if they could contribute money towards the operation. Iris, one of our volunteers, moved by Tony's sincerity and desperate situation, gave him two hundred dollars, though she didn't have much herself.

Several weeks after Tony's impassioned plea for prayer, he didn't show up for our Friday or Saturday meetings, which was atypical for him. When we didn't see him the following week either, John asked Vasili, one of the Romanians to whom we had grown close and who had learned some Hebrew, what happened to Tony.

"Didn't you hear?" Vasili answered. "Tony was borrowing money from lots of us. Not till the end did we begin to suspect him. Then all his stories fell apart, and we understood he was lying. I heard the Israeli police were after him and that he was arrested when trying to leave the country."

If Tony had succeeded in fooling his countrymen, then maybe we weren't as gullible as we felt.

המקום

Unfortunately, this wasn't the first time we were duped nor would it be the last. Though John has a gift for discernment and for seeing behind people's facades and masks, we often tend to be trusting and even naïve. And con men tend to be types like Tony—friendly, charismatic, and smooth talking.

"One thing we have to do is to coordinate with each other when we give money to needy people. Although we prefer to donate anonymously, if I'd known that Iris had contributed so much money which she barely has, I would have told her that we already gave Tony a large sum," John told me. "And what else makes me feel bad is how I followed him to the building site where he works and loaded the building materials into our van."

"What were you thinking?" I couldn't believe John had done that.

"I wasn't thinking," John replied. "I hate to imagine what would have happened if the police had come by. What would I have said? Next time I'll know better. Do you remember that Israeli man who came to the Shelter a few years ago? I can't remember his name—Meir maybe—but like Tony he had a charming personality. He wore a suit and said he'd come to Eilat for business and had meetings with hotel managers and the mayor. When he went out, he'd carry a briefcase that he said was full of his plans.

"He hadn't gotten around to paying us yet and I wondered, with all his connections, why he was staying at the Shelter. One of our guests came to the office and said money had been stolen from his wallet and he suspected this guy because they were in a room together. But we still didn't have evidence until two volunteer girls from Christ Church Guest House in Jerusalem arrived and when they saw Meir, they turned pale and took me aside to talk. Apparently he'd stayed at their place for a month and took off without paying. So I called the manager there, confronted our friend, and that was it. Of course he denied everything and thankfully he'd only been staying with us a day or two. He took off immediately and was gone with thankfully little damage."

Many times worse was a man who used the Shelter for years for his deceptions. We had known him since the Sinai and considered him one of our best friends. Although he often showed signs of instability and of being overly friendly and improperly affectionate with women, we and others who knew him dismissed our doubts by saying he had a warm and friendly nature. Furthermore, the fact that he traveled a lot made it hard to follow through on our misgivings.

When some years ago this friend appeared to be more agitated than usual, John invited him for a heart-to-heart conversation in the desert. John, unable to draw out of him the reason for his unrest, suggested he see a professional counselor, to which he agreed. The counselor, however, also wasn't able to penetrate his shell. But not long afterwards he had a breakdown and confessed to having sexual relations with women in our congregation as well as others around the world. When news of his confession spread, many women came forward saying they had been sexually harassed by this so-called brother. We took years to recover from our pain and sense of betrayal.

"Better a thousand attacks from outside than one from inside," John said. "I read that in *Matthew Henry's Commentary*."

הַמַּקְלֵט

Gradually fewer and fewer Romanians were working in Eilat and coming to the Shelter meetings. We heard that they were able to work for higher wages in Spain. Vasily, one of the last of the group to remain, joined us in the hostel activities and desert hikes because he was alone and had learned Hebrew. He still sends us cards a couple of times a year written in Hebrew with Latin letters, having learned to speak but not to write.

Although the next major people group to come to the Shelter was more distant geographically and culturally than the

Romanians, they became more entwined in our lives. And in the meantime, Shelter guests came and went, as did our quest for a permanent license.

Entering the house after one of his regular visits to the municipality's licensing office, John poured a glass of water from the jug in the refrigerator and sat down. "I spoke to Esther again, the one who tried to fine us for handing out books when she was a city inspector. She has worked her way up and is now on the building committee. She still can't stand us and what we believe—it's like a personal vendetta for her. But she doesn't have the final word, and in the meantime we keep receiving yearly licenses. Every day we're open is a gift."

19. Chicken Feet & Dog Liver

"I know it's important that a hostel meet basic health standards," John said, entering the house after his morning in the Shelter, "but sometimes they ask the impossible."

"What d'you mean?" I asked.

"You know how the Department of Health inspects us every year before issuing a new license? This morning two men came and said that the ceilings on the girls' rooms are too low and that room thirteen needs its own bathroom."

"Were they nice about it? Did they give a deadline?"

"They were okay but said they'll close us down if we don't comply. There's no way we can raise the cement roof so we'll have to lower the floor. I'm thankful we've got a good team of volunteers here now."

Maintaining an old structure like the Shelter requires constant upkeep, but John thrives on building projects. He finds it hard not to jump into the hard physical work, but due to his bad back he tries to take a more supervisory position, a challenge for an active guy like John. He enjoys working with a crew, seeing the place clean and attractive, and utilizing staff's capabilities.

Thus, the day following the health inspectors' visit, John and his team began breaking up the floor tiles and hauling hundreds of bucketfuls of dirt out the front gate. They built two steps down from the entrances of each room. Tiling specialists laid new floors.

As a result, the Department of Health was satisfied; the Shelter stayed open; and the rooms felt more spacious.

Adding a bathroom to room thirteen was more of a problem. Our smallest room, its two bunk beds already filled up much of the space. We had considered this problem before, because those sleeping in room thirteen had to use the bathroom in one of the larger dorms or walk around the corner to the toilets in the boys' section.

Once we had a honeymoon couple stay with us, which demonstrated this inconvenience. After vacationing in a hotel for a few nights they had wanted to extend their vacation, so being friends of ours they checked into the Shelter. Our staff remembers the young bride sweeping out of room thirteen in her lacy white negligee and over to the bathroom in room twelve where eight women were sleeping.

"We can't let the hostel be closed down, but I'm going to wait till we come home from our trip to Turkey to tackle this problem," John told me. "Leaving just one bunk bed in the room seems like a waste of space."

We had a family tradition of taking each of our children on a trip abroad for their bar or bat mitzvah. Now it was Moriah's turn and we had decided to go to Turkey. A friend, whom we had met in Nueiba and had later helped me after Racheli was born, was living with her family in Istanbul where they taught English. We visited them as well the extraordinary landscapes and caves of Cappadocia, the travertine pools of Pamukkale, and the ruins of Ephesus. One night we stayed in a hotel where the bathroom was so small that we practically had to sit on the toilet to take a shower.

"That's it, Jupe!" John exclaimed, emerging from the shower with a towel around his waist. "I've got it!"

"Got what?"

"If they can do it, we can too."

"Do what?"

"Put a bathroom into a small room," John said smiling.

We came home and John immediately went to work adding a narrow bathroom to room thirteen. The bunks are closer together, but at least guests don't have to step outside to use the bathroom.

הַמְקֵקָט

In the spring of 1995, while at the stationery store near our house, I stood next to some Oriental men who were trying to make themselves understood in an unfamiliar language. Not only did we rarely see Orientals in Eilat but I sensed they weren't ordinary vacationers. Since the days when John and I used to walk around Jerusalem's Old City meeting people and inviting them over for a meal and Bible study, we've made it a game to guess people's origins. Americans are easy to spot, and we can often differentiate between countries in Europe, but we had had little experience with people from the Far East.

Nevertheless, having sympathy for foreigners and trying to be helpful, I joined the exchange at the store. The men spoke no English, but through hand motions they finally bought what they wanted and, equally important for me, I discovered they were Chinese.

"Guess who I met in the stationery store?" I asked John as I entered the house and without waiting for an answer continued, "Chinese! I wonder what they're doing here."

"Did you talk to them? Invite them to the Shelter?" John asked.

"They seemed nice enough but didn't speak English. And they didn't seem like regular tourists."

A few days later John came home from one of his rounds of the building sites giving Bibles and books to the Romanian workers.

"How'd it go?" I asked.

"Great! We met a bunch of new guys who said they'll come on Friday night. But guess who else we met? Those Chinese of yours. Turns out they've been brought over as construction workers like the Romanians. I saw loads of them. Most don't speak English, but there's a translator with every group. I invited them to the Shelter. I was planning on going soon to Victor in Jerusalem to get Romanian books, so I'll ask him if he has anything in Chinese."

The next week at Yanetz Publishing, John filled the back of our van with Gospels of Luke as well as Billy Graham's *Peace with God* and *The Secret of Happiness*. Afterwards, when John entered the office, Victor invited him for a cup of coffee. John shared with Victor about the growing work among the Romanians, and the weekly Bible study at the Shelter.

"And what's more," John added, "last week I met some Chinese workers. You wouldn't have anything in Chinese would you?"

"Interesting that you should ask," answered Victor. "A couple of days ago a Chinese brother from Singapore was here bringing a gift from his church for our work. Daniel Ong's his name—a nice person, and he left me his card. I'll call and you can talk to him."

Victor dialed Daniel's Israeli cell phone number and passed the phone to John, who explained our dilemma—what appeared to be hundreds of Chinese workers in Eilat with no literature in Chinese and no one to explain to them the good news.

"I don't speak Mandarin," Daniel told John. "But I have a friend here in Tel Aviv who does—Wee Chow Leng. I'll get in touch with him."

When Daniel contacted Chow Leng, they considered their options: either a five-hour drive or a one-hour flight to Eilat. In comparison, Singapore is so small that a half-hour drive is considered a long journey.

"Traveling to Eilat was something out of this world," Daniel told me years later when we were reflecting on the beginnings of the Chinese work. "But the Lord has a different way of seeing things."

After speaking with Chow Leng, Daniel called John back. "We can fly down to Eilat this coming Friday," Daniel offered. "Do you think you could gather some of the Chinese together?"

Things were moving quickly, the way John liked. We had just met a new, unreached group from communist China and already had a meeting planned for them. I wondered what Daniel and Chow Leng were doing in Israel.

John picked up Daniel and Chow Leng from the small Eilat airport. While driving among construction sites to invite the Chinese workers to the meeting, the three men were able to get to know each other a bit. John found out that Daniel was working for the Singaporean government and that Chow Leng had an import/export business.

An hour later the Chinese workers filled a large portion of the Shelter's courtyard. They sat transfixed as Chow Leng interpreted John's message for them.

When the meeting was finished, Daniel and Chow Leng looked at each other. "I don't know about you," Daniel said, "but I'm coming back next week to help these Chinese."

"I was thinking the same." Chow Leng turned to John. "Expect us again next week."

We hadn't known much about Singapore, but learned that it was a small city-state at the southern end of the Malay Peninsula with strong bonds to Israel, particularly in the military and business areas. Being surrounded by over two-hundred million Muslims, Singaporeans identify with Israel's position.

The common language in Singapore is English with a distinct accent, which the locals call *Singlish*. Daniel's mother tongue, however, is Malay while Chow Leng's is Mandarin. Both felt connected to Israel because of their deep love of the Bible. Beyond their professional reasons to be here, they felt God had a purpose for them in Israel.

We invited the workers to come the following week for a special Chinese meeting in our house.

הפטרה

At six thirty the next Saturday evening more than fifty Chinese workers came in and filled our living room. With rough, simple faces, dressed in pleated slacks with belts pulled up to their waists, and because it was winter, a suit jacket or sweater, the men had an old-fashioned appearance. The smell of perspiration mixed with cigarettes and Chinese food hung over the room.

We began by offering them glasses of juice and cups of tea along with sunflower and pumpkin seeds, popular snacks in Israel. Later we learned that the Chinese preferred them over cookies and cakes. Our children withdrew to their rooms while John and I sat in the back. Daniel stood up to introduce the evening and was followed by Chow Leng giving a Bible message in Mandarin.

Though not understanding a word of Chinese with its rising and falling tonal sounds, John and I couldn't mistake the men's interest, and I enjoyed gazing at their faces. As Westerners we sometimes think that all Orientals look the same with their dark eyes and straight black hair, yet when I observed each man I could see his unique features and body build.

Keeping this first meeting short, Chow Leng finished with a prayer and a promise to return in two weeks. After the workers left, we had a few minutes to sit, relax, and review the evening before John drove Daniel and Chow Leng back to the airport.

"Unbelievable," Chow Leng shook his head, smiling.

"Looks like we'll be coming down here often," said Daniel.

John, having figured out where the workers lived, determined to follow up with them by building networks with the translators and group leaders.

Similarly to the Russians and Romanians, the Chinese were blank slates as far as the Bible or any religion was concerned. Since Mao Zedong's founding of the People's Republic of China in 1949, he had made it his goal to eliminate religion. Through his "Great Leap Forward"—a large-scale economic and social reform project in which an estimated forty-five million people died—and the Cultural Revolution, the communists had succeeded in erasing most religious practices. As previously, we found this created advantages for the gospel because we didn't have to pull out weeds before sowing the seeds of God's Word.

הפסקה

Our Saturday evening Chinese meetings grew into a routine. John picked up Daniel and Chow Leng at the airport; the children knew to clear out of the living room by six thirty; and I added bags of sunflower seeds to my shopping cart.

After a few weeks of commuting to Eilat for half a day's visit, Daniel and Chow Leng bought packets of ten plane tickets.

"This is preaching the gospel in its raw form: Christ came, was crucified, and rose again," Daniel told us in his usual understated way.

Many men accepted the Lord as their Savior, and the new Chinese believers had a hunger for the Word of God. Daniel and Chow Leng encouraged the men to write down their questions in a notebook during the week as they read their Bibles, and many basic issues arose: How do I live as a follower of Christ? What does the Bible say about Jesus? What are His commandments? What are His promises? On Shabbat Daniel and Chow Leng tried to provide answers.

John learned a few key phrases in Chinese: "*Ni hao ma?* (How are you?)," "*hen hao* (very good)," "*zai jian* (goodbye)," "*xie xie* (thank you)," "*Yesu ai ni* (Jesus loves you)," and "*yi, er, san, si* (one, two, three, four)." He especially liked greeting the Chinese with "*Ni chi wal le ma?* (Have you eaten yet?)"—a traditional greeting harking back to the times of food scarcity in China. And at Chinese New Year he was adept at saying "*sing nee-ann koo-why ler* (Happy New Year)." The Chinese didn't always understand John's accent, but he never failed to draw smiles.

John had quickly discovered that a translator or supervisor

accompanied every group of Chinese workers. Although many learned rudimentary Hebrew during their time here, the laborers were simple men from the countryside who spoke no English and thus a translator was indispensable on the building sites as well as after work. Especially in the first years, China was still restricting contact between their citizens and foreigners, and some of the leaders were members of the Communist Party whose job description included isolating the workers from harmful, outside influences, such as the Shelter.

We discovered their prohibition against mixing with us when we suddenly didn't see a group of men who had been coming regularly on Friday evenings for some weeks.

"Something feels fishy," John told me. "I'm going over to where these guys live near the Peace Café to find out what's happening."

When the leader told John that the men were forbidden to come to our meetings, even John couldn't argue with him. We found that the actual enforcement of this ban depended on the leader, and thankfully the restrictions lifted through the years as the Republic of China became more open.

The Chinese came in groups organized by Israeli manpower agencies and lived in camps according to the building companies. Though some were larger and others smaller, all the camps' living conditions were similar, and when we visited we felt we had landed in China. Hundreds of men lived in Eilat's largest camp which consisted of rows of trailers on a fenced supply lot in the industrial area. The caravans, with clotheslines strung between them, were divided into two sleeping rooms with bunk beds and provided little privacy.

The men hung posters above their beds of whom I guessed were modestly dressed Chinese singers or actors. Chinese music rang out from all directions, with what to my ears sounded like high, shrill voices, lots of stringed instruments, and a different musical scale.

A shower room occupied a central location, and while in

the smaller camps the men prepared their own food, the larger groups had a dining room with dedicated cooks. After chopping piles of cabbages, onions, chickens, or whatever was on the menu, the shirtless cooks threw the food into enormous woks and blackened pots. The distinct smell of Chinese food infused all the quarters.

The men, maybe because no visitors ever came to their site or else it was usual in China, habitually walked or sat around in their underwear. I felt uncomfortable, but they didn't seem to see a problem. In fact, the whole camp made me uneasy at first.

"How can they house these guys in such conditions?" I asked John when we returned home from one of our visits. "Isn't it treating them as subhuman? No Israeli would agree to live like that. And leaving their families for years, too."

"I've been talking to Yang," John answered, "and he said that in China they also leave home to work in another province and live in camps. I don't know what those places are like, but they only go home once a year at Chinese New Year. So maybe they're used to it."

Yang, our first Chinese friend and one of the early believers in Jesus, was the leader of a group of tilers who were laying red marble in the Moriah and Herod's Hotels as well as working on the new mall. Educated as an engineer, Yang spoke English exceptionally well and his whole demeanor and finer features set him apart from the workers.

Yang arrived in 1995 and stayed in Israel, his first overseas position, for two years. When he was sent back to Eilat sixteen years later by the mammoth Chinese construction company for which he currently works in order to bid on our new airport, we were thrilled to meet up again.

"What made you start to believe?" I asked him when we sat down together over a meal. After all these years I could only remember parts of Yang's story.

"Life was lonely; international phone calls were expensive, and we didn't have video chats in those days. After work we'd cross the street to the bar, drink Goldstar beers, and go home to bed. That was all we had—work and sleep. Then I met John and found a better place: a home with people to talk to."

"And what attracted you to the faith?" I continued. "Reading the Bible?"

"It was John. He was so warm-hearted toward us. I couldn't relate to the Bible in the beginning. I thought it had nothing to do with us, because we have our own history in China, and the Bible is about Israel."

"Had you heard about the Bible before?" John wanted to know.

"I knew it existed, but in China it was just one of many options—like Buddhism. In the early 1990s our government was totally opposed to Christianity and said that missionaries were part of the invasion. I hated the Communist Party, though, and used to argue with my father and mother who were both members. I considered the Party to be hypocritical: they spoke beautiful words and made promises, but did nothing. Robbers, I called them."

Yang's father served as a general on a submarine in the Chinese navy. For his loyalty and ranking he received a comfortable apartment in Qingdao, a large coastal city in Shandong Province southeast of Beijing. However when he retired and the young leaders showed no respect for him anymore, his thinking changed and he turned against the Party.

"At first I didn't like to read the Bible. Although my English was poor and I didn't understand much, I was attracted to people's testimonies about their faith. Slowly, I began to think that the Bible wasn't just a story, because a fable wouldn't cause people to live a pure and honest life. I saw that many people died for their faith and you don't do that for a story. I began to consider it seriously."

Around the time that he was beginning to believe in God and the Bible, Yang had knocked on the door of our house one evening, terribly agitated.

"I came back to Eilat last night from Tel Aviv where the big boss gave me the salaries for all my men in cash, five-thousand dollars," Yang told John as he sank into a chair. "When I entered our camp, I found that two men had been fighting and that one was in the hospital. I hurried there and when I finally returned to my room, the money was gone. I don't know if I lost it or if someone stole it. You know how hard we work, sixteen hours a day, so I was exhausted. How can I face the men?" Yang bent over, holding his head in his hands.

"First, let's pray," John said. "And then you have to go to the men, persuade them that you're telling the truth, and assure them that you'll pay them back slowly as you get paid. They'll believe you. It's written in the Bible that God works all things together for those that love Him. He can even use something awful like this. And start reading the Bible I gave you. It changed my life and will change yours too."

Yang walked out of our house more confident than when he entered. As we had already noticed, he had a good relationship with the men up to this point. They trusted him to keep his promise, and every month he was able to return portions of their salaries. Moreover, Yang put his trust in the Lord.

"I realized that after this incident the workers' love for me was gone; our connection wasn't the same," Yang explained to me. "We all left home for money and it became so important to us—the number one priority in our lives—that I didn't have friendships with the men any more. I asked myself if money really brings happiness and saw that at the Shelter our relationships were different."

After several months of frequent visits, Yang showed up one day with a smile on his face. "I've decided I want to be called Timothy," he announced.

"Why Timothy?" John asked.

"Paul is Timothy's spiritual father. You're my Paul."

Ren and Wang were two other leaders with whom we became

friends at the same time as Yang, though not to the same degree. They also dropped by our house and were interested in the Bible. Wang, a quiet, sincere man whose round, wire-rimmed glasses made him look like a scholar, often spoke about his wife and daughter whom he missed greatly. He didn't seem disturbed about China's one-child policy, even though his only child had a learning or mental disability. We didn't understand the exact problem. But Wang's love for his daughter shone in his smile as he spoke about her and showed us her picture.

Wang's group of workers was working on the new mall in Eilat, shopping centers having suddenly become popular in Israel.

"In Yantai we have much larger malls and hotels," Wang told John.

Wang didn't seem like a boastful person, but knowing nothing about China at the time, I had a hard time believing that a city I'd never heard of could have such elaborate buildings. Later I was astounded to see the scope of architecture and development in China.

Then, there was Ren. With his broad smile he was unusually tall and well-built for a Chinese. Like Wang, he was from the city of Yantai in Shandong province. He loved to swim and frequently came with us to the beach. The Chinese love of seafood, however, proved dangerous for Ren.

While we were enjoying a Shabbat afternoon on the beach with our family and friends, Ren staggered out of the sea groaning and grasping one hand with the other.

"Sit down. What happened?" John sprang into action. From our experience, the Chinese were not demonstrative with their feelings and didn't show their pain.

"A fish," Ren gasped. "I cornered him, but he stung me."

Corner a fish in the sea? Since when does the sea have corners?

"How did it look?" John questioned him.

"Like a fish with feathers."

"A lion fish," John said. "Get in the car. I'm taking you to the hospital. They're poisonous but not deadly like stone fish."

Following an injection from the doctor in the emergency room, Ren became himself again after a few hours.

הפסקה

"I've got an idea," John suggested as we were organizing our house for one of the Chinese meetings. "I'm going to tell Yang to come early next week with some guys who like to cook. He can give me a shopping list and they'll cook a meal for everyone. What d'you think? Food brings people together."

"Sounds complicated and a mess," I answered, "but sure, why not? We enjoy Chinese restaurants, and I like to cook stir-fry. Maybe I'll learn something."

Stores being closed on Shabbat, John came home from the supermarket on Friday with boxes of vegetables—cabbage, carrots, mushrooms, onions, cauliflower, green onions, parsley, bean sprouts, and more—as well as various kinds of meat, and rice of course. Six men showed up early Saturday afternoon, rolled up their sleeves, and went to work: first spreading the food all over our large kitchen table and then each taking a knife and beginning to chop.

"Do they really have to smoke while cooking?" I complained to John. For years we had asked smokers to step outside onto our porch. I understood that John was delighted to have an entrance with the Chinese and was trying to be culturally sensitive, but smoking while cooking was not only unsanitary, it stank up the house.

"I'll talk to Yang."

To my amazement, a multi-course meal was ready in less than two hours and the kitchen was spotless. I discovered new elements of Chinese cooking, different from the food we ate in Chinese restaurants—no egg rolls, sweet and sour chicken, or chow mein. Furthermore, instead of stir-frying everything together as was my style, they produced many dishes, each with one kind of meat and vegetable and different seasonings. The more entrees, the more respect accorded the guests. And the soup, usually a clear broth, came last.

"Clears the palate," Yang explained.

That wasn't a problem for me, even though I was used to hot and sour or wonton soup before the meal, but I found the chicken feet floating around in the bouillon neither appetizing nor tasty.

"Healthy and good for the bones," Yang added.

John quietly slipped his chicken feet back into the pot.

"Must be an acquired taste," I said.

Some workers invited David, a volunteer, to eat at their camp, and he enjoyed a delicious dish of liver and peppers. Three days later the translator asked him, "Do you know what you ate?"

"Do I want to know?" David asked.

"The workers caught a dog by the dumpster. You ate its liver."

We had many delicious meals, both at the camps we visited and when they cooked at the Shelter. Dumplings, a dish we had never seen on a restaurant's menu, became one of our favorites. We loved eating the mouth-watering dough pockets, but also watching the whole labor-intensive process: preparing the special mixture of flour and water, rolling the dough across the table, filling and sealing the dumplings with a specially seasoned ground meat mixture, and finally boiling them. Grasping each dumpling with chopsticks, we dipped them in soy sauce and popped them whole into our mouths, the juice dribbling down our chins.

Through the hundreds who came to meetings at the hostel and our home, deep friendships with the translators, and countless shared meals, the Chinese became an integral part of Shelter life for many years. While remaining at home in Eilat, we entered into a new world and unfamiliar culture, and the door also opened for our first overseas trip besides the United States and Europe.

20. Visits to Court & to China

I noticed John didn't have the usual spring in his step when he returned from the post office, so I poured him a glass of water.

"They want to close us down," he muttered. "It's the same story: they claim we're violating zoning regulations."

He plopped into his favorite chair, re-reading the letter from Eilat's engineering office. "I'm ordered to appear before the Building Committee in Beer Sheva. I'm not a guy for committees, but I'm not giving in. I don't ever want to be sorry and think I could have done more."

Though in the late 1990s and early years of the new century we focused our attention on the Chinese workers, life continued in other ways too, including our ongoing quest to receive a permanent license for the Shelter.

"What about contacting Yossi Cohen, the lawyer who ran for mayor on an anti-religious platform?" I suggested. "He'd probably be sympathetic." In Israel, political parties are often based on levels of Jewish orthodoxy or secularism. "His son is in Yonatan's class and his wife exercises with me."

Wasting no time, after lunch John walked over to Cohen's office around the corner from our house. Eilat is an informal town with everything close-by and appointments unnecessary. Soon John was home again, his manner changed.

"A nice guy," John said. "He seemed understanding—not just in it for the money—and thinks we have a good chance. He'll drive with me to the meeting next Monday."

I imagined John having an interesting three-hour ride. He was glad to have his own attorney, knowing that the lawyer from city hall would be there as well as Esther, who seemed to find special delight in giving us fines for handing out books on the beach or on the boardwalk—an activity that isn't prohibited under Israeli law. With no formal education or qualifications, Esther had used her connections to become the chairwoman of the Building Committee.

When Cohen entered the courtroom and saw the committee members and the red-haired judge with a *kippa* (a yarmulke, a platter-shaped cap worn by religious Jews), he turned pale, and sitting down next to John, he leaned over and whispered, "This doesn't look good."

After the opposition claimed that the Shelter was located in an area not zoned for commercial enterprises, Cohen stood up and presented his case. "The Soldiers' House, the Melony Hotel, and the Sports Hall, all commercial enterprises, are in the same neighborhood. Before Mr. Pex opened the Shelter it was already used as a hostel for hotel workers."

The judge turned to John and asked, "Can you please explain to us why the municipality has a problem with you?"

John reasoned he had nothing to lose. "We're Messianic Jews and non-Jews, Your Honor. We believe in Yeshua as the Messiah of Israel. Have you read Isaiah Chapter Fifty-three?"

The blood left Yossi Cohen's face a second time.

"I barely have time to glance at the morning newspaper." The judge sounded frustrated, and the hearing soon ended.

The trip home was quiet with the lawyer falling asleep. But within a few weeks John received a phone call telling him to come pick up a letter at the engineering office.

"Our problems are over!" John declared, waving the envelope in the air as he walked through the door. The letter stated that the regional committee in Beer Sheva had awarded us "a change of status."

Little did we know that although Beer Sheva had approved our request to continue operating the Shelter, those in Eilat led by Esther, would continue to torpedo our legitimacy as a hostel with all the weapons in their arsenal. Years later we were still struggling with their excessive and unrealistic demands for structural changes.

הטקסט

Life continued also in the sense that our family was growing up. Nannies lived with us when the children were small, and later our volunteers were like older siblings. But the day came when Joshua finished his three years of army service and wanted to work as a volunteer himself. In time, Racheli, Moriah, and Yonatan also joined the hostel team.

I knew that children often worked with their parents in businesses and ministries, but I wondered if it wasn't hard for John having Josh on staff and treating him the same as other volunteers.

"Not at all," John told me. "He fits in great. He grew up with the hostel."

Josh acknowledged that his position was different, including sleeping at home instead of in the volunteers' room on the premises. However, he often hung around the hostel, even when he wasn't on duty, and he had no problem working under his father.

"One of my vivid memories," Josh later told me, "is of Jeff and Dennis poring over the guest book like a chess game, sometimes for half an hour, moving people from one room to another to make place for everyone. Then Abba would walk in and say, 'None of this works,' and quickly sort things out."

Charlie from Germany showed up during Josh's time as a volunteer at the hostel. Tall, blond, and bearded, Charlie looked like the stereotypical picture of Jesus and called himself "Charlie Love-alution." He always wore sunglasses, even when inside, and spoke slowly with deliberation and authority even when saying something off-the-wall. Charlie told Josh he had come to Israel for a Rainbow Gathering—a temporary "intentional community" (as they call themselves) with roots reaching back to the 1960s counter-culture. Begun in the United States, the Rainbows aim to practice peace, love, freedom, and community, as opposed to popular culture, capitalism, and consumerism.

But for Charlie, things went terribly wrong. At a Rainbow Gathering in Ein Gedi, a lush oasis by the Dead Sea, twenty people were sleeping in a small area when they woke up and found that one of the family members had been murdered. After an extensive police investigation, Charlie came to the Shelter distraught and looking for a quiet place to rest.

"You can stay free for one night," John told him, and on the side said to Josh, "If I don't set a limit, he'll never leave."

Josh felt bad, but Charlie wasn't upset. He continued to come to our Friday evening meetings and the Bible studies for a while but eventually vanished.

הפקעת

On John's trips through the north of Israel to distribute Romanian Bibles at construction sites, he discovered much larger camps of Chinese workers than those in Eilat. But, although some had thousands of Chinese, the layout and living conditions of the camps were similar—like a ghetto.

John invited Daniel and Chow Leng to meet him at the camps after the men returned from their work, having first asked permission from the camp's boss to gather the men for a gospel meeting.

By this time the authorities in China had relaxed their restrictions and the leaders invariably agreed.

Large groups of men would listen with rapt attention, most for the first time in their lives, as Daniel and Chow Leng explained our belief in one God, the Bible as His Word and our authority, and Jesus who came to save and give us new life.

After one of his trips handing out Bibles, John arrived home just in time to hug the children, hear their adventures, and pray with them before they went to bed. He took a shower and propped himself up with pillows on our bed.

"One thing Mao did right," John reflected, "is to teach the Chinese to read and speak Mandarin. Everywhere we go, the workers happily receive Bibles. It's amazing."

When John went to building sites he had to be careful that the bosses didn't think he was encouraging the workers to slack off and leave their positions to come and take Bibles. He made sure to first find the Israeli supervisor and after a friendly chat and the offer of a Bible and literature in Hebrew, most had no objection. Often they were glad to see someone interested in their laborers.

At a new neighborhood near Jerusalem, when the Israeli contractor saw that John had a Chinese speaker, Mark, with him, he pressed John to stay a few minutes longer to help solve a problem.

"You've come at exactly the right time," the contractor told John as he nodded at an Israeli woman arguing with the Chinese leader. "Her family was one of the first to move into the new building and now she says her dog has disappeared."

"Ask him if he's seen my dog," the woman begged John in Hebrew. "It vanished yesterday. We've looked all over. My kids are crying."

John interpreted the message to Mark.

Mark passed the message on to the Chinese.

The leader frowned and spoke in Chinese.

"He says he's sorry," Mark finally explained, "but his men ate the dog."

The woman became hysterical.

The two Chinese launched into a long discussion. Then finally Mark explained, "He says they didn't know it was forbidden and asks if you have a list of rules for this country, so they'll know what to do and not to do in the future."

"Read this book," John said, handing the Chinese leader a Bible. "You'll learn everything here."

The rest of the Chinese workers also asked for a Bible.

מקדש

As our relationships with the Chinese expanded, God provided us with a series of Mandarin speaking volunteers. For a time, the Chinese became the largest group at our Friday evening meetings at the Shelter, and these volunteers could interpret John's messages as well as interact with the workers throughout the week.

Wan from Hong Kong, spoke Cantonese as her mother tongue but quickly adapted to Mandarin. She worked together with David, a new immigrant from the States, and despite their dissimilar backgrounds and cultures, they fell in love and later married in Hong Kong—another "Shelter couple." After their wedding they returned to Eilat where David continued serving at the Shelter. When their beautiful baby was born in the Eilat hospital, we felt like grandparents.

Linda, also from Hong Kong, moved to Jerusalem to study at the university. She rented a room above the Mandarin, a well-known Chinese restaurant, and eventually married Billy, the Chinese manager who had Israeli citizenship.

מקדש

As Chinese workers in the center of the country became believers in Jesus and grew in their faith, Daniel and Chow Leng became busier. They rented a building for their meetings in the south Tel Aviv neighborhood where many foreign workers gathered after work, and in Haifa held Bible studies at a Chinese restaurant.

Daniel and Chow Leng began organizing Chinese New Year events for the workers from around the country, and we sent our Chinese up in buses. Everyone received a meal, listened to speeches, enjoyed entertainment, and watched the official People's Republic of China broadcast on a large-screen television. At the peak of the Chinese era, Daniel and Chow Leng rented the enormous basketball arena in Tel Aviv for this purpose.

The Chinese New Year became a key date in our calendar as we realized its significance for our Chinese friends. In China, families gather together even when that involves traveling hundreds of kilometers by train and bus. Also called the Spring Festival, they wear new clothes, light firecrackers, eat special foods, and give gifts of money in red envelopes. The Chinese in Eilat became homesick for their families and country at this time, and in the days off they received from their Israeli bosses, they attempted to replicate some of their customs and atmosphere.

We celebrated our most memorable Chinese New Year in Eilat's largest camp numbering hundreds of workers, which had been spotlessly cleaned and decorated with huge, shining red posters printed with black Chinese characters. Food and alcohol were abundant, and after dinner we were treated to an elaborate program of speeches, singing, dancing, and skits using home made floats: a sort of talent show.

"It's like being in China," I said to John.

"We should go there," John replied.

"You said that about Russia and Romania too, but I'm ready when you are."

הפסקה

The bulk of our Chinese contacts were with construction workers and their leaders, but a number of scientists who were studying and working in Eilat also came to our meetings. Tim and Polly, here with their young son, worked at the Inter-University for Marine

Sciences in the field of fish genetics. (Like many Chinese, they had English as well as Chinese names, and we never knew how they were called in Chinese.) Curious about our faith, they used to visit Wan and David on Friday afternoons where they could get their questions answered and with whom they became friends.

On one occasion after Tim and Polly watched a science film dealing with their area of expertise, how patterns in nature point to God, Tim decided that it was reasonable to believe in God. Through further study, both parents and their bright, multi-lingual son concluded that Jesus was the Messiah and Savior, and their lives changed radically.

Busy with the Chinese church in Tel Aviv, and since we now had Chinese volunteers at the Shelter, Daniel and Chow Leng didn't fly to Eilat as often. They did, however, continue to come for the special, joyous occasions when groups of thirty, forty, or fifty men who, having decided to believe in Jesus and wanting to express their faith publicly, chose to be baptized in the Red Sea.

The wide smiles on the faces of these simple laborers were unmistakable. As most of them didn't possess a bathing suit, they either took turns using the same one or entered the water in their underwear, being careful to remove the bundle of cash they often carried in a special, built-in pocket. As part of the celebration, John prepared a tall stack of his famous pita on the fire, followed by hot dogs and chicken wings. The Chinese snatched the wings from the grill and ate them while they still looked red and bloody to me.

"Never mind," John told me. "They're enjoying themselves and we've got food at home."

הקמצן

Our Chinese period at the Shelter overlapped the Romanian season. Many of the workers, especially outgoing ones, learned Hebrew during their stay. The enterprising men found private jobs after their regular work and needed basic Hebrew to communicate and negotiate their wages. When these Chinese and

Romanians met on Friday evenings at the Shelter, they spoke in their common language—Hebrew.

The Africans, though not in large numbers, also continued to dribble into Israel. One burning hot summer afternoon in July when John was home taking his siesta, one of our volunteers phoned.

"Come quick!" she said. "An African has been following me around for half an hour with a Chinese after him. Both are upset, and I don't know what they want."

John quickly switched from resting to action, and ran to the hostel. The African, perspiring profusely, was well-dressed in a pair of slacks and a button-down shirt; the Chinese was in his work clothes. The Chinese pointed to the African and tried to explain something to John in Chinese and limited Hebrew. John picked up the word *shekel*.

The African kept twisting his head and darting around with his eyes. "Do you speak English?" John asked him.

He nodded.

"So what's going on?"

The African looked at the ground.

"Do you believe in Jesus?" John asked, knowing that most of the Africans in Israel were at least nominal Christians.

"Yes."

"So why's he following you?"

The African told John his story—a familiar tale with a new twist. His Holy Land tour with a group of pilgrims had ended in Eilat. When their bus stopped outside the supermarket, he saw his chance for escape, obviously having made previous plans. He left his suitcase on the bus and apprehended the first person he saw—the Chinese worker—and asked to be taken to the Shelter, where his friend had said he would meet him.

Whether the Chinese was kind-hearted or couldn't escape the grip of the large African, he knew of the hostel and stopped a taxi for both of them. Upon arrival, the Chinese paid the driver fifteen shekels, and the African made a dash from the taxi straight into the first open door he saw, fearful the immigration police were on his trail.

The Chinese followed, wanting his fifteen shekels back, while the African, already paranoid, couldn't understand why the Chinese stuck with him so closely. John quickly sorted out the puzzle, paid fifteen shekels to the Chinese who happily went on his way, and gave the African a Bible. His friend shortly came to collect him.

הפסקה

With tens of thousands of Chinese workers in Israel we experienced tragedies, too. When Gao, a laborer from Shandong Province, became depressed, he could no longer work effectively. Chinese workers paid thousands of dollars to receive permits to work in Israel, usually received as loans from family members. Israeli manpower agencies with their Chinese counterparts were the principal beneficiaries. His boss knew that sending Gao home would mean the inability to pay back his loans and an even worse punishment for a Chinese: losing face. Yet after several warnings he had no choice but to terminate Gao's contract. Gao chose to take his own life rather than having to meet his wife and family in this humiliating position. He was buried in the Eilat cemetery in the presence of his fellow workers, Daniel and Chow Leng, Shelter staff, and representatives of the Chinese embassy.

Ba was one of a group of workers who used to come to the Shelter meetings, yet we didn't know him personally until he was struck by a taxi while riding his bicycle to work. When John and David heard from Ba's colleagues that he was hospitalized with a serious head injury, they began visiting him. After finally being released, Ba suffered debilitating headaches which prevented him from working. His friends cared for him for a short time until their contracts finished and they returned to China. Although Ba couldn't imagine remaining in Israel without his friends, he was suing the taxi driver's insurance company for compensation, and we all agreed that he would never receive the money if he left. So Ba moved into the Shelter.

John became Ba's driver as well as his advocate. We found him a lawyer through *Kav La'Oved* (Worker's Hotline), an Israeli nonprofit organization dedicated to protecting the rights of disadvantaged workers. John drove Ba to appointments with neurologists in Hadassah Hospital in Jerusalem and to his lawyer in Tel Aviv. When the insurance company offered him a pittance and Ba was tempted to go home to his wife and family in China, we convinced him to stay and wait for a fair settlement.

Ba, with a mustache and a thick head of hair in an early Beatles style, became part of the Shelter community. He improved the little Hebrew he already knew and also learned English. With plenty of free time, Ba began to read his Bible, and like Yang, was touched by the compassion and generosity of the staff. He joined the volunteers at ten o'clock when they cleaned the hostel and at the Bible study that followed at eleven o'clock. When John needed tiling done, Ba immediately volunteered. In his quiet and humble way, Ba slowly became a believer.

"You must be patient," John encouraged Ba. "All things work together for good for those who love God. They're required to pay you, and you'll finally go home and can start your own business."

Ba's long-suffering finally paid off, and when he received the good news of an eight-thousand dollar payment from the insurance company, we had a party at the Shelter before he flew back to his village in the northeastern province of Liaoning.

When we were engaged with the Russian immigrants, John dreamed of packing our van with Bibles and sailing on a ship to Odessa. I pictured myself spending a few days to track down my family's roots in the villages around Kiev, from where my mother's father, Morris Kramer, had left as a young boy for America. But it never happened—we had the Russians here to attend to, and our children were young.

With the wave of Romanian construction workers, I envisioned visiting some of the men who had returned to their quaint, forgotten-by-modern-times villages and standing in the square at Timisoara where the revolution had begun. But this trip also never came to pass.

By 1998, though, when Josh was in the army, Racheli had just graduated from high school, and only Moriah and Yonatan were at home, we were offered a plane ticket to China—our opportunity to look up Chinese friends and for the first time, travel outside the U.S. and Europe. After landing in Beijing, we began with a thirty-six hour train ride to Ulan Bator, Mongolia, where we met a former Shelter volunteer who was working at an eye clinic. From there we traveled to Yantai to visit Wang and Ren, and then on to Qingdao where Yang waited for us.

"You'll be on your own?" asked one of our Chinese friends in Eilat. Foreign independent tourists were uncommon in those days.

"Why not?" John answered. This wasn't our first trip abroad.

In fact, though, we did face challenges, like searching for the train to Mongolia in Beijing's enormous train station where the signs were only in Chinese and no one spoke English. And being kicked off the train on the Chinese-Mongolian frontier because our travel agent had told us we didn't need visas. Stuck in a tiny border post with a dozen houses, we slept in the home of the chief immigration official until being repatriated to the Chinese side where we were issued visas.

Ren and Wang took us to visit one of the workers from Eilat, in an area officially closed to outsiders. He brought us to his parents' traditional village house, where the *kang*, a heated sleeping platform with a stove underneath, occupied half of the main room. The communist village chief joined us, and the women prepared a multi-course meal on a wood-burning stove, including their specialty: deep-fried silk worms.

"You're the first foreigners to come here," the mayor told us, spitting chicken bones onto the floor. He seemed proud to think that through our presence his village had jumped up a few levels in its rating among the millions of Chinese hamlets.

Following the meal and with just a few hours' notice, they managed to organize a church service in this nondescript, left-behind village. We all crammed into one of their homes with mostly women in attendance, as we understood was common in China. After only knowing Chinese men in Eilat, I enjoyed finally meeting women.

Ren and Wang also arranged for us to go to the home of Gao's (who had taken his own life earlier in Eilat) widow who, despite her poor living conditions, cooked an elaborate meal for us, arranged on a low table on the kang.

Our trip ended in Hong Kong where we met up with Wan, our volunteer who was at the time engaged to David. We gained a new appreciation for the cultural distance she would have to travel, and after we came home we had a better understanding of the mentality and background of the Chinese workers.

On our second trip to China in 2004, Zhu and his son met us at the Beijing Airport and served as our tour guides. Zhu had come to Eilat as the translator for a group of thirty workers, heard about the Shelter, and began coming to our meetings. In time, Zhu became convinced that the Bible had the answers to his questions, could help him to be a better person, and meet his deepest needs. He became a believer, and when he eventually went home to Anhui Province he worked as an English teacher and joined a small, unregistered house church together with his wife.

A highlight of our second trip was visiting Ba in his village and attending his church. Sleeping on the kang in his home, we could hear pigs grunting in their sty throughout the night—a happy sound because Ba had used the money from his insurance settlement to invest in pigs, allowing him to support his family.

In common with the foreign workers, Daniel and Chow Leng also eventually left Israel. After four years, Daniel returned home to Singapore. Chow Leng stayed three years longer before moving to Canada.

"The work with the Chinese was a season given to us," Daniel shared with me later. "We came, we saw, we caught it, and then moved on to other opportunities. Our continuing challenge is to see a season coming, grasp it quickly, and be blessed."

21. Trail Angels

"What about trying the Sinai again?" John suggested. "Maybe they've taken my name off their black list." We had scheduled a few days' vacation and were trying to decide where to go.

Though after the Sinai was returned to Egypt we continued to visit and bring clothes and food to our Bedouin friends, the Egyptian authorities were neither happy with such contacts nor with the Bibles and cassette tapes we distributed. John had been refused entry a couple of times, but feeling the need for a rest, and with the Sinai such an attractive and close-by option, we decided to make another attempt.

המקלט

Guests who enter the Shelter for the first time often speak of the peaceful atmosphere. They see the sukkah with its palm-branch roof, colorful rugs, and low sofas, and the carpet-covered stage with a hammock. They see people sitting in small groups engaged in conversation, playing guitar, or sharing a meal. Moreover, I believe visitors sense something beyond the physical aspects of the facility.

For the staff, though, who both live and work within its high, white outer walls, the hostel can feel like a pressure cooker where volunteers, long and short-term guests, local friends, and weirdos from the street mix, interact, and form a community.

Mary, a former volunteer, calls the Shelter a pirate ship. "John is the captain," she wrote to me. "During the cleaning, we spray torrents of water all over and swab the deck with squeegees. The staff room brings to mind a boat with its wood paneling, and on Friday we cook in giant pots for the crew. We often resemble a rough and tumble crowd of pirates, especially with folks like Jox who once showed up wearing a black bandana decorated with a white skull and crossbones.

"Like a ship, the Shelter is constantly being repaired or held together by the gang—painting projects, as well as fixing lights, blinds, doors, toilets, and desert coolers. We travel the world (the world comes to us, rather) and gaze out over the hostel wall, aware of enemy pirates who may come in and try to take over. We deal with people who are like stowaways and have even rescued a few who seemed to have been lost at sea. In our free time we sit around singing and drinking 'ale' (coffee)."

Thanks to our changing crew, each one bringing new talent and enthusiasm, we're able to keep floating. The volunteers come and go—for three months, six months, a year—but the captain remains. And the five-minute walk between the Shelter and our home provides enough distance to maintain our stability and sanity.

Because the hostel is open from early morning till midnight 365 days a year, our other strategy is to take periodic breaks. The desert, which touches Eilat on all sides except where the Red Sea laps at the town's edge, is both easily accessible and for us an ideal retreat. The absolute silence, lack of man-made objects, and stark, empty landscape never cease to quiet my soul.

הַמִּקְלָט

On this particular day in February 2004, the Egyptian authorities looked at my passport and waved me through, but when they checked John's name in their computer, the officer apologized and told John that he didn't know why, but John wasn't allowed in Egypt.

Having prepared the staff to manage for three days without us, we didn't consider returning home, so after overcoming our disappointment we changed direction and headed north in our Chevrolet Blazer. We planned on traversing the Negev Desert to Kadesh Barnea, the spot where the nation of Israel disobeyed the Lord after the exodus and were forbidden to enter the Promised Land for forty years. But through other unforeseen twists in our plans, we ended up in Ein Zik, an oasis far to the east of our objective.

Arriving after dark and sleeping on a mattress next to our car, we woke at dawn to find ourselves in a dazzling location of rugged brown hills and a sparkling blue sky providing a backdrop to the spiky, green palm trees. As we began exploring, we saw a young couple emerging from a small dome tent in the middle of a winding path, never imagining that they would point us in a new direction and bring a different clientele to the Shelter. Since we didn't see any other cars I wondered how they got there.

"We're on the Israel Trail," the young man told me. "We left Eilat eighteen days ago and hope to reach Kibbutz Dan in another month."

I remembered reading about the Israel Trail, a thousand kilometer (six hundred mile) path from the Egyptian to the Lebanese border, but had never met anyone who had walked it. Impressed and curious, we peppered them with questions. "What do you eat? Where do you sleep? What about water in the desert? How heavy are your packs?"

Instantly, John and I knew the reason why we hadn't been allowed to enter the Sinai and had ended up in Ein Zik instead of Kadesh Barnea: in order to meet this couple and to walk the Israel Trail. We enjoyed hiking around Israel and discovering out-of-the-way places, and lately had been feeling the need for a longer get-away, but this would be a giant leap from anything we had ever done. Yet, walking the Trail sounded like the perfect way to spend time with each other and with God—out in nature in the land we loved—while sharing our faith and meeting a diversity of people.

We were in reasonable physical condition, but with John turning sixty in two years we didn't want to wait long. So focusing on our goal, I began researching, reading, planning, and dreaming. I found a book in Hebrew called *Shvil Israel* (Israel Trail) and an outdated website. We bought backpacks, hiking books, a tent, sleeping pads, and walking poles as well as the fourteen topographical maps covering the route.

Recognizing that we wouldn't want to sleep out every night and that this would be an opportunity to connect with family and friends in the rest of the country, I made a list of those who lived along the Trail and called to ask if they would be willing to help us. In order to share our vision with people we met, we produced a small, colorful pamphlet explaining who we are, why we were hiking, what we believe, and extending an invitation to stay at the Shelter. Furthermore, I decided to keep a journal for the purpose of later writing a book about our journey.

One of our biggest challenges was finding someone to replace John at the hostel while we would be gone. Our daughter Moriah was on staff, having finished her two years of compulsory military service and the customary post-army trip (volunteering at an orphanage in Kenya) and felt she could manage, together with the volunteers.

With all obstacles cleared, we began our hike in February 2005 and after forty-two walking days, we finished on our thirtieth wedding anniversary, March 21st. We climbed over mountains, through valleys and streams, in the rain and scorching sun, in deserts and forests, next to kibbutzim and Bedouin villages, along the edge of Jerusalem, and through the center of Tel Aviv. We spoke to Bedouin shepherds, Orthodox Jews, fellow hikers, and those who picked us up hitchhiking. We developed a new appreciation for characters in the Bible like Abraham who walked from Ur of the Chaldeans (Iraq today) to Canaan; Jesus who went from Jerusalem to the Sea of Galilee numerous times; and Paul who trekked all over Asia Minor. Our prayer life deepened, as well as our trust in God to supply our daily needs.

Elated at having fulfilled our dream and unwilling to end this pivotal event in our lives, in the bus and plane on the way home I already began thinking of ways to prolong our experience. Writing a book would be another tremendous challenge and a jump beyond the newsletters and few magazine articles I had written, but I was eager to share with others not only our adventure but lessons I had learned.

Aiming to minimize the amount of water we would have to carry, we had begun earlier in the season than most hikers and so met only thirty-five through-hikers on our journey. On our final day we met a young woman who was just beginning her trek, and as we spoke she mentioned that she had attended a Shvil preparation lecture in Tel Aviv.

"They gave us a list of Trail Angels," she told us.

"Trail Angels?"

"People who want to help hikers, like by supplying water or offering a place to stay."

On the spot I decided we would be Angels. I could tell that the *Shvilistim* (Trail hikers), mostly young folks who had just finished the army, were the kind of guests we enjoyed: nature-loving, open-minded, and friendly. With its abundance of pubs, bars, and discothèques, Eilat often attracts people looking for action rather than peace and quiet, and from experience we have learned those people don't fit in at the Shelter.

The backpacking world travelers we began with weren't coming as much to Israel any more. Israel has become an expensive country; our popularity has plummeted due to politics and the media; and more exotic locations such as Vietnam and Chile have become accessible.

Offering ourselves as Trail Angels would not only bring us a new/old sort of client, but after receiving help from our personal angels, I wanted to bless others on their journey. And networking with other Shvil hikers could help us keep the spirit of our trip alive.

I found a telephone number in Tel Aviv to register.

"What kind of help can you offer?" a woman asked me.

"We'll give a free night to those finishing the Trail."

"How many people can you accommodate?

"Unlimited."

"How far in advance do they have to notify you?

"No notice necessary."

"Other kinds of help? Caching water? Driving?"

"Let's leave it at that." I put down the phone, feeling excited.

הפסקט

Rebecca and Nir, a couple who gave us one of our first opportunities to be Trail Angels, showed us the potential of our new guests. From New Zealand and Israel, they had originally met in Africa and then walked the Shvil together. Although Rebecca's family were believers, she had left that path, while Nir grew up in a family deeply rooted in the Galilee.

With no immediate plans, Rebecca and Nir decided to stay around longer and do a diving course. Nir soon began attending Bible studies and having long talks with Jeff about our faith. At one point, after spending several days studying the prophecies in the Tanach about the Messiah, Nir became convinced they were speaking about Yeshua, but couldn't understand why the rabbis don't accept Him—the same question I had asked when I began reading the Bible.

"Why don't you go speak to a rabbi?" Jeff suggested.

Nir, acting on Jeff's recommendation, went to a nearby synagogue. He asked questions and spoke to the rabbi for three hours until the rabbi became angry with him and Nir left. When he returned to the hostel Nir told Jeff that whereas at the Shelter we welcomed his questions, the rabbi only became upset.

Rebecca initially kept a distance. However, after staying for over a month, Nir and Rebecca both committed their lives to Yeshua. When they left the Shelter, they went to work at the Bet Immanuel Guest House in Jaffa. We kept in touch with them long enough to hear that they went home to her family to get married.

As Trail Angels we were thrilled to see two hikers discover belief in God and to wed, and in the case of Avi, a tall, well-built young man from Tel Aviv, we became saving angels. Previously, we had no idea what kinds of trouble people could get themselves into on the Trail, and how we would end up rescuing them.

When Avi, carrying a big brand-new backpack, showed up at the Shelter in August 2006 and announced his plan to begin the Shvil the following day, John warned him that it was too hot.

"I'd planned to start in the north, but it's dangerous there now with the *katyushas* [rocket artillery] falling," Avi explained. Israel was in the middle of a war with the Hezbollah in Lebanon.

"I'd take my chance with katyushas any day over this heat," John told him. "I live in Eilat."

"My mother and grandmother also told me not to do it, but I just finished the army paratroopers, and have time now."

"At least take my phone number and call if you need help."

Avi left at dawn with six liter-and-a-half water bottles in his pack. While sitting on the beach in the late afternoon, we were putting on our masks and snorkels when John's phone rang.

Although barely audible, John recognized Avi's voice. He had run out of water over an hour before, but deep in a wadi with no cell phone reception, had no choice but to continue climbing until one stripe appeared on his device.

"I can't go on," Avi stuttered.

"Where are you?"

"After the cleft with the cables."

"You're not far from the road."

"I can't walk another step."

"Hang on. We'll be there soon."

John, who was having problems with his Achilles tendon and couldn't hike, drove Thomas, our athletic Dutch volunteer, and me to the trailhead. With Thomas packing four liters of water, we ran down the trail and found Avi huddled in the shade of a boulder. I held a bottle to his lips and helped him to drink slowly so that he wouldn't throw up, a danger when someone is dehydrated. Then Thomas slung Avi's pack on his back and supported him with a strong arm as we made our way back to the car, step by step.

Needless to say, that was the end of the Israel Trail for Avi, and the following day he had recuperated sufficiently to return home. His mother surprised us some days later with a phone call.

"Thank you for saving Avi's life. I, too, believe that it was God who saved him."

הפסקט

After settling back into life again, I soon turned to my book project and spent a year writing *Walk the Land: A Journey on Foot through Israel*, having to fit my new avocation into an already full schedule. Finding a publisher and editing took another year, and the book was later translated and published in German, Dutch, and Hebrew. I'm encouraged by interest and emails from around the world, and as people ask for help organizing their own trek on the Shvil, I'm happy to answer questions and share my experiences.

When Michael and Eloise, relatives from Holland, came with their six-week-old baby and planned to hike for eighteen days, we helped them in the area near Eilat with water and food. On their third evening, we arrived early at the campground so that John could prepare *pita* and *poike* (a one-pot stew cooked over coals) while I hiked up the trail to meet them.

I wondered how Michael and Eloise were managing with the thick sandstorm raging such as occurs several times a year in Eilat. I braced myself against the strong winds while dense yellow dust erased the mountains, and I squinted in an effort to keep the sand out of my eyes.

I passed many Shvilistim as I walked, and later ten joined us at our camp.

"Do you think our tent will hold in this wind?" Eloise asked.

"The wind usually drops following the sunset," John answered. "And you can always sleep in our van with the baby."

After enjoying John's sweet, Bedouin-style tea, Ziv, Dan, and Natan, three friends, began discussing their water situation. Ziv and Dan decided to hike to the next community, fill up their bottles, and return.

"It's too late," John warned them. "I've enough water for you to drink tonight."

"It's only a kilometer," Ziv insisted. "We need water for washing, too."

John explained that actually it was at least three kilometers away over a high hill, darkness would soon overtake them, and walking in the sandstorm would slow them down. Nevertheless, they stubbornly took off. Later, while lying on our backs looking at the stars in the immense spread of sky over our heads, Natan's phone rang.

"It's Ziv," he said to John. "They're lost and out of water. Could you drive me to find them? I'll pay for the gas."

"Forget about the gas. Let's go!" John said.

I said a quick prayer, wondering how they would find someone in the middle of the desert in the dark. But after they drove a couple of kilometers down the rough track, Natan spotted a light stick—the kind they use in the army—stuck in the ground and pointing up the hill. John began negotiating the car slowly up the steep, rocky incline until he could proceed no farther.

Grabbing a bottle of water, Natan jumped out of the car and far up the ridge spotted the faint glow of another stick. When Natan reached him, Ziv was alone, collapsed on the ground, and hallucinating. Natan immediately called Dan to say he had found Ziv, and later back at camp after he'd recovered enough to speak, Ziv told us what had happened. When Dan had seen that Ziv couldn't continue, he had gone on alone.

"You were right," Ziv told John. "It was far. You saved my life."

It's not every day we have the chance to save someone's life; but we've been able to help many Shvilistim who come to the Shelter—more than a hundred every fall and spring season with the numbers growing—in other ways. We've driven out to the Trail to take a recorder to a girl who forgot her musical instrument, an opportunity for John to make pita for twenty hikers sleeping at the first campground. And we had two girls who walked in a circle around Eilat before calling John to bring them back to the hostel.

Our volunteers, having heard our Trail stories, appreciate the accomplishment of finishing the trek and welcome the hikers warmly, offering them a meal and the use of our washing machine (better than having their stinking, unwashed clothes piled in a corner). The Shvilistim bring a lively, fresh energy to the hostel. They enjoy the atmosphere, ask questions about our community, and often return to stay with us again.

הפסקה

The 2006 Lebanon War that disrupted Avi's hiking plans also transformed the Shelter for a time. Rocket attacks from Lebanon into Israel have been a chronic plague in the lives of Israel's northern residents since 1968. The First Lebanon War in 1982 brought temporary relief, but after Israel's withdrawal from southern Lebanon in 2000, Hezbollah took control and intensified the cross-border attacks. Though we live in the same country, what happens in the Galilee doesn't usually affect our lives in Eilat.

So even when Israel's ongoing conflict with Hezbollah turned into an all-out war in July 2006, with over one-hundred rockets a day being fired at Israel, we didn't anticipate changes at the Shelter. Slowly, though, as life under the shellings became intolerable and our defense minister ordered all people in the north—one million residents—to stay near or in bomb shelters, desperate phone calls to the hostel began.

Ultimately 250,000 civilians evacuated their homes and relocated to other areas of the country, including hundreds finding their way to Eilat. While the first choice was to stay with friends or relatives, not everyone had that opportunity, so municipalities out of the range of missile fire opened community centers and schools for the internally displaced people. When our local high school became available, whole families moved into classrooms: sleeping on mattresses, using the toilets and sinks in the boys' and girls' restrooms, and eating food provided by volunteers. Shelter staff began going to the school to organize activities for the children, bored after the novelty of being in Eilat wore off, and one evening John prepared pita for everyone on a campfire next to the soccer field.

Despite the extreme heat, July and August are busy at the hostel because Israelis as well as people from abroad have their vacations at this time. Nevertheless, we tried to squeeze in as many refugees as we could. A Russian-Israeli family with two young children from Haifa, who had narrowly escaped a hit on their building, heard about us and asked if they could shower at the Shelter after having been using the outdoor showers at the beach. When a room became available, they moved in. After the hostel was full, and friends of friends called us, we invited them to stay at our home.

The rockets didn't discriminate between religions or backgrounds, and we hosted Jewish, Druse, and Christian families, all traumatized by having to abandon their homes, concerned about damage while they were gone, but thankful to find a safe and welcoming haven.

One of the last families we accommodated was Michel and Samia from an Arab village in the Galilee with their six daughters.

"We didn't want to leave home," Michel explained, "but from our porch we could see the *katyushas* whizzing by and hear the booms."

The Russian-Israeli family returns regularly to visit us. Michel and Samia have received us in their home with typical Arab hospitality—giving up their bedroom for us and preparing a feast. Our families' lives became more entwined the following summer when we invited their two oldest daughters to Eilat to meet an urgent need, for a wave of Arabic-speaking guests surged in like a tsunami and penetrated straight to our hearts.

22. From Sudan to Zion

"I saw some of those tall Africans again." John remarked when he entered the house.

"Me, too," I said. "Wonder where they're from; probably not Nigeria or Ghana. They're too dark to be from there."

It was May 2007, and we had recently begun noticing men, women, children, and babies on our streets whose appearance was unlike any people we had known.

Gabriel solved our mystery when he entered the Shelter a few days later. "I'm a refugee from Sudan," he introduced himself in perfect English.

"Sit down. Have a cup of coffee," John welcomed him. "How did you get to Eilat? Why Israel? Where do you live?"

"I have to return to work, but I'll be back," Gabriel explained in a serious, quiet voice. "I just wanted to find the Shelter."

The next time Gabriel visited, he brought with him several countrymen, and their story unfolded.

We never dreamed then that Gabriel would become a dear

friend and the Sudanese an integral part of our lives.

I asked Isaac, one of Gabriel's friends, why they came to Israel. I remembered Sudan as an extremist Muslim country that harbors terrorist groups and enforces the sharia law.

"In southern Sudan we are mostly Christians," he explained. "The fanatical Muslims who hate Israel are also killing our people. We escaped as the children of Israel did from Pharaoh and his army. There's a chapter in the Bible about the Sudanese coming to Mt. Zion."

Sudanese on Mt. Zion? Even after thirty-three years of Bible reading, I couldn't recall that passage.

"You can read for yourself," Isaac said and opened his Bible to Isaiah Chapter Eighteen: "*Woe to the land of whirring wings along the rivers of Cush, which sends envoys by sea in papyrus boats over the water. Go swift messengers to a people tall and smooth-skinned, to a people feared far and wide, an aggressive nation of strange speech whose land is divided by rivers ... At that time gifts will be brought to the Lord Almighty ... to Mount Zion*" (verses 1, 2, & 7, NIV).

I could see his point. Cush was the ancient name for Sudan. Our new friends were obviously tall as well as smooth-skinned, having little body hair. Their tribes were constantly fighting one another, matching the description of "an aggressive nation."

"Sudan is the 'land divided by rivers' because the White and Blue Niles meet at Khartoum, the capital," explained Isaac.

Whatever the original meaning, many Sudanese found encouragement from these verses in their struggle as refugees in Israel. Gabriel and Isaac told us they preferred life here with its uncertainties to what they had endured.

"These must be the ones Jox has been talking about," John said to me after Gabriel and his friends left.

With his dreadlocks, creased face, and dusky skin, Jox used to drop by our tent when it was on the Aqaba beach. He not only looked like a Rastafarian (member of a spiritual movement advocating use of marijuana and forbidding the cutting of hair) but he acted like one too—stoned and spaced out. Jox, a free spirit, liked to travel and added the hostel to his circuit, sometimes away for weeks or months before reappearing.

I found Jox's rambling narrative hard to follow, but slowly understood that he had run away from Nubia Province in Sudan and had supported himself as a musician in the Sinai before becoming one of the first Sudanese to cross the border. The Israeli police immediately placed Jox in jail, but eventually released him, and he received official United Nations refugee status.

Beyond his roaming around Israel, at first Jox's disappearances usually meant he was drinking or getting stoned with friends. But everything changed after he started to believe in Jesus. Jox moved into the Shelter and sat for hours in the sukkah reading the Bible and joining others in making music on the guitar or drum, both of which he played better than anyone we knew. When he vanished after that, he told us he was visiting Sudanese in prison—refugees who were beginning to sneak across the border by the same route he had taken.

הפליטים

Due to the ongoing civil war in Sudan since 1983, thousands of South Sudanese fled to neighboring Egypt, but as refugees they lived in the worst neighborhoods and worked in the most menial jobs in a country where much of the native population lives in poverty and is unemployed. They had no recourse when employers refused to pay or abused them, and they lacked access to proper medical care. The Egyptians' prejudice against dark-skinned people added to the refugees' hardships.

The hope that the United Nations would resettle them in Australia, Canada, or the United States enabled them to hang on. Yet the process was impossibly slow—virtually nonexistent. In December 2005, during a peaceful demonstration in front of the United Nations headquarters in Cairo, Egyptian police killed dozens of men, women, and children, and the first of the current wave of refugees began crossing the frontier into a country of which the only news they had heard in both Sudan and Egypt was negative to the extreme.

When the surge began, Israel faced a dilemma: with Sudan being an enemy state, Israel considered its citizens a security threat and felt justified sending them to jail. Our government, however, also realized it couldn't keep stuffing prisons full of refugees; human rights organizations protested that this went against the Geneva Convention; and Holocaust survivors such as author Eli Wiesel maintained that we have a moral obligation to help people fleeing genocide, as the Darfur conflict was defined.

Consequently, without a clear plan or policy, the Israeli government began to release some of the refugees to kibbutzim and moshavim where they were allowed to work, reasoning that the refugees would be under a type of house arrest while making themselves useful. When they heard that the kibbutzim employed refugees, the hotel managers in Eilat had a bright idea. Desperately short of workers, but unable to find enough Israelis willing to work as dishwashers or cleaners, they concluded that the Sudanese could fill those positions while still being secluded from the rest of the country. It seemed a perfect plan: the refugees received salaries, housing, meals, and even child-care, while the hotels found cheap labor.

"Where else do refugees have it so good?" I asked John when we came back from visiting the holiday-village-turned-refugee-center near Eilat where many lived. "In Afghanistan, Chad, Pakistan, Congo, and other places they live in tent camps or slums, while in Eilat they have jobs and apartments."

In time, however, we realized that the hotels weren't charitable organizations with altruistic motives. In some cases the money deducted for the refugees' expenses was more than they earned and left them in debt to the hotel. Neither did the favorable attitudes from Israelis last.

In this connected world of cell phones and email, the refugees' friends and families heard about the first-class circumstances awaiting those who succeeded in jumping over the border. We, as well as the refugees, realized that Israel couldn't accommodate all the poor Africans who wanted to flee here—potentially millions.

"As more come, it won't be good for those of us already here," Yien, one of our friends, told us early on as they continued to stream across the border.

Not only did most Israelis come to view the refugees as "illegal infiltrators" (the phrase the media and politicians used), but the Bedouin who had smuggled the Sudanese through the Sinai for a minimal fee, started seeing in the refugees a lucrative source of income and began torturing and extorting them, to extract the maximum amount of money.

For us at the Shelter, however, we knew that God had called us to help those we were meeting and to treat each one as a human being created in His image. As I studied my Bible, I found many references to "alien" and "stranger." I read in Deuteronomy 10:18-19: "The Lord defends the cause of the fatherless and the widow and loves the alien, giving him food and clothing. And you are to love those who are aliens, for you yourselves were aliens in Egypt."

הַמִּקְלָט

A nonprofit organization from Tel Aviv opened a day care center for the children of the Club Hotel's employees. Short of helpers, the group turned to the Shelter, and suddenly a new area of service opened up for our volunteers. What could be more fun—or tiring—than playing with cute little African children for a few hours?

That was when the two oldest daughters of Michel and Samia, who had come to Eilat to flee the katyushas the previous year, responded to our plea for Arabic-speaking aides. While faithfully helping with the children by day, in their free time they participated in meetings at the Shelter and The Eilat

Congregation, and Maria developed a relationship with Andrey, a young man from a Russian background. Two years later John and I were guests of honor at their celebration in the Galilee, and John officiated their wedding at the Shelter.

When Mansur, our Arabic-speaking staff member, decided to organize a Fun Day for the children and some of the mothers, our family and volunteers participated along with Gabriel. Because many Sudanese had arrived barefoot, one team bought them sandals and then toured the Underwater Observatory. The rest of us cooked lunch at our house, and afterwards we all met on the beach.

The children loved the water, and it's a good thing we had plenty of adults as well as air mattresses, since they had never been swimming before. An Israeli woman, sitting on the beach nearby with two little girls, bought popsicles for everyone. The kids loved playing soccer even though they didn't always seem to be playing on teams. My heart was drawn to one young boy who, while missing one of his legs below the knee, enthusiastically hopped around after the ball.

Collapsed on our sofa at the end of the day, John said to me, "Gabriel told me this was the best day of his life."

"For a guy thirty years old?"

"We'll do this again and find ways to reach the adults, too."

"I'll take Avraham, that boy without the leg, to get crutches tomorrow."

"Mansur's friend knows a doctor who may be able to make a prosthesis."

"But crutches in the meantime."

הפסקה

As I tried to understand the conflict that had driven our Sudanese friends from their homes, I found Gabriel a good source of information, together with the Internet and books I ordered. Roughly two million people had died as a result of war, famine, and disease caused by the First and Second Civil Wars. Four million people in southern Sudan had been displaced at least once (and often repeatedly) during the conflict. Darfur is a separate hostility because, though the population is Muslim, they are black Africans who are also being killed by government forces.

As Gabriel opened up and shared his life story, including his daring crossing of the Sinai Peninsula, I understood that he belonged to a sub-group of refugees called the "Lost Boys." With their villages being bombed, and forced to flee from their homes, groups of children escaped to large refugee camps in Ethiopia and Kenya; the U.S. ultimately accepted some as asylum seekers, and a number of books were written about them.

As I read these books hoping to gain insight into Sudanese culture and history, I felt moved to tell the stories of Sudanese who came to Israel, though I was unaware in the beginning of the complexity and amount of work involved in my undertaking. Naturally I first turned to Gabriel, recording his testimony on my small tape recorder and praying that God would lead me to others. I eventually included another man and three women, including a woman from Darfur who had suffered horrifically.

In 2011 Cladach Publishing produced my book *A People Tall and Smooth: Stories of Escape from Sudan to Israel*. As the animosity among the Israelis toward the African refugees grew, I was thankful to have HaChotam Publishers publish the book in Hebrew in 2013.

הפסקה

John's cell phone rang one afternoon while we were sitting on the beach. "Thirty-three Sudanese just came over the border without clothes, food, or bedding." The Fattal hotel chain housed their workers at the former Kibbutz Eilot guest house, a few kilometers north of town, and the kibbutznik overseeing the refugees, a colleague of John's from his years at the experimental station, called us when she needed help.

"I'm coming!" John replied. "I'll see what I can find."

John began by going through his closet. "I've got too much stuff anyway," he said as he emptied his shelves.

In the old days we had the "Bedouin Box" in the Shelter garden where neighbors and friends could bring their old clothes, and we in turn brought them down to our friends in the Sinai. When that door closed for us, John took the clothing along with Bibles and books on his trips to the Russian caravan camps. After the Russian immigration slowed down, we found that the Romanian workers would package up large parcels of clothes to send home. Now the Sudanese became the recipients, and when we sent word out to friends around the country, clothing poured in.

Since the Sudanese worked in shifts, any time we drove to the kibbutz we found many people hanging about outside. Though the scenery wasn't the same, in spirit I felt transported to an African village—women and children sitting on patchy grass, men around wooden picnic tables or leaning back on white plastic chairs, and happy screams of children running around. Papers and plastic bags blew by, with broken toys and empty soft drink bottles scattered on the ground.

The Sudanese were needier than any previous group we had encountered. The Russians, though they needed translators, were educated and had the Immigrant Absorption Ministry backing them. The Romanians seemed to manage with no help from us, and the Chinese had jobs and interpreters to guide them. But the Sudanese were refugees, totally on their own. Furthermore, unlike the other groups, they had multiple children and pregnant women among them. Taking a woman to the pharmacy for baby formula and diapers, another family to the used clothing store, a couple to the supermarket, or a child to the doctor, occupied more and more of our time.

Since all were apparently Christian and had suffered so much, we assumed they would be interested in reading the Bible with us. Unfortunately, within a short time we discovered that they were Christian in name only. Even when some of the Sudanese themselves started church services at the kibbutz, few attended.

John came home for lunch one day after taking a dozen little children for vaccinations at the mother-and-baby clinic. "I've got an idea, Jupe" he said. "We'll have our morning Bible studies with the Sudanese at the kibbutz instead of the Shelter, and the staff can come with me. Some will play with the kids so the parents can listen, and Tom will take his guitar. We'll go there evenings, too, for the ones who work in the morning."

"What about the Friday night meetings?" I asked John.

"Yeah, that too. We'll get the Sudanese there by picking them up and driving them to the hostel."

So, using our van and Blazer, we began shuttling the adults and children to the Shelter for the Friday meetings.

"I feel like a *matatu* [the crowded minibuses used as shared taxis] driver in Kenya, except that I don't have a conductor to keep order," I said.

After a couple of months we decided to rent a bus, though that introduced other issues. The first week the bus driver showed up at the kibbutz parking lot at seven o'clock p.m. as John had requested, loaded the handful of waiting Sudanese into his bus, and took off. Unfortunately, another forty or fifty people continued to straggle in for the next half hour, surprised the bus hadn't waited for them.

"Gotta work this out," John said to me.

Bringing the Sudanese to the Shelter was the first challenge. Keeping any kind of order once they arrived with thirty or more young children and babies scampering around under foot proved nearly impossible.

"I'll keep my message short," John said to me before the second time they came. "These kids aren't used to sitting still."

In the past we had enjoyed hearing and learning songs in Russian, Chinese, and Romanian, but when fifty Sudanese stood to worship the Lord in Arabic or in one of their tribal languages, a tangible excitement filled the courtyard. Was it because they were our most recent people group, or was it the pounding drumbeat accompanying their voices, their striking appearance, or the simple, repeated African choruses? In any case, all heads turned, cameras pointed, and hands clapped as we joined our new friends in praising the Lord. Jox provided the rhythm, beating the large drum that Racheli had brought back from Uganda with a long, thick wooden spoon.

Another problem arose following the meeting when the children ran outside, having quickly finished their food and leaving big portions scattered on the floor. After a few weeks of their yelling and racing around in the garden and street in front of the hostel, our neighbors complained. I could understand, especially when they started throwing rocks at each other. We did our best, though not always successfully, to contain them.

23. Trouble In Zion

Some of the Sudanese came straight from the border to the Shelter, having heard about us from their friends, and if we had space, we put them up until they found other accommodations. When Joseph arrived he told us that in his sprint across the frontier in the middle of the night, he had lost track of his wife and two little boys, ages two and four. Having heard harrowing stories of the crossing, often under a barrage of bullets from Egyptian soldiers, we could picture Joseph's predicament, so John began phoning people we knew who helped refugees.

Unbelievably, we not only located Angelina, Danny, and Sunny at our friends' place in Moshav Kadesh Barnea, but within a day the family was together again in Eilat. Our thrill of orchestrating a family reunification soon turned sour, however, when we saw Joseph and Angelina going out during the day, little Sunny crawling out of the window between the blinds, and we realized the parents had locked their sons in the room. When Joseph began appearing drunk at the hostel, John told him to leave, and

Angelina moved to the kibbutz with Danny and Sunny.

In the meantime, the Fattal Hotels saw a need to open a day care center for the Sudanese children on the kibbutz. Moriah and Tom, our recently married daughter and son-in-law, had moved into an apartment next to the Sudanese housing, and Moriah's studies in education as well as involvement with the refugees made her the perfect candidate to run the program. Moriah rose to the challenge of starting the center—equipping it with toys and furniture, finding helpers, communicating with the children who only spoke Arabic or their tribal language, and explaining the arrangements and ideas to the parents, most of whom likewise didn't speak English. Our volunteers often went there to help.

Little Sunny was one of Moriah's children in her day care center, and when she would see him and Danny wandering around alone at all hours, she used to take them home. John often brought the two brothers to our house for a meal, bath, hugs, and playtime.

The Department of Education opened a school for the Sudanese children, but after school, with most of their parents working and because they lived in tiny apartments, the kids had little to do, so our home and the Shelter became their hubs. The Sudanese had crept over the border with only the clothes on their backs, but once they began working, they eagerly acquired cell phones, video cameras, fancy clothes, and other accessories offered by a modern society. For the boys this meant bikes, and soon our yard turned into a bicycle parking lot. Our food consumption spiked also; teenage boys have good appetites.

Members of our family took different approaches to helping. "I like buying them things and taking them places," John told our children when they voiced their objections. "They're from Sudan and never had anything."

"But Abba," Racheli and Moriah said, "you didn't spoil us, so why spoil them? You can't let them do whatever they want."

"I'm like their grandfather," John insisted. "Grandparents

don't discipline, they show them love and acceptance. That's what they need, and a safe home where they're welcome."

No wonder the Sudanese called John *Abouna*, a term of respect meaning "our father."

I felt caught in the middle and sought a balance. But even John realized we needed to make changes when our neighbors complained about the noise, and worse, when someone broke into their storage shed and they accused our boys.

"We understand you want to help," they told us, "but we shouldn't have to suffer."

I knew they were right; I wouldn't want my neighbor's house being turned into a teenagers' club either.

"From now on, keep your bikes at the hostel," John informed the boys.

הפסקה

When a friend of ours from Beer Sheva asked if Akalino, a Sudanese man who suffered from psoriasis, could come to the Shelter, John readily agreed. But after his arrival, we found that Akalino would sit on the bomb shelter outside the hostel's gate all day, with a forlorn expression on his face, scratching his skin. Even in the burning summer heat he dressed in long sleeves and pants to cover his sores, and didn't interact with the rest of the Sudanese. John sympathized with this refugee who had a friendly, round face, and reminded us of a leper from biblical times.

Unemployed due to his psoriasis, Akalino had no health insurance, so John went to the dermatologist and explained Akalino's plight. Wanting to help, the doctor wrote a prescription for some expensive creams, but if anything, Akalino felt worse.

"The only solution for your friend is a prolonged stay on the Dead Sea," the doctor advised John when he returned.

"We saw how it helped Adriaan," John reminded me when he came home. So we bought a tent, put blankets and food in the car, gave Akalino some money, and dropped him off at a beach on the

Dead Sea on our way up to Jerusalem a few days later.

"Do you think he'll last here?" I asked John as we waved good-bye.

As we drove into the parking lot on the Dead Sea on our way home, I strained my eyes looking for Akalino's tent. Not only was he still there, but he seemed happier than usual. His psoriasis hadn't cleared up yet, but Akalino had hope.

We began stopping to visit Akalino on every trip to Jerusalem. The next time we saw him he had found a job arranging the beach chairs. "Will you keep my salary for me?" he asked John.

Slowly Akalino's sores disappeared and his money accumulated. On following visits he introduced us to his friends, and his broad smile spoke more than words. When after four years Akalino decided to return to South Sudan, he came to say good-bye and to collect the money John had saved for him: eight-thousand dollars.

הפסקה

Our life became so interwoven with the Sudanese that our new volunteers couldn't imagine how previous staff had kept busy without having children at the hostel every day. Interacting with the little ones (because even eight or ten year olds showed up with their younger siblings in tow), teaching guitar to Abdullah and Dongdiet (who both went on to become accomplished musicians), playing backgammon and other games, learning English and Hebrew from each other, and just trying to keep order, kept our staff busy.

Every Shabbat we loaded twenty, thirty, or forty children and adults into our cars and drove to the beach—a continuation of the Fun Day. They loved the pita and hummus, snacks, cookies, and watermelon, and playing in the water. Volunteers and friends stepped in as lifeguards.

Besides being babysitters, guitar and swimming teachers, mentors, and youth leaders, our staff taught English classes.

Observing the refugees' desire for education, we started lessons in our home, reminding me of the days when we had to clear out our living room for the Russian and later the Chinese meetings. Two volunteers, having willing spirits though they had never taught English, spent hours preparing lessons for the beginning and intermediate levels. My friend, a retired high school teacher, instructed the advanced group. Later, when two Sudanese men began their own English learning centers in rented apartments, we disbanded the classes in our home and the staff taught there.

One volunteer, Mary, viewed this as training for a possible career choice—teaching English as a second language. Jasmin, from Switzerland but living in England, heard about the English school, came to the hostel, and immersed herself in the vocation and the Sudanese community. Though she slept at the Shelter, we rarely saw her.

After a few months, Jasmin, with light, copper-colored hair and alabaster skin, wanted to talk to John and me. She came to our house with Yien, one of the Sudanese leaders, whom I had interviewed for my book.

"We're beginning a relationship," they announced, looking at each other and smiling with the unmistakable look of young lovers.

Though we appreciated their openness, the differences in their backgrounds and cultures, and Yien's uncertain status as a refugee concerned us. Nevertheless, love and the conviction that they were meant for one another prevailed, and their relationship grew until the day that Yien and Jasmin announced their engagement.

According to Sudanese tradition, they organized an elaborate party in the meeting hall on the kibbutz which included speeches, blessings, flags, suits and ties, and lots of food. Jasmin and Yien exchanged vows in the presence of the Sudanese community, Jasmin's parents who came from Switzerland for the occasion, and The Eilat Congregation members.

Two months later they married in Sudan and amazingly,

thanks to much prayer, Yien received a visa to join Jasmin in England. Later they moved to Addis Ababa, where Yien studies at a Bible school. They now have a beautiful, sweet, smiley, milk chocolate-colored little boy named Joshua.

הַמְקֵרוֹ

Avraham received his prosthesis and was soon genuinely playing soccer. People who meet him don't notice his missing limb. When he goes to the beach, Avraham pulls off his black plastic leg, bounces over the sand and across the pier, takes a hopping start, and dives into the sea together with his friends. His gentle manner and bashful smile charm everyone Avraham meets, including the physicians and orthopedic technicians who have donated time and services to help him. Avraham has grown rapidly since he arrived in Israel at age eight, thus every year he travels to Tel Aviv to be measured and fitted for a new leg. With South Sudan suffering an enormous health care shortage, we pray he'll be able to remain in Israel at least until he stops growing.

Abdullah (which means "God's Servant"), and Dongdiet always spent much time at the Shelter. Among the oldest of the Sudanese boys, they sought the company of our volunteers while learning the Bible, guitar, drums, and English. Because the Sudanese school, substandard for all the children, offered nothing for Dongdiet and Abdullah, Dongdiet became a teacher there while Abdullah volunteered at the Shelter.

"I'm glad Abdullah's at the hostel," John told me, "but he's seventeen and should be getting an education."

Through many phone calls, interviews, and much patience we eventually succeeded in getting Abdullah and Dongdiet accepted at the prestigious Sde Boker Environmental High School where they not only completed their matriculation exams but made deep friendships. At their graduation ceremony we observed the impact they had had on fellow students, their families, and teachers, and felt like proud parents, especially as we watched Dongdiet on stage as master of ceremonies.

Dongdiet's musical path recently carried him to heights we could have never imagined when school friends suggested he audition for the Israeli version of American Idol, and he reached the stage of the last fourteen contestants. Dongdiet's participation generated much media attention due to his background, and with his quiet, humble manner and ability to answer difficult questions, not to mention his singing, he became a role model for the refugees.

Danny and Sunny's home situation continued to deteriorate, and they shifted between their mother and father. One spring evening when John was visiting Joseph on the kibbutz—Angelina had left for Tel Aviv—he met the social worker.

"Danny and Sunny can't stay with their father any longer," he said. "I wonder if Moriah and Tom could take them, or else we'll send the boys to a children's home."

"I'll talk to Moriah and Tom," John answered. "And we'll pray."

Married only a year and a half and with no children yet, Moriah and Tom felt pulled to these two little brothers and had already spoken and prayed about this step. Although they knew that they would have to make a huge leap from sympathizing, feeding, bathing, and playing with them once in a while to being their parents, they believed that God had brought Danny and Sunny into their lives for a purpose.

The following day the boys moved in with John and me for a few days until Moriah and Tom came down from Sde Boker, their current home. Danny and Sunny seemed so vulnerable; I couldn't believe I was suddenly responsible for a four and six year old. What foods do they like? How would they feel when I put them to bed? Did they miss their parents? We communicated in Hebrew which they spoke passably, but they stuttered when excited or upset.

Foster parenting, challenging under any circumstances, takes on new dimensions with refugee children. Even usual tasks such as registering them for school or taking them to the doctor require perseverance. Yet in a loving environment Danny and Sunny have flourished. They call Moriah and Tom *Ima* (Mother) and *Abba* (Father), John and me *Saba* (Grandfather) and *Savta* (Grandmother), and they adore the blond little sister and brother who have since been added to the family.

We have adjusted to Danny and Sunny's complicated situation, the uncertainty concerning their future, and continue to pray and place them in God's hands. Several times we thought they would leave us. Having a living biological mother and father, they may not remain in our family forever.

הַמַּקְדֵשׁ

Jox, though he had visited the early arrivals in jail, wasn't interested in the current wave of Sudanese: despite being from the same country, he came from a different tribe and background—Muslim rather than Christian—and had already lived many years outside of Sudan. Increasingly, however, he entered into the Shelter community, and we celebrated with him in the sukkah when he received his Israeli identity card. However, when Jox began losing weight, wincing in pain, and gripping his stomach, John became concerned and urged him to go to the doctor.

"He says it's ulcers and gave him medicine," John told me after Jox came back from another doctor's visit. "But this has been going on too long."

Therefore, unfortunately, by the time they discovered Jox's pancreatic cancer, the prognosis was that he had a few months to live. Nevertheless, as we watched Jox slowly weakening, we observed his spirit soaring—no complaining, bitterness, or depression. Even when too weak to walk, Jox asked to be carried to the Friday night Shelter meetings.

On a hot July evening, John and an oncologist friend went to visit Jox, who was now slipping in and out of consciousness.

"She said it's a matter of hours," John told me when he came home. "But something amazing happened: while I was praying, Jox suddenly sat up in bed and said, 'Jesus Christ, the same yesterday, today, and tomorrow,' before lying down again and falling asleep."

In the morning Walter called to say that Jox had passed away shortly after midnight. Shelter people and Jox's Sudanese friends attended the funeral in the cemetery on a hill overlooking the Red Sea and the Mountains of Edom. A few speeches, prayers, and lots of music accompanied Jox as he was laid to rest.

הפסוע

On July 9, 2011, after a drawn-out struggle, South Sudan became an independent country. In Juba, the new capital, as well as in Eilat, the South Sudanese celebrated with speeches, flags, music, dancing, and food. Would they return home to help build their new nation, or remain in Israel? South Sudan, plundered by the North, devastated by war, with little infrastructure, and one of the poorest countries in the world, had little to offer except patriotism and the call to pioneer. Most chose to wait and save more money before eventually going back.

They soon discovered, however, that the choice wasn't theirs; when Israel's Minister of Interior decided to implement his vision of a migrant-free Israel, he began with the South Sudanese who were technically no longer refugees. The Immigration Authority started rounding them up on the streets and within a few months, more than a thousand were "voluntarily deported." Many human rights activists demanded that though most wanted to eventually return, they should be treated in a humane and dignified manner and be given time to prepare.

On Wednesday mornings, some of us would gather on the main street where buses stood to transport the Sudanese to Ben Gurion Airport and from there to Juba. Dressed in their finest, girls' hair plaited, a guitar hung over a shoulder, suitcases piled high, with baby strollers and televisions, they told us in fluent Hebrew that "We still love Israel" and assured us that, though they would miss us, they would be okay.

The end of another era at the Shelter? Not completely, because some have petitioned to remain in Israel for humanitarian or medical reasons—Dongdiet's family, Avraham's because of his leg, Danny and Sunny because of their family situation. Nevertheless the majority is gone, and Friday evenings at the Shelter are strangely calm and less chaotic without so many children running around, playing, and shouting.

We chat on the Internet and speak regularly on the phone to Sudanese friends. Their lives have undergone extreme change: dwelling in shacks without running water and electricity, suffering from rampant dysentery and malaria, and having few opportunities for employment. Several among those who lived in Eilat have died, while others have left for Ethiopia or Uganda, or returned to Egypt. But as refugees, they've learned to be resilient, and their voices sound hopeful and positive.

The Sudanese touched our lives deeply. I told John, "I don't think it's because they're our latest group and we've forgotten how attached we were with the others, but I think it's because of the children. The Russians, Romanians, and Chinese didn't have their kids with them. ... And it's because of Danny and Sunny."

When I'm asked how many grandchildren I have, I always include the boys. Danny's face lights up when I tell him he's my first grandchild. Whether they stay in Israel or eventually return to Sudan with their biological parents, they will remain part of our family.

Will we host another people group at the Shelter? Nothing will surprise us, and we pray to always be prepared.

24. EPILOGUE: Musings and Memory

"I decided to volunteer at the Shelter when I was sixteen and visited here the first time," Joy began her farewell speech to volunteers, Eilat Congregation members, and guests, the usual Shelter mix: Jewish and Arab Israelis; immigrants from Russia and Ethiopia; Sudanese and people from a dozen other countries. Having enjoyed trays of tasty lasagne, a huge vegetable salad, plus a cheese and fruit tiramisu, chocolate frosted poppy seed cake, and cream puffs, everyone stopped their conversations to listen.

"My mother had worked here twenty-five years ago and wanted to share her love of Israel and the hostel with my father, me, and my brothers. The whole trip was great, but our week at the Shelter was one of the best holidays I'd ever had, so that's when I knew I'd return when I finished high school."

"Tell us your highs and lows," John asked. Sometimes called "roses and thorns," all staff answer this question before they leave.

"I'll begin with the lows," Joy answered. "I wasn't used to all the conniption [sometimes converted into an adjective, this term is used lightly at the Shelter] people. My first week we had some odd people, and I freaked out. But later I could take it, even when they were really crazy and yelled at me. I've learned a lot."

"And highs?"

"Too many to count. But mainly the people. The way you accept volunteers into the community. I've made so many friends and hope to be back soon."

"How do you keep going?" a guest turned to me. "Getting close to people and then always saying good-bye?"

"It's our life. Better to get to know people and part, enriched by our time together, than to never have met."

הסקלמ

Life-changing events often originate in imperceptible ways; only later we realize a new era has begun. When Guy suggested that John rent Rachamim's house, we never imagined we would still be running a hostel thirty-six years later, that the Shelter would host guests from over ninety countries, and that dozens of men and women, old and young, would begin new lives here and be freed from their pasts.

Back then, we had no clue that the Iron Curtain would fall in 1990 and that our hostel would absorb new immigrants from the former Soviet Union. With China at that time isolated behind the Bamboo Curtain, we never dreamed that thousands of Chinese would visit our hostel and some would become our best friends. In 1978 we could gaze out our window at the Jordanian city of Aqaba a few kilometers away, but it was inaccessible to Israelis. Little did we know that Jordanians would be guests in our hostel and that they would warmly welcome us in their homes.

In a world where wars rage all around and where distrust, discrimination, and discouragement reign, the Shelter has been an oasis of hope and reconciliation, a beacon shining on a stand, and "a shelter and shade from the heat of the day and a refuge and hiding place from the storm and rain" (Isaiah 4:6, NIV).

How can a person attempt to describe and summarize thirty years of working and growing with the Shelter? Open seven days a week for 365 days a year, guests, staff, and people groups come and go; children grow up; our city changes; but the hostel has assumed an entity and personality of its own. Anything I write is inadequate to encompass all our experiences and the people we have met.

הסיפום

I conceived this book in stages as we sat around with former volunteers and friends reminiscing and telling stories. Someone would inevitably say, "We need a book." For years I had many reasons to believe I wasn't the one to write it: I was too busy; I believed that the world didn't need more books; I hadn't spent as much time at the hostel as the volunteers; and I thought my English wasn't adequate after living so long in Israel.

But slowly the idea began to germinate in my mind, and I couldn't escape it. I realized I had more time since the children left home; I could use other people's memories to refresh my own; and the computer and friends could correct my English. I began the Shelter book in 2004, but after writing twenty-five pages, took a break to hike the Israel Trail. The journal I kept became the basis of my first book, the writing of which was another journey. When I thought to return to the Shelter story after publishing *Walk the Land: A Journey on Foot through Israel*, we were deeply involved in the South Sudanese community, and I felt compelled to write *A People Tall and Smooth: Stories of Escape from Sudan to Israel*.

Thinking I'd incorporated enough about the Shelter into those two books, I tried to forget about my first writing project, but it wouldn't leave me alone. When after rolling the concept around in my brain for a long time and finally feeling ready to begin, I found myself thinking, dreaming, talking, and imagining the book at all hours and with nearly everyone I met.

At this stage I began to discover truths about memory and its limits. How could I accurately record events from the distant past which percolated to the surface of my mind as indistinct colors, shapes, or smells? John and I often had dissimilar versions of past incidents. I enjoyed talking to John and others about the old days, but could I write a book based on inevitably inaccurate recollections, particularly because I'm a precise type of person?

Furthermore, I realized that different memories shine out for each volunteer. I gradually understood, however, that as the author, I write from my point of view and recollections, though I wanted to be careful when telling about other people. For this reason I double-checked as far as possible with those involved and have changed some names for protection.

The Shelter is an amalgam of all our volunteers. Each one adds part of themselves to forge a dynamic, evolving community. Similarly, when two people marry, each member of the couple changes as a result of the union, and together they become something that neither was before. Their interactions, exchanges, and conflicts produce growth and transformation. As the years pass, the initial love matures and deepens.

I am thankful for the privilege of being involved with the Shelter all these years, yet I know we could never have succeeded and continued without our staff. Daily, they interact and deal with guests and those who stop by. They create the warm atmosphere that visitors feel when they enter and that draws them back.

I hope our volunteers and friends will find that these pages reflect their experiences even if I haven't described situations in which they were present. And I pray that people who haven't visited the Shelter will be challenged and encouraged by this story of how God uses ordinary people to participate in His extraordinary work.

25. POSTSCRIPT: Best News in a Zillion Years

"God doesn't hurry, but He's never late," Viju, an Indian friend, wrote in response to my group email.

Having begun nine years previously, put it aside, and plodded away steadily for a year and a half, I finally finished writing and re-writing my Shelter memoirs. Cladach Publishing was an answer to my prayers when they accepted the book and committed to publishing it before our thirty-year anniversary reunion in December 2014.

Yet one problem still nagged me.

Would the hostel actually be open for the celebration, or as the municipality threatened, would we be shut down? A year earlier they had given John a list of demands that had practically guaranteed our closing: break down the sukkah and construct a parking lot; remove the shack; build a bomb shelter. And only a few weeks previously they had added a new condition: station a guard at the front gate.

"I'm going to postpone making these changes as long as

possible," John had told me at the time.

"And what about the license?"

"If we can't stay open as a hostel, people can still come to us. It will just be different."

Though I couldn't understand how that would work, I continue preparing for the festivities.

Two months before the license renewal deadline, John picked up a registered letter at the post office. He immediately called me.

"Hey, Jupe! You won't believe it. I got a letter from the city hall saying they've given us status as a small business."

"What's that mean? We've got the license?"

"No, much better. We don't even need a license. Wait for me with lunch. I'm going to our accountant to have her read the letter and make sure I understand correctly."

When John came home we read over the letter together, and he told me that he was going to bring cakes to our accountant and architect who had both helped and supported us through the years. He also called Marvin, our lawyer in Haifa.

"You have no idea how truly happy I was to hear about the Shelter receiving status as a small business and being exempt from all the paperwork that you had to deal with over the past zillion years. This is the best news to come out of Eilat that I have heard about to this date," Marvin emailed back.

All week John walked around as if in a dream.

"What will you do with all your free time?" I asked. "Now that you won't be running around between offices? And you'll miss the secretaries and clerks you've gotten to know through the years."

I sent an email to friends who had been following our struggle for the license and praying with us, to share with them the good news.

"What a story of grace on the one hand and perseverance on the other. A great reminder that 'not yet' is a perfectly reasonable and necessary answer to prayer despite the fact that we tend to think that 'yes' alone is evidence of God's attention to our petitions. As for John's free time don't let him be tempted to take up golf!" Stuart wrote back.

Unbelievable, except by God's mercy.

Acknowledgements

First, I want to thank all our volunteers for giving of their time to join the Shelter community: And not only your time, but your hearts, ideas, and lives too. We couldn't do it without you.

Thank you to the many friends who willingly shared their hostel experiences with me: I tried to write the stories accurately as you related them and as I remember and hope you feel satisfied with the results.

To my husband, John: These stories and memories are yours as much as mine. Thank you for your patience as I threw questions at you day and night, and for being my sounding board. We've had an amazing forty years together and I look forward to a bright future.

To our four children, Joshua, Racheli, Moriah, and Yonatan, as well as their two spouses, Sarah and Tom: You have been an integral part of the Shelter story. Thank you for your encouragement as I wrote this book, often by simply asking how it was going and listening to my answers.

To our seven grandchildren, Danny, Sunny, Noya, Amalia, Shilo, Gili, and Boaz: You are the joy of my life. Thank you for all the smiles, laughter, and sense of amazement you give to us.

Thanks to my parents, Harry and Velma Galblum: Through your example, I learned about hospitality, tolerance, and the excitement of traveling to discover new places and cultures. You also instilled in me a love of reading.

To Polina Lozhkin, who spent hours editing and polishing my manuscript: You found the right balance between correcting mistakes while leaving my voice and style intact. Thank you.

Thanks again to Catherine Lawton and her team at Cladach Publishing for choosing to publish this book: It's a pleasure to work with you, and I appreciate your encouragement and help along every step of the way.

Finally, thanks to the Lord my God, from whom all good things come and who has everything in His loving hands, who called me to Come, invited me to Stay, and continues to Celebrate with me.

About the Author

Judith Galblum Pex was born in Washington, D.C. but has lived with her husband, John, in Eilat, Israel since 1976. They began the Shelter Hostel in 1984. John, from Holland, is the pastor of the Eilat Congregation, a multi-cultural, non-denominational fellowship.

Judith and John are the parents of four grown children and happy grandparents of seven. In her free time, Judith likes to travel, hike and camp in the mountains around Eilat, snorkel in the Red Sea, read, take pictures, and spend time with family and friends.

Judith is also the author of *Walk the Land: A Journey on Foot through Israel* and *A People Tall and Smooth: Stories of Escape from Sudan to Israel* (both through Cladach Publishing).

Learn more online at:
http://www.judithpex.com
http://www.shelterhostel.com